Bishop

Florence Clemens

TO BE YOUNG WAS
VERY HEAVEN

TO BE YOUNG WAS
VERY HEAVEN

Marian Lawrence Peabody

Illustrated with Photographs

BOSTON

HOUGHTON MIFFLIN COMPANY

THIRD PRINTING   R

Bliss was it in that dawn to be alive,
But to be young was very Heaven!

WORDSWORTH, *The Prelude*

FOREWORD

In no sense of the word is this to be considered an autobiography. That never entered my head in all the eighty years I have kept a diary. The book came about because I was merely following in the steps of my forebears in keeping a journal. I was not so much a doer as an onlooker on life, and as my paths led me to some variety of peoples and places, bits of my journals found their way into print from time to time as the eyewitness account of some incident.

I should like to thank Mrs. Norman Hapgood, Jr., who helped me make one book out of eighteen volumes of diary.

Marian L. Peabody
Somesville, Maine, July 1966

CONTENTS

~§

ILLUSTRATIONS

❧

TO BE YOUNG WAS

VERY HEAVEN

CHAPTER 1

BOSTON BEGINNINGS

~§

Some years ago, when I didn't consider myself really old enough to be helped across the street, a tall young traffic officer I had never seen before came over and took my arm to lead me across, through the traffic, to my house. He said as a greeting, "I'm sorry for you folks who used to live in Boston when it was nice"! I was surprised and quite moved by this remark. Boston *was* a lovely place to live when I was a girl—Boston and Cambridge, and Bar Harbor in the summers—and that is the reason I want to tell you about it.

I was born in Boston in 1875—one hundred years after the start of the American Revolution. My parents were staying with my grandmother Mrs. Frederic Cunningham on Chestnut Street awaiting my arrival. This occurred on May sixteenth, which was the day of Boston's celebration of the centennial, and my father took time off while awaiting my appearance to see the procession marching down Beacon Street.

Those were the days of exploration and expansion. There was a feeling of excitement and optimism in the air as pioneers spread out in all directions over the vast continent. My grandmother, who lived almost in the shadow of the beautiful Bulfinch State House with its golden dome, referred to it often as "The Hub of the Universe." (In those days the State House was painted yellow and had not acquired its marble wings. When they were added the Bulfinch center became red brick, and that is why the architect Ralph Adams Cram called it a "ham sandwich.")

My father, William Lawrence, then twenty-five years old, who had been working in Philadelphia since his graduation from the Theological School, had just received a call to the busy industrial city of Lawrence, Massachusetts, to take charge of the Episcopal church there. This call pleased and interested him as the city had been founded by and named for his grandfather and great uncle, Amos and Abbott Lawrence. They were partners in the textile business in Boston, and highly respected, so that when they decided to dam the Merrimack River and build factories there it caused great interest and some dire prophecies. The project was successfully accomplished, however, and considered a marvel of engineering, and the Atlantic & Pacific Mills, the largest in the world at the time, were built along the river's edge.

Abbott Lawrence, who had been the moving spirit of the venture, became a member of Congress and later Minister to England. Amos, who was my great-grandfather, remained in Boston and became known as one of the first "philanthropists," in the latter part of his life giving away nearly four-fifths of his income. The biography of him written by his son William in 1855 was an unusually popular book of the day. Many years later John D. Rockefeller, Jr., told my father that it was this book which so interested *his* father it made him realize for the first time the joy and benefits of sharing his wealth. Mr. Rockefeller, Jr., said, "I was brought up on Amos Lawrence and his good life." How surprised and pleased Amos Lawrence would have been if he could have known that he was the inspiration of the great Rockefeller Foundation which has done so much good all over the world!

*

My recollections of our life in Lawrence are meager. We lived at first in Jackson Terrace, which was above the lower town and reached by granite steps. As I remember it, there were a few mansard-roofed houses surrounding an oval of green. Below the Terrace and not far away was the church, facing the common. Across the common the mill hands lived, and it seemed as if the police wagon (which our nurse called the Black Maria) was continually dashing around the common in that direction. There was so much fighting and drinking among the English mill hands that even we children heard about it, as many of them were my father's parishioners.

Two sisters, Julia and Sally, followed me before I was four years old, and the rest of the household consisted of a nurse, a cook, and a colored man named Harry who drove the horse and buggy. The Jackson Terrace house proved extremely cold, and my father decided to build a modern one, which in that era meant "Queen Anne." This was not far away on a side street with about an acre of land and was much more comfortable and convenient. It also had a stained-glass window—much admired by me, who up till then had only seen them in church.

The Reverend Leighton Parks, coming to visit us, inquired the way to our new house as he left the horse car. The conductor said, "You can't miss it. It's the ugliest house on the street." And what amused Dr. Parks was that he came directly to it! Another frequent visitor and great favorite with us was Phillips Brooks. We had never seen anyone so big and tall, yet so interested and friendly with children.

Julie was always the most conscientious of us girls. In fact my recollection is that she was thought to have too much conscience—a typical New England trait—and it was remarked upon often as "Julie's conscience."

One of my earliest recollections is of the time when we were perhaps five and four, and a young lady came in the mornings to give us lessons. At the end of the hour or two we received a

tiny slip of paper with "good" written on it—that is to say,
Julie did usually and I did sometimes. There came a day when
I received one and Julie didn't and I rushed to tell of my
triumph, calling out, "I got a 'good' and Julie didn't!" Of
course my exultation was quickly squelched when I was reminded how often Julie got one and I didn't, and she had not
boasted of it.

Our summers were passed at Nahant—at first with my grandfather and grandmother Lawrence in their large house on a
point overlooking the harbor. Later we had our own house
between my grandfather's and Mr. Henry Wadsworth Longfellow's. These three houses were near where the Boston boat
docked, bringing home the businessmen, among them my
grandfather and uncles, who went back and forth by boat every
day. We never had dinner until the boat got in at three o'clock,
but "Mr. Vickers," the butler, always put fruit and cake on the
dining-room table, under domed covers of wire netting, for us
children or anyone who was hungry before that time.

My grandmother, Sarah Appleton Lawrence, who was tall
and stately, "took her constitutional" walking on the broad
piazza which went all around the Nahant house. The roof to
the piazza was supported by pillars made of trees with their
branches still on them and thoroughly sanded so they were
rough and unpleasant to the touch. This architectural curiosity
always puzzled me and still does.

Grandpa was shorter than Grandma. He felt this so keenly
that he didn't like to walk beside her in spite of his tall hat,
and I believe he had lifts put in his shoes for special occasions.
He was always immaculately turned out, and when he took me
on his lap to see his beautiful repeater watch and hear its chimes
and bells, I noticed a delicious clean smell of bay rum. Sometimes he would take out his crocheted silk purse, with the silver
rings and spangled fringe on the ends, and give me a tiny gold
dollar.

My grandfather once showed me my great-grandfather's diary

written in a hand so small and fine that I was fascinated and immediately started my own diary in a small neat hand and have kept it up—the diary—off and on ever since, but, alas, not always in the small, neat handwriting.

The three youngest of my father's five sisters were still living at home at this time. They rode horseback, swam, and watched my father, Dr. James Dwight, and Richard Sears play the new game of tennis. Nahant was the first place in the country to have a tennis court, which was on the lawn of my great-aunt Emily Appleton's house, and Mr. Sears later became national singles champion. I was surprised many years later to see my father's racquet of that era in a glass case in the hall of The Country Club in Brookline.

Occasionally a huge box would arrive from Worth's in Paris for the young aunts, and we children had the thrill of seeing the glittering contents tried on and admired. Mr. Benjamin Porter, the fashionable portrait painter, made several portraits of my pretty aunts before he was satisfied with the results. There is a famous Sargent of Aunt Harriet, which I copied in my painting days. Her daughter, Charlotte Denny, has my copy and she says she likes it better than the original, because when Aunt Harriet had it done she sailed over for the sitting and her nose was red from the sun, and that's the way Sargent painted it. When they expostulated he said, "I have to paint what I see." I don't know why he couldn't *not* have done it, because in my copy she hasn't a red nose.

I think two of the aunts got married while we lived with Grandpa. Aunt Sue married William Caleb Loring, who became a judge. She and Uncle Caleb, we discovered, in their courting days, used to sit behind a great rock on the shore, on which our nurse put us up to painting "Lovers' Retreat."

In 1883 we moved from Lawrence to Cambridge, where my father was to be professor and later dean of the Episcopal Theological School. He had leased the house of Mr. Ernest

Longfellow, son of the poet, at 108 Brattle Street. Mr. Longfellow was an artist and had built a large room onto a comfortable square house for a studio. This room had a stage at
one end and to repay the hospitality of their kind friends who
had welcomed them to their new home, my mother gave a party
and arranged some very pretty *tableaux vivants*. I remember
them to this day. It was the first time I had been allowed to sit
up late.

The studio rather baffled my parents at first, as Mr. Longfellow had painted frescoes around the high walls, depicting the
four seasons by life-size figures of young men and women very
scantily clad and certainly not suitable for a clergyman's study.
After many plans had been discussed, my mother ordered four
six-foot stretchers made, which she covered with some decorative imitation leather, fashionable at the time for wall covering
and considered warmer and richer than wallpaper. These were
fastened securely over the four seasons and we all felt it made
an even handsomer room.

After four years in this house my father was able to buy the
beautiful old Hastings place next to Craigie House which was
still occupied by the Longfellow family though the poet had
died. This was a beautiful house but needed some work before
we moved into it. In my diary for 1888 I wrote:

> Papa and Mamma are about discouraged about our
> house. Two men left off working on it because they got
> mad, and the gas man shot himself, and Papa afterwards
> found that the pipes were too small.

Ten days later came moving day.

> *Nov. 17, 1888.* Moved over to our house which is still in
> the most awful state. The 3rd story is all that's done. The
> men are working all through the rest of it. It is going to
> be very pretty, I think, and everybody says so.

Dec. 1, 1888. All the mantlepieces are up now and the study and parlor seem to be in a hopeful condition.

From my window I could see straight out across what is now Longfellow Park to the Charles River. That park was made to set off Craigie House which had been Washington's Head-quarters so there would be nothing between the house and the river. Now it's just a narrow strip and there are houses on either side, but from our house and the Longfellow house you used to look right down to the river. At high tide ships would go moving along just as they do in Holland. We would even see three-masted schooners going upstream.

This house, in which my two brothers were born and from which my sister Julia was married, we have always thought of as "home." It adjoined the grounds of the Episcopal Theologi-cal School where my father was assistant to Dean George Zabris-kie Gray, our neighbor on the other side.

At breakfast time we would see President and Mrs. Eliot bicycling up Brattle Street, and a little later elderly Miss Palfrey on her tricycle with its enormous wheels. Another neighbor whom I remember very well was James Russell Lowell, in his dapper English clothes with beaver hat and spats, boutonnière and cane. He had long side-whiskers and made a most elegant bow.

When we first came to Cambridge, horsecars rumbled by, a source of great worry to me as the poor horses had to struggle so hard to start the overloaded morning and evening cars. If there was ice and snow a third horse was added, to my great relief. When there was sleighing, all the children of the neigh-borhood went "punging," which meant jumping on the side-board of the tradesmen's sleighs—sometimes five or six of us to a side, and all shouting gleefully as we rode along to the merry sound of sleigh bells. Sawin's Express and S. S. Pierce had the best pungs. There is one sport which has gone for-ever! We had our own comfortable sleigh and pair driven by good-natured John Herlihy, but a ride in that was no excitement.

We had all kinds of fun in winter, and I described some of it in my diary in 1888 and 1889.

> Very cold but beautiful. Good sleighing. Trees very clear against the sky. After school and lunch went tobogganing as usual on Gurney's Hill. Had 23 rides and got dumped lots of times. I was the only girl who went over a big jounce in the middle of the coast. I went with Reggie and we flew way up in the air. Mamma said I ought not to have done it for I might have got spinal trouble.

> Beautiful, beautiful day. Went up to Gurney's Hill where there were about 50 children tobogganing. I did not bring our toboggan today, but I was asked to go down twenty-four times and it is a lot of exercise to walk up. Strafford took me down till he had to go home, then Harry, and he let me steer, and then Arthur asked me to steer him down, and I landed him in the lower branches of an apple tree!

Our first year in Cambridge Julie and I went to a small school of boys and girls kept by Miss Staples, a roly-poly little lady who tried to make us talk French and learn geography and arithmetic. The brightest boy in our arithmetic class, Fred White, kindly did my problems for me and I considered him a genius. At the end of the year I was elected Queen of the May and sat on a throne with crown and scepter of daisies, having had my hair "frizzed" for the occasion. After that year, I went to Miss Ingall's school for two years, and then Julie and I went to the new Cambridge School on Mason Street in the present grounds of Radcliffe.

*

My grandfather and grandmother Lawrence lived at Cottage Farm which is now the Longwood section of Brookline. My grandfather named his place Cottage Farm and the railroad took the name for its station. The bridge now known as Boston University Bridge was then called the Cottage Farm Bridge. After the Civil War, a large library with deeply recessed windows was built onto the Longwood house, and in the stone around the windows were cut the names of the battles of the war—they are still there, though the house has been moved into a corner of the old place and the rest cut up into many house lots. Here we often stayed and always came for Thanksgiving and Christmas parties.

Grandpa also had a farm at Chestnut Hill overlooking the reservoir. It was the land now occupied by Boston College but was then beautiful farming land with an old farmhouse on it. My grandparents went there to stay between seasons, but in my day it was more often occupied by a newly married aunt and uncle. Aunt Susie Loring had the family dinner there on Thanksgiving in 1887:

In the morning we went to church. P.M. we played Prisoner's Base on Hawthorne Street. In the evening we went to the Farm to dinner. Seventeen were there. First course, raw oysters; second course, thick and thin soups; third course, two kinds of fish; fourth, patties; fifth Turkey, cranberries, celery, potato and peas; sixth, ducks, rice birds and salads; seventh, Plum Pudding, four kinds of pie, wine jelly and Charlotte Russe; eighth, ice cream and cocoanut cakes; ninth, fruit and candy. Julie, Amos, and I sat at a little table. In the middle of dinner Amos had to run up and down the stairs so that he could eat some more and he also took his vest off, it got so tight.

The next day's diary begins:

I am not very well—neither is Papa. I had my music lesson but did not go out.

I was twelve years old when I began keeping a diary. All my family were great diary-keepers, and it seemed a natural thing to do. Besides, I thought life was so exciting and interesting that I wanted to keep a record of it. There was that Christmas party at the Longfellows, for instance:

> I cannot describe the beautiful scene that met our eyes when we were marched into a large parlor with lots of other boys and girls. They had got a sleigh into the room and a great St. Bernard was harnessed to it with strings of evergreen. In the sleigh among the fur robes and presents was Santa Claus and in his arms was little Allston Dana dressed as a fairy. Mrs. Ole Bull was playing the piano and the servants who were standing by the door were jingling sleigh bells. After getting our presents, we had supper and afterwards a magic lantern and finally the Virginia reel.

Early in March of 1888 I was writing:

> Helped them to get ready for the School Fair. It looks very pretty. They have a lemonade-well made of birch bark with a pole and iron buckets—an orange tree on which all are blood oranges but one and whoever gets that one gets a prize—and a Post Office and you pay five cents to get a letter. All the paper dolls I made were sold in the first ten minutes and all but one to boys and I have got to make a lot more. At five a fiddle and harp came and we danced and then the boys treated to ice cream and cake.

> *March 13.* This is said to be the biggest snow storm since 1851. The railroads are all blocked and the people in

New York who want to telegraph to Boston have to cable
it to London first and from there to Boston. We waded
along to school as best we could. The crust began to freeze
so we went coasting before our music lessons.

March 14. It is surprising how much damage this storm
has done. It is said to be worth $20,000,000. In New York
500 dead people are waiting to be buried for they can't
get out of their houses.

March 16. Went to school and Dancing School. It was
the last day, so it was unusually fine. There must have
been more than 100 people looking on. Miss Carroll
pulled me out to the middle of the floor to help her show
how to point your toes. My dress was white lawn with
elbow sleeves, long gloves, and three blue bows. For the
first German I was No. 8 but in the second I led.

Our dancing school was held in what is now the Coop on
Harvard Square—one flight up. The next year I had more of
an adventure at the last class.

Eight boys had asked me for the German but of course
I had to take the first one who asked, but once four boys
bowed to me at once and I did not know which was first.
When I was dancing right in the middle of the room suddenly my petticoat dropped off and I had to rush for the
dressing room, dragging it after me. (I had four petticoats
and two bustles on.) It was very embarrassing.

Two bustles may seem more than enough for a young person
of thirteen. One was a little sort of cushion, I remember, and
the other was a great big one, made of hoops and covered with
white muslin.

That same spring of 1888 we had especially lovely *tableaux vivants*. This was one of the favorite ways of entertaining people in those days. Children might have a magic lantern, or a juggler, but the grown-ups would have private theatricals or tableaux.

After supper the people began to come to our tableaux. About one hundred students came and a few girls from Boston. The tableaux were beautiful. Miss Fosdick was Brunhilde. Miss Hopkinson looked pretty spinning in a casement window and Mr. Sam Eliot (her fiancé) as a troubador handing her a rose through the window. Then came the Pears soap advertisement, a life-size cardboard of the old woman scrubbing the little boy and this received much applause. The last one was the prettiest. It was supposed to be up in the clouds which were made of white mosquito netting but looked very natural. In the midst of these was a young girl sitting on a silver crescent moon looking down on an owl who sat beside her. The light was thrown onto the girl whose white robes seemed to melt into the clouds. After the tableaux we had supper and the girls all sat around with a half a dozen men around each which must have pleased them. I had ice cream and did not get to bed till eleven o'clock.

Thursday. Miss Fosdick took all her Essay Class to the Peabody Museum to see the things that came out of the mounds. It was very nice and interesting and we saw some horrible mummies, etc.

April 30. Really hot day. We put on thinner shirts and stockings and left off flannel petticoats. Went to Mrs. Dixwell's and put flowers in May baskets and then Martha and I left them around. I gave one to Baby who has been sick and it brightened her up.

Nov. 5. In the evening Papa took us into town to see the torchlight procession.* We called first on Mr. Phillips Brooks who had christened me as a baby. The procession was miles long and *beautiful,* especially a certain division in white satin trimmed with gold and golden helmets, who marched wonderfully. The fireworks were fine too. We drove home but a lot of people had to walk, the horse-cars were so full.

Nov. 8. Harrison is elected President but I wish Mr. Cleveland had been on account of the Tarriff.

Dec. 2. Julie and I went to the Deanery to try on dresses for the missionaries.

Dec. 3. We all went down to Pachs to have our picture taken. Charlie Young was down there waiting. He evidently had been acting as he was dressed in pink and blue and silver spangles.

Spring 1889. Julie and I went to the Parkers' party. I left my slippers in the carriage so I had to wait till Papa brought them back before I could go into the room so then everybody rushed up and I had four partners for the German and four for supper and it was great fun. Papa and Mamma went to dinner in Boston and to see Uncle Caleb and Aunt Sue [Loring], Aunt Hetty and Uncle Fred [Cunningham], and Aunt Harriet and Uncle Augustus [Hemenway] all dressed up for the Artists' Ball at the Art Museum. They said Uncle Caleb looked like a big red barrel, but there was a very complimentary description of him in the Herald. Aunt Harriet had on one of those high peaked fools-cap-like headdresses with a veil coming out of the top so she could not sit up in the carriage but had to lie on Uncle Augustus's lap with her headdress out the window.

* It was the election day on which Benjamin Harrison won the presidency.

June 13. After passing the night in Medford, I went
with Grandma L. to Longwood where John met me and
we drove to Cambridge and I am sorry to say I broke the
new whip. The lash got caught in a tree but it was my
fault.

June 18. The picnic came off at last and was even more
scrumptious than I expected. Prof. and Mrs. White and
Mrs. Abbott chaperoned but they didn't pay any attention
to us at all. Eliot [Goodwin] and I walked away up the
brook. Coming home in the barge we all sang and yodelled.

June 19. We had a tennis party and ice cream. About
20 came and we played on the students' court as well as our
own.

June 26. Elinor Meyer (my cousin)* has sent me some
dresses from Paris and they are down to my ankles.

The next winter was my last at the Cambridge School.
When school started I wrote:

I am taking Algebra, Greek History, English Literature,
German, French, and Drawing. I had Geometry last year
and loved it and wanted to go on with it but they made
me take Algebra and I see no sense in it or use for it at all.

At the end of the year Miss Brewster was leaving for good, and
we gave her a gold watch. I had to present it and she seemed
much touched.

That year I also had my first trip to New York.

Papa, Mamma, Julie and I all went to New York. We
arrived there in time for dinner at the Fifth Avenue Hotel.

* Alice Appleton had married George von Lengerke Meyer, later Ambassador
to Italy and Secretary of the Navy. Elinor was his youngest sister. [Ed.]

Then we went to the theatre. Miss Ada Rehan acted and
I think she is lovely. The next morning we took the elevated railroad and went and saw the Statue of Liberty.
We did not go out on the water as it was bitter cold and
the sea was very rough and grey but we just looked at
her and also Brooklyn Bridge and Castle Garden. Then
we went to see Cousin Jessie King, then Grace Church,
and then Tiffany's and Stuart's and Sypher's and other
stores. Sypher's I thought the most fascinating, because
the things there were all old.

P.M. We looked through the Metropolitan Museum and
drove in Central Park and called on Mrs. Gray and Mrs.
Zabriskie after going through the Roman Catholic Cathedral. In the evening we went to Daly's Theatre again and
saw Ada Rehan in "As You Like It". It was simply beautiful. In the morning we came home after a fine trip. Julie
vomited twice in the cars.

March 14, 1890. Here I am with the worst cold I have
ever had, lying on the sofa in our beautiful parlor with
the firelight casting flickering light on our pictures, busts,
screens, old cabinets, palms and rubber plants. I have
been reading "Quentin Durward" with the banjo beside
me for an occasional diversion. But now Clara comes in to
light the gas (the electricity being out of order again) and
this peaceful hour, the first I have had for weeks, is turned
into hard reality and I must do my algebra and German.
I feel awfully discontented with myself because, though
I have been to chapel nearly every day this Lent, I don't
see that I have improved any. Sundays after church I have
been to walk several times with Harley Parker. He is
awfully nice, and also with Hal de Wolfe and Bert Dibblee.
They are all older boys. They were going to ask me to go
to the big toboggan slide in the evening but Mrs. Dibblee

told Bert she was sure Mrs. Lawrence would not allow it.
All the girls go with boys but I have to wait till Papa can
take me so all last week I only went once, but that was the
night Bert was going to ask me so he asked me down all the
time and as soon as we got back to the top someone would
be waiting to take me down again and oooh! it was fun!
There was a gorgeous moon and the air was fine and crisp.
Poor Papa dumped the Miss Horsfords and cut his face. It
has been a beautiful snowy winter. We have been sleighing on the Brighton Road several times to see the fun and
the racing, and one day when I sleighed in to the dentist's
Boston looked just like a carnival. Commonwealth Avenue
was full of beautiful sleighs dashing past with one or two
men on the box. It was lively and gay, all but the dentist
part.

Easter was a lovely day as usual. I went to the 7:30
service. There were about eighty people there and the
church looked beautiful. Then we had nine people to
breakfast and back to the 10:30 service, when the church
was crowded. Mamma gave me a new Liberty scarf to wear
and we all had violets on in our pew. Two Theologs came
to lunch and at four was the children's festival which
Ruth* attended all in her best white silk coat and pink
feathers.

A little later I wrote:

I had some gaiety every night last week but will only
write about the play at Kitty's. How excited we were beforehand, shaking in our shoes. Strafford did not know his
part very well but what he did know he acted finely. I
wore a muslin dress, leghorn hat with pink roses around

* my youngest sister then.

it, and pink sash. It went off very well on the whole but they left out Grace's part entirely and had to go over the last half twice to get her in. I had Eliot for supper and Harry [Dibblee] for the German. He expected to go home with me but Bob W [alcott] had asked first, and I had him for the Virginia Reel and he also engaged me for the German next time. Grandma Lawrence thinks we go to too many parties.

Tues. Sally went in town to the Horse Show this afternoon and her talk at supper was so lively about it that Mamma suggested we should all go this evening, so we prinked up and took a car to the Mechanics Hall. We met Mr. Ned Burnett and he got us a box at balcony prices. We saw lots of friends and relations through our opera glasses. One poor horse jumped 5 ft. 11 inches. It was awfully exciting. Sometimes he would rush at it and then not dare go over. Sometimes he would jump it and then fall on the other side, but sometimes he would clear it and then everybody would clap and stamp. I thought it was *very* cruel so we came home.

March 3. We went in town to lunch with Theresa Davis. Twenty-five girls were there, all older than I. I did not know many but was introduced to them and found some very nice. Amy Lowell* was staying there. She is the fattest girl I ever saw.

May 16 was my fifteenth birthday and I got lots of lovely presents from everyone, the best being from Grandma Cunningham, her beautiful dark blue enamel Swiss watch with the diamond star set in the case and all hanging on a beautifully designed gold chatelaine.

* the future author and poetess.

CHAPTER 2

CHILDHOOD IN BAR HARBOR

ﻌﻪ

W HEN I WAS ELEVEN we tried an experiment, renting a cottage
at Bar Harbor, Maine for the summer. We all became so enthusiastic about the island of Mount Desert that it has been
our summer home ever since. It seemed to us to have everything—wonderful climate, scenery such as we had never imagined and also a great variety of interesting people from all over.

I fell in love with Bar Harbor at first sight. How well I
remember the thrill of the first mountains I had ever seen!
Then the first glimpse of the rocky, thickly wooded islands in
beautiful Frenchman's Bay completely took my breath away.

My father had been coming to Mount Desert since he was a
Harvard freshman to visit his friend George Minot in the Field
(the Minots had one of the first summer cottages, on the shore
in an open space still called the Field). My mother, busy with
young children, had never come and indeed never wanted to,
as she had an idea it was a rather wild place where girls from
New York and Philadelphia walked up mountains "swinging
their arms"! In Boston you kept your hands in a muff in winter and in summer clasped over a purse or card case at your
waist. So my young father came alone for a short holiday and
—perhaps thinking it would be considered strange to come

without his wife—said little about his family and had a very
good time!*

After this first visit to Bar Harbor in 1886 we continued to
come almost every summer for the rest of our parents' lives.
We first rented the Shingle Cottage on Mt. Desert Street where
we children played croquet on the grass patch in front and
watched the three pretty Sturgis girls, beautiful Lulu Morris,
and fascinating gypsylike Marie Scott tripping back and forth
between Lynam's Hotel and the Parker Cottage next door to
us. We greatly admired these young girls and copied their costumes for our paper dolls.

After two years of renting, my father built a house on School-
house Hill at the head of Mt. Desert Street, just below the
summer home of his cousin, Frank Lawrence. Some years later,
Cousin Frank's house was struck by lightning and burned to the
ground.

Moving to Bar Harbor or anywhere else was something of a
feat. We always took with us four horses, a cow, a dog, and a
bird—and usually a baby with all the necessary paraphernalia
that goes with one. We kept a buckboard on the island, and
took up with us a little yellow wagon with a rumble behind
which we had in Cambridge. The town carriages we left behind. Nearly every afternoon on the island we would go for a
drive. We could take a *different* beautiful drive every day of
the week.

We had our first sleeper trip at the end of that first summer:

> On the train we made friends with the conductor and
> a lady passenger. She slept in one berth with her *two*
> children and a man and his wife on top of them.

* One of the pretty girls he picnicked and "went rocking" with was Grace
Revere who afterward married the famous doctor, Sir William Osler. A picture
book of rhymes, written and illustrated by two of his classmates (now in the
Jesup Library collection and at the Boston Athenaeum) depicts Miss Revere
being assisted over the rocks by a young man with an Alpine staff and ribbons
flying from his sailor hat.

The easiest and most delightful way to make the trip was by boat, provided the night was clear and fair. But shortly after we started going there, a good train went to Hancock Point near Ellsworth, and there everybody was put on a fast steamboat and ferried across Frenchman's Bay—one of the most beautiful short trips in the world. One hated to leave the deck with the wonderful scenery, even to go below for an excellent breakfast, but the clear bracing Maine air by that time had given us such an appetite that we usually succumbed to the smell of good coffee coming up the companionway.

Mr. Rich, our nice old caretaker, was on the wharf to meet us, among shouting cutunder men* and expressmen who put our many trunks on low drays, and off they would go racing each other up the hill to the town. We, on our buckboard, and Mr. Rich driving the maids in his cutunder, would get to the house in time to receive the expressmen when they came and direct them where to take the heavy trunks which they carried on their backs up two or three flight of stairs! The reason there were so many stairs was because the house was on the side of a steep hill. It was Swiss Chalet type with heavy timbers and two piazzas or loggias—one on the first floor and one on the second—running all across the front of the house. My room was on the top floor with a superb view, over all the treetops, of mountains and sea.

On the other side of the house was a view across Frenchman's Bay to the blue Gouldsboro hills, and this view was often compared to that at the Bay of Naples. Beneath us in front was the town and the harbor with the Porcupine Islands, and in summertime many yachts and usually a number of men-of-war of both the United States and the British Navy. Many Washingtonians as well as Philadelphians summered in Bar Harbor to get away from the heat at home and most of the Embassies followed them for the same reason. My mother's friends often

---

* The cutunder was a four-wheeled carriage often used as a taxi.

warned her of future difficulties in bringing up daughters in both Cambridge and Bar Harbor. I think still that through the gay nineties and up to and through the maligned nineteen-twenties Bar Harbor was probably the most delightful place in the world.

I should like to describe our ways of getting about. There was the cutunder, a surrey with or without "fringe on top" which turned around in a smaller space than most four-wheeled vehicles. Dogcarts, having only two wheels, swung around easily. Buckboards were practically impossible to turn, some having four seats, each holding three people besides the driver up in front. Buckboards had two or sometimes four horses. They were very springy, and it was fun to go bouncing over the roads singing "Rig-a-jig and away we go!" We would jump out and walk up the steep hills to save the horses. It was easy to jump on the step again and sit down. The only drawback was that three on a seat did not work out very well as there would be one girl between two boys or one boy between two girls. A Cleopatra's Barge was better. In it we all sat around the edge of a big wagon like a boat, which rested in summer on wheels, in winter on runners. The driver was up on a high seat in front and there were many rugs, and fur robes in winter, so that some could sit in the middle too as well as around the edge.

Motoring is the dangerous sport of the young nowadays, but we used to "go canoeing" on any sort of day, our escort often standing to paddle, and I, for one, could not swim a stroke! We also climbed the cliffs at the Ovens and Otter Cliffs, the favorite picnic spots, and we jumped the chasms by moonlight, stumping each other to do more and more dangerous things.

The summer I was thirteen, my cousin Elinor Meyer and I went to a picnic given by the Laurie Masons.

Phoebe McKean and Isabel January were there besides Marion [Mason], Cousin Lou Mason, her two sisters and Cousin Laurie Mason and a maid and butler. We went to the Ovens and Elinor and I undertook to climb up the cliff over one of the caves and then stumped the others to, but they didn't. It was really terrible and lots of times I thought I would fall and be killed. When we tried to catch hold of a rock or a stump, it would give way and so it was perfectly awful. I had a lovely time, and it was a very good meal.

How well I remember the little mossy path leading to Otter Cliffs. As we picked our way through the thick woods, the roar of the sea and the surf and the mournful sound of the bell buoy grew louder and louder until we emerged on the high flat shelf of rock, dotted with bluebells in every chink, on which we had our picnic. Afterwards came the ride home through the Gorge on a three- or four-seated buckboard, three on a seat, bouncing along and singing at the top of our lungs— the pair of horses taking the hills at a gallop, which we were told was what they preferred to do.

Every year the United States North Atlantic Squadron visited Bar Harbor. When we were first there, Admiral Gherardi was in command. He had two sons a little older than Julie and me, so that we spent much time, at their invitation, on the ships or on excursions in the ships' barges or launches. The barges were huge, heavy boats rowed by about sixteen sailors, and it was a pretty sight to see the oars all going straight up in the air at once, as we approached the ship or dock. Later on our warships were accompanied by the British Bermuda Squadron and then there were gay times indeed and beautiful parties in the large galleried ballroom in the Kebo Valley Club.

When I was twelve, I noted in my diary for August:

> Papa hired a boat and we rowed out to the warships.
> Halfway there a man yelled out of a passing steam launch,
> "If you want to go aboard the *Yantic* ask for Mr. Jones,"
> but we told him we would rather go on the *Richmond*
> because it was the biggest and the Admiral's. So we did
> and an officer showed us everything and was very kind and
> explained it all. When we were ready to get off, he said we
> had seen everything unless we wanted to go up the rigging.
> Uncle Fred came to dinner. He has just been towed in
> on his yacht *Clytie*. Uncle Caleb is here too on the *Vixen*
> and he and I and Mama and Rev. William Huntington
> went for a drive in our buckboard. We have a telephone
> now, which Mamma finds convenient to order with.

When we were still in Shingle Cottage, the Leffingwells were
our nearest neighbors and we played with the Leffingwell children. Old Mr. Leffingwell was the rector. He was a saint, and
looked it, with his deep-set eyes, erect carriage and long white
beard. I always thought the prophets might have looked like
him. His was a very humble character, and he shrank from
preaching to the big summer congregation. My father knew
how he felt and had told him that he would preach for him
if he needed him at the last moment. Accordingly Mr. Leffingwell would announce, "Next Sunday the Rev. Mr. Lawrence
will preach *unless* I can find someone else in the meantime."

For fifty years, through many changes in the church and in
Bar Harbor, our family half filled the west transept of St.
Saviour's. In those days, they had camp chairs on either side of
the aisles every Sunday to accommodate the crowd. Once, when
the great preacher Phillips Brooks was staying with us, my
father would not let any of us children go to church because he
wanted our seats filled by people who might never have heard
him.

In 1889 I wrote:

> Julie and I went to the 11 o'clock service with Papa. There was a baptism and Mr. Leffingwell turned to the congregation and said, "*Should* the child cry, let no one be embarrassed."

That was the same summer I saw President Harrison:

> Went down town to see the President. The *Sappho* came in all dressed up with flags. I got on a high post and saw over everyone's heads but he was not much to look at. He is to stay at the Blaines'.

I expect I thought the sea serpent more exciting:

> Mr. Kane saw it yesterday just where we had been rowing, right near Bar Island, and Cousin Frank saw it once and wrote about it in a magazine. They both said it had a head like a camel.

Those were the great days of flower parades—of ladies driving their own phaetons completely covered with flowers, from the horse's ears to the groom's seat in the back—including the lady herself who wore a dress to match or contrast with the flowers she had chosen for decoration.

There were also canoe parades, a couple in each canoe under a canopy of flowers. These parades were held off the attractive clubhouse of the Canoe Club on the bay side of Bar Island. Some of the summer visitors equaled the Indians in their prowess, notably Mr. Llewellyn Barry and my cousin George Derby, one of whom usually was in the finals of the races against the young son of Big Thunder, who seemed to be the head of the local Indian tribe.

The Indian village was where the baseball field now is. We used to go from tent to tent buying sweet-smelling baskets and admiring the cunning children and papooses. Lovely young

Alice Shepard (later Mrs. Dave Morris) went every week to
give the Indian children a Sunday School lesson.

We early settlers have been up Green Mountain (now called
Cadillac) in various ways. First by cog railway to a hideous
cupolaed hotel on the summit; then on foot, always the best
way to appreciate the scenery; then by the "carriage road"; and
finally by motor. One beautiful full-moon night early in the
century a few of us in a buckboard, chaperoned by young Mr.
and Mrs. Dave Morris, drove slowly up the mountain, shivered
on the top until the Vanderbilts' butler (up there with the rest
of their household) gave us some wood and matches for a fire,
after which we thoroughly enjoyed the moon over Eagle Lake
and then the dawn and sunrise over the sea, returning to the
Morris's with a great appetite for a six-thirty breakfast.

In my fourteenth summer my diary begins:

I am writing sitting on my platform with my casement
windows open and there is nothing between me and the
mountains and sea but woods, and today is so clear it looks
as if I could throw a stone over the tree tops and almost hit
the mountains. There was a gorgeous rainbow yesterday.
It stretched across Newport Mountain over the ocean and
onto Sheep Porcupine and the colors in it were most
beautiful.

July 18. The Eastern Yacht Club came in and also four
of the U.S. Atlantic Squadron, including the beautiful old
square-rigger, *Kearsage.* The village is full of officers and
sailors and handsome private carriages and buckboards
tearing around corners.

Papa hired a boat and an Indian and rowed out to the
Baltimore. We were bobbing up and down under the side
of the great monster when Papa called up and asked if

Commodore Schley* was aboard, and when the Commodore himself answered Papa said who we were and he gave us a very urgent invitation to come aboard. He introduced some of his officers and then he took us all over the ship himself. He is Southern and he called Cousin Lucilla "my dear little woman" and he took Sally and me around the waist and called us "Dear." He was a great talker, telling us all about everything. He was one of those who rescued Lt. Greely of the Northwest Passage.

July 22. The Amorys had a very nice tennis party. All the boys were nice, especially Horace Stebbins whom I had not met before. In the evening I went to what Mrs. Leffingwell called a "Frolic" at the rectory and we played games and acted charades. The next day our tennis club met—15 girls and I am the youngest. That evening Marion Mason had a supper and dance but the harp, fiddle and fife they had engaged to play just went off with their money and never came, so we all went over to the Malvern and danced in the ballroom.

August 7. Mamma had a tea for Mr. and Mrs. Richard H. Dana† who are staying with us. About 75 people came. Julie and I, dressed in white, passed things around. I got all talked out and very tired. Admiral Gherardi, Commodore Schley, and Capt. Bronson all came in uniform.

August 26. The Squadron has gone and Uncle Robert Amory went with it on the *Baltimore* to New York, where they are going to drop him and pick up the President and

* Commodore Winfield Scott Schley of Spanish-American War fame. [Ed.]
† This was the son of R. H. Dana of *Two Years Before the Mast;* Mrs. Dana was born Edith Longfellow, the "Edith with golden hair" of "The Children's Hour." [Ed.]

bring him to Boston for the Grand Army celebration, and
then they take the body of Ericsson* to Sweden.

August 27. Went off on an all-day excursion on Mr.
Fairman Rogers' beautiful steam yacht. Mr. Rogers is
Nannie Gilpin's uncle so he took about fifteen of her
friends. We had a very swell lunch in a very pretty dining
room.

It was the next summer that we learned to ride horseback.

Julie and I take riding lessons this summer of Mr. Ryder
of Washington who taught Grace Train, and she often goes
with us. I had never ridden before and the first lessons
were *awful.* I was scared pink but now I love it, and think
it is the best of all sports—cantering up and over the hills
and riding across Sand Beach.

In a few weeks I proudly noted:

Rode around the Breakneck and *jumped* over some very
low fences—and enjoyed it!
Grace Train, Alice Barney, Julie and I took a ride of
three hours. Those whose horses would go took them into
the ocean at Sand Beach. Liesberg would *not* go, the
breakers were very high and he didn't like the look of it.
I jumped a lot today and Mr. Ryder was very complimentary.

Admiral Gherardi and the ships were in again and early in
the summer I wrote:

One morning he sent his barge in and we went out to
see the morning drill which was very pretty. After it Sally

* John Ericsson, the famous engineer. [Ed.]

and I fired off the 6-inch guns with a sub-caliber cartridge. We fired at a target in the water 300 yards away and hit it several times to the surprise and delight of ourselves and the Captain of the Gun.

Grace and Julie and I went in the Admiral's gig with the Gherardi boys to see the boat race from the flagship. It was a perfect day and the harbor was full of yachts, launches and canoes. The band on our ship played all the time and the races were great. The crew were *so* excited. They climbed up in the rigging and even were on top of the masts. They had bet all their money on their ship and were sad when the *Enterprise* won the first race. The *Philadelphia*'s boats were larger and heavier than the others so they were slower but the crew kept cheering even though they were losing their money steadily. After the races the sailors were waltzing together on the quarterdeck. One couple were dressed up as a gentleman and lady and acted ridiculously but the officers laughed and applauded them. We stayed on board till the sun set and the moon rose and then came home on the barge. We raced the barge of the *Despatch* and beat them. It is pretty when the flags go down; the band plays the National Anthem and all the men stand and uncover.

Wednesday. 19th. I went to the disembarkment and drill of all the sailors with Alice Wilmerding, granddaughter of Secretary of the Navy Tracy, at the Kebo Valley Club. There are two squadrons in now—the White and the North Atlantic—eleven ships in all and two Admirals.

We never wanted summer to end. One year I wrote on our return:

We arrived at Nahant at 6:30 A.M. and Papa went right to Boston. It is an awfully windy day and the harbor is green and choppy and the surf is fine. I went down to see it and thought how wonderful it must be at Schooner Head or the Derbys' place where we always go on picnics and run out on the rocks and back again with a big wave after us and often catching us and wetting us through. Here the yachts were dripping their bowsprits and the Cup Defender *Volunteer* had housed her topmast and was splashing about like a cork with men in yellow tarpaulins running over the deck.

Oh! Nahant is so tame after Bar Harbor!

CHAPTER 3

SCHOOLDAYS IN BOSTON

❧

In the late fall of 1891 my sister Julie and I moved from Cambridge into Boston to pass the winter with Uncle Caleb and Aunt Sue Loring on Hereford Street, returning to Cambridge for weekends. Aunt Sue, I think, felt we needed a little polishing up, and more social contacts, which the big city could give. Uncle Caleb was a member of Boston's leading law firm, but nevertheless I only too often took him on in argument. I have never been noted for my tact, though I admired the quality in other people, if it did not include flattery, which I despised. I had read Jevons' *Logic* and found it absorbingly interesting. It seemed to clear things up and give you something firm to stand on. Finally Aunt Sue took me aside and said, "You *must* not argue with your Uncle Caleb!"

I may as well admit now that I never hit it off as well with Uncle Caleb as did my sister Sally whose turn to live with them came two or three years later and who did not argue, and laughed more enthusiastically at his jokes.

Julie and I had been put in different schools. Julie walked to Miss Winsor's but I boarded the little horsecar that ran from Hereford Street down Marlborough, around Arlington to Beacon and then to Charles, where I got off and walked up Chestnut Street to Miss Folsom's School. There I received in-

struction from Professor Kittredge of Harvard, Professor Dewey
of M.I.T., Frau Grote, a wonderful German teacher, and others.
At one I went home again in the same car. It had straw on
the floor to keep your feet warm and a little old driver and an
old conductor, both bearded, who took the fares and pulled
the bell rope to "stop" and "go." It looked like the Toonerville
Trolley.

In the afternoon we had riding lessons in the New Riding
School on the Fenway. Mr. Busigny was the instructor, and we
were told he had been a French cavalry officer. This was easy
to believe. On his beautiful horse he looked like a fine eques-
trian statue which should have been in a city square. He was
an expert at schooling horses and fascinating to watch. The
trouble with Mr. Busigny was that he made his pupils cry, and
having heard this, I was on my guard. Months passed, however,
and he was very nice to me. But one day toward the end of the
year when I always lose my pep anyway, he kept us trotting
around and around the ring. We rode sidesaddle, of course,
and were taught to rise to the trot. We went on so long and
I got so exhausted that finally I pulled out to rest. Immediately
he called out, "What ees ze trouble, Miss Lawrence?" I said,
"I have a pain in my side." This he found so funny that he
bowed back and forth on his horse in laughter and said, "Trot
some more and you get over your pain." After that he lost his
charm for me.

As I remember, riding only took two afternoons a week but
we had music lessons and practicing to do, and the usual den-
tistry, etc., and Aunt Sue was also particular to see that we
called on our aunts and great-aunts and grandmothers occasionally, so our time was filled up. They were very kind about
taking us to the theatre, too, alone or with a couple of boys.

We went to see Booth and Barrett in *The Merchant of
Venice*. Booth was Shylock and splendid though hideous.

Barrett was Bassanio and seemed rather stiff but of course his part was hard. Gobbo was fine and awfully funny.

Mamma, Sally and I went to see Mansfield in *Beau Brummell*. It was all *perfection* but the first two acts were thrilling. The last two very sad of course, and it was the first time I ever cried at the theatre. I have been buying photos of him ever since.

I actually went to see Duse. All New York has been thrilled by her and tickets are from $10 to $20 apiece. The first play was *Cavalleria Rusticana* and Duse looked the picture of despair and so pale and ill one would not think she could live an hour but in the second play (*La Locandiera*) she was the most gay and bewitching coquette. One would think her the most healthy and happy young woman and yet in a day or two she had broken all engagements owing to illness. She really is an invalid and has to use a cane to walk.

There was music too.

We went to hear Paderewski and really he is marvellous! The Music Hall was jammed with people standing all around. There is something fascinating about him. He is so foreign and so indifferent-seeming to what people think of him. They say he plays a wonderful game of billiards at the Tavern Club.

And there were new and exciting pictures to see.

Papa took Mamma, Julie and me in to see "The Angelus" and the Russian pictures.* The Russians were huge, violent and vivid. "The Angelus" was beautiful and very different and peaceful."

* "The Angelus" by Millet and some war pictures by Vereshchagin.

After dinner Uncle Peter [Peter Chardon Brooks] showed
us all his new pictures by a man named Monet which have
just arrived. He has always had a house full of paintings
of the Barbizon School, but these are very different and
very impressionistic so they cannot be hung near the others.
He had them in the front hall and all up and down the
long staircase. I thought they were lovely, so light and
sparkling and sunny. They were mostly of the Riviera
and the Mediterranean Sea, a lovely shimmering blue.

These were not only among the first Monets anybody had
seen in Boston, they were also the first Impressionist pictures.
So many of Uncle Peter's Barbizon pictures were very very
dark. But these were so bright, it made a great stir.

This was also the year when I went to the Friday Evening
dancing class at Papanti's. Every girl of fifteen or sixteen went
to the Friday Evening if she could get in, and danced with
freshmen from Harvard and some sub-freshmen. When they
were seventeen they went to the Saturday Evening, and danced
with sophomores. The classes were run by the mother of one
of the girls, and Mr. Papanti—tall and thin and old and lame
—just stood around and apparently did nothing. Mamma had
gone to his father's classes in the same hall and *he* really *taught*
dancing and played a fiddle, I believe, at the same time. The
hall was on Tremont Street just a little further downtown than
Park Street Church and up two winding flights of stairs. It had
a spring floor that gave an extra bounce to the dancing. I have
never heard of one anywhere else and I have always wondered
how this one happened to exist. It was wonderful for dancing,
especially for something called the Boston, which was really the
waltz but with a lot of bounce to it, and we went swooping and
swinging around the hall in a delirium of delight.

The Boston was a local thing. Nobody at first had heard of
the Boston outside of Boston. It was our way of doing the waltz,

and may have started because of the spring floor. The German
(or Cotillon) usually began about one o'clock. Everyone took
seats around the hall. The leader was apt to be one of a few
gentlemen who were used to doing it, and he and his partner
would ask the first eight or twelve couples (depending on the
size of the party) to go out and dance, giving each person a favor.
After dancing a short time they would break off and each would
take a new partner by giving their favor to anyone they liked in
the hall, making sixteen or twenty-four couples. Shortly they
would return to their seats, and the leading couple would then
ask another eight or twelve couples to do the same thing, and so
on until everyone had had the chance to go out and give a favor
to someone. Of course the more favors you got the more pleased
you were.

You waltzed in the cotillon, or you might do various figures
as they do in folk dancing or perhaps a polka or two-step. If the
hall was big and it wasn't crowded, the leader of the cotillon
would let other people come and ask you to dance, and that was
called "privateering."

After my first evening at Papanti's I wrote in my diary:

> I was awfully frightened and my heart went pit-a-pat
> when I went up those long stairs and heard the music. The
> dressing room was full of girls and I had been introduced
> to some before, but they didn't seem to remember me.
> Luckily Bob Walcott and Rodman had engaged me for the
> first two Germans. They were the only boys I knew but
> several boys got introduced and seemed very nice. It is
> great fun dancing on a spring floor and to a band.

By the end of the season I felt more at home:

> The last day of dancing school and I led the German.

My partner brought me a big bunch of roses but the
matron made me give them to Mamma who was looking
on. I had a fine time and my dress was much admired
and I had my favorite fan, my lucky blue chiffon with
silver spangles dotted on it.

We had some merry parties at Christmastime that winter.

There were eighteen of us in a Cleopatra's Barge and it
was fine sleighing and a beautiful moonlight night. We
went to Lexington and had supper and danced in Massachusetts Hall; at nine we started for home. We had four
horses but it was a long pull for them. We met lots of
other parties and they tooted their horns and yelled at us.

Spent the night at the Joys' in Groton. They have a big
house and all the rooms are wainscoted up to the ceiling
and carved and have old portraits and tapestries on them.
Also there are statues and armor and bronzes around the
rooms. They have a dining-room and a butler and a breakfast room but nobody came down to breakfast but the
governess.

At the end of my first winter in Boston, Julie came down
with scarlet fever. It was supposed that she had tonsilitis and I
was sleeping in the same room with her. Nothing could have
been more inconvenient for everybody: Grandma, who lived
next door, had gone to California, and Aunt Sue and Uncle
Caleb were about to sail for Europe in two weeks. Mamma and
Papa were entertaining the Irish Archbishop of Armagh and
his daughter, Miss Alexander, in Cambridge. Mamma had to
leave them and move into Grandma's house with me, but she
passed most of her day in Cambridge seeing that things went
right. Julie took a long time peeling and had to stay alone with

her nurse at Aunt Sue's for many weeks, but she did not mind as she adored her nurse and felt very sad when she had to come home and leave her. I spent a long and lonely two weeks of quarantine. I could not go to school or anywhere and nobody would speak to me, but it ended at last, and what a relief it was to have escaped the fever!

I was sixteen when I started teaching Sunday School at St. John's Chapel next door to our home in Cambridge. I wrote:

I have ten boys of nine or ten years old. Half of them are very good but I have no time for them as it takes all my wits to look after the others. One is very cunning but a terror. With most, a sweet smile and lifting of the eyebrows will suffice, but with him this has no effect. They call me "teacher" and say "Please, marm" whenever they speak—that is, all but John Ross who says such funny things and asks impossible questions.

However, I managed to stick it out, and at Easter I wrote:

Sunday School festival and it was all I could do to manage my ten little boys and their noisy mite boxes as we all marched in singing carols.

Here are some of the good times and bad times from those years before I came out.

Sept. 1892. We just had a cholera scare. It started with the Russian famine and has been rife in Europe and lately many ships have arrived in N.Y. with ten to twenty deaths on a voyage. Everybody had to pass through a long quarantine. The cabin passengers were very upset at a quarantine of twenty-one days, so Mr. Morgan bought an old Sound steamer and took the passengers to Fire Island,

which the Government set aside for the purpose. Then the
Fire Islanders objected so the Government sent soldiers
there to quiet them. Altogether there was an awful time
trying to keep the sick and the well and the suspected
apart, but the health authorities did a good job and only
about ten cases got into N.Y. and none to Boston so far,
though the streets are all sprinkled with chloride of lime.

Dec. 1, 1892. Aunt Sue took Julie and me to the matinee
Eddy Sothern gave for the Vincent Hospital. He and Miss
Derby have started a Club called the Vincent Club of
girls to help the Vincent Hospital (a small hospital for
women with women doctors). I was one of the girls who
was asked to the first meeting at Mrs. Derby's, and now
there are forty and they were all to go as a body to this
first benefit performance, but Uncle Caleb thought it was
dreadful for forty girls to go together and wouldn't hear of
my being one of them; so Aunt Sue took me with these
others, none of whom belong to the Club, so of course it
looked as if I didn't, when in fact I had been one of the
starters!

They were very busy days, sometimes too busy. There were
times when the doctor said I was anemic and gave me an iron
tonic.

Danced steadily all evening but suffered for it by lying
awake all night. Bromide seems to do no good and I feel
very weak and ratty. I think I am doing too much with
riding twice a week, music twice a week, painting once
and lots of homework for school.

Christmas, 1892. We had the family dinner on Xmas and
all the afternoon I drew appropriate dinner cards. We sat

down eighteen at our big round table with exactly even men and women. Aunt Sue, as usual, proposed passing a kiss around, which was done amid much laughter, with the exception of myself who refused to kiss Lawrence Brooks. Vickers (Grandfather's butler) thought it very funny, especially when Uncle Amory, turning quickly to kiss Mamma before she was aware of it, embraced the salad bowl.

Jan. 23, 1893. I was in an electric car when I saw the huge headlines in the papers which almost everyone was reading, "Bishop Brooks is Dead"! I simply couldn't believe it. How everyone will miss him!

Thurs. I tried to go to the funeral but it was an impossibility. The crowd was solid all through Copley Square. I stood on the corner of Clarendon and Bolyston for fifty minutes waiting for Papa to come for me, but he couldn't get there. Papa was working over the funeral all of the last three days. He thought it would be nice to have the coffin carried by Harvard boys, so he asked Charlie Cummings, Harley [Parker], Nelson Perkins, Lincoln Davis, Bob Emmons, Davy Vail and Sam Chew to do it. As I could not get near the church I went to Mt. Auburn. It was a gorgeous day with snow on the ground. The funeral was so long that many could not walk to the grave in time for the service. But we were very near and so could see and hear it well. The Harvard boys came slowly down the plank walk straining under their heavy load. They had to go up some slippery, narrow stone steps, lift the heavy metal coffin* over a narrow iron gate, and then turn it

---

* It had to be a metal coffin because Bishop Brooks died of diphtheria. He was six foot three and stout, he must have weighed nearly three hundred pounds. None of the pallbearers ever forgot the weight of that coffin.

completely around. At one point it was really awful as
Sam Chew, deceived by the boughs of evergreen over the
grave, fell in. With a terrific effort he pulled himself up
again and they managed to lower the coffin and really per-
formed their difficult task in a very dignified manner. The
service was read by his brother and the day was so cold
and still that his voice carried well to the sad and silent
crowd all around.

Sunday. Papa preached his memorial sermon and it was
very fine. The church was draped in black and I cried as
silently as possible, mostly because I knew Papa felt so
badly.

Feb. 22, 1893. Julie and I went up to stay at the James
Lawrences' [in Groton]. We were to have gone yesterday
but both had colds, but we started up today in spite of a
bad snowstorm. Jessie, the maid, went with us. Cousin
John Lawrence was on our train and when he found no
one at Ayer to meet us, said he "felt responsible" so, when
a sort of pung finally came for him, he kindly took us
along. We hoped Jessie would get back to Cambridge
somehow and climbed upon the pung, sitting with our
backs to Cousin John and the man. The horses had to
walk of course through the very deep snow and after an
hour or so we were pretty wet and uncomfortable. Our
veils and shawls had blown off and my hat kept blowing
first one way and then the other pulling my hair, which
was white with snow and looked like an old witch's.
I yelled to Cousin John to ask how far we were and he,
looking like a snow man, said, "About half way" and
then we tipped over! Cousin John and the man found
their feet, picked up the rugs and then came to where
J. and I were lying helpless in the snow. They pulled us

up and dragged us to the slanting sleigh. The snow was up to my waist and felt very cold slipping down my legs. In about two hours we got to the Homestead and, after changing our clothes, went down to lunch. In the evening we went to the play at the school.

April 10, 1893. This has been a hard week. Ma and Pa went to New York and left me in charge. Grandma C. is with us but is sick and Wednesday she was *very* sick and I went twice for the doctor and she wanted a nurse, but I did not know how to get one and was very worried. She is better now but Sally has been hard to manage. She had tonsilitis but was better and kept teasing and threatening to go out. So finally I said she could go for an hour. She came back in two hours, all perspiration, and said she had been playing baseball with the boys, so I said she could not go out again, but when I drove home later in P.M. there she was in Hubbard Park playing with a lot of boys and girls.

Spring, 1893. We saw a little horse trying to get a heavy cart full of wood out of a rut in the road. The man kept whipping him and the horse kept struggling and finally, with the help of a passerby, got it out. I noted the name on the cart and wrote to the S.P.C.A. and got a very polite answer saying they would attend to it. I have seen many horrid and cruel sights this winter of horses struggling with too heavy loads and slipping and falling because their shoes were not sharpened but it is hard for a girl to interfere with an angry driver, especially if there is a crowd of men around as there sometimes is, and doing nothing to help.

May 4, 1893. Papa was elected Bishop of Massachusetts! We feel proud but rather blue about it. He has been thinking it over for some time but finally they persuaded him to do it. Today all the theologs in a body, about all the ministers in town and many Cambridge people came to call and there were innumerable telegrams and letters. The bell has been ringing steadily since six excited students rushed in to tell us the news. Reporters keep coming and want more and more photographs and we wonder if we will have to leave this beautiful house just as we had settled down we hoped for good. However, nothing is settled yet.

Harvard was an important part of our life in Cambridge—my father was connected with it in some official position for over fifty years. We used to go to the games, and the boat races, and the Hasty Pudding show every year. Class Day was always a high point, a wonderful day like the one I described in 1892.

June 24. Though undecided early, it was gorgeous by noon. My dress was organdy muslin with blue in it and blue bodice and sash. Very stylish. Even Papa approved. Mamma had not seen it till today—it was all my own idea. It had a train and elbow sleeves, trimmed with deep lace. My hat was trimmed in front with white ostrich plumes and was immense, which did not make dancing any easier. Papa and I went to the Gymnasium Spread. This was the best ever, a prettily decorated hall, plenty of room to dance and splendid music. The snappiest band I ever heard. Even Papa thought it was great when they played "Ta-ra-ra boom-de-ay." I started off at once with Arthur, then Rodman, Frank White and never stopped a second as people came up and wanted the next and next. Even law students would say, "May I have the last half of the next?" etc. Finally I had to cool off and went out on the lawn and had an ice with R. Walcott. Lots of couples were there sitting at little tables. After this splendid time Papa, Julie and I went to the "Tree." This was very pretty and exciting. The little grassy enclosure around the Tree was packed. Julia Marlowe sat right in front of us with Olia Bull.* The seniors had a terrific struggle to get the flowers which circled the big tree far above their heads. They climbed on each other's backs and finally the wreath was bare and all the flowers gone. Hal de Wolfe gave me some he got, which I wore with great pride.

It was just before my eighteenth birthday (May 1893) that I wrote:

Today I am very nervous as the family seems to think I have the mumps and I have a lot of nice things I want to do. I would not have the doctor come to decide the question as I intend to go to the dance tonight even if I have the cholera.

As it turned out, I may have had the mumps, for they returned to plague us a little later as you will see.

* The daughter of the well-known violinist, Ole Bull, celebrated as "the Musician" in Longfellow's *Tales of a Wayside Inn:*

> *The Angel with the violin,*
> *Painted by Raphael, he seemed.* [*Ed.*]

CHAPTER 4

THE CHICAGO EXPOSITION, 1893

✍§

M*ay 30, 1893*, Pa's birthday, and we started for the Chicago World's Fair at 8:00 A.M. Papa had invited a group of friends to share a car on a special train with us. They are Mr. and Mrs. A. L. Hopkins, Mr. Edward L. Davis and Lillie, Mrs. Colt, Mrs. Beach and Miss Lizzie Beach of Providence, Mr. Percy Brown and daughter, Cousins Frank and Lucilla Lawrence, Mrs. Payson and Elinor and Cousin Gus Amory. Miss Beach is very pretty and attractive. Mr. Davis keeps us laughing all the time and Mr. Hopkins, they say, tells good stories in the smoking room.

May 31. Things are not quite so cheerful today. First we are four hours late owing to Mr. Montgomery Sears's private car having had a hot-box. Also I was told not to mention the fact but Sally has the mumps! Fortunately she had been put in the stateroom with Mamma and Papa. After a long day, we arrived after midnight in a terrific rainstorm and the train was so long that we were far outside the station—if there *was* one. I never saw such a mess of frantic people, umbrellas, barges and mud in my life. Not very good for Sally's mumps!

June 1. Aunt Emily and her sister, Miss Silsbee, called
to take us to the Fine Arts Building but Mamma had to
stay to look after Sally. I can't attempt to describe this
beautiful building, the superb statuary outside and the
beautiful dome inside. A month is not too much to devote
to this building alone. The Russian rooms were not
quite finished and the pictures immense with startling
sun effects. Miss Silsbee did not consider them good
but I liked them. Then we looked at the French Exhibit,
which was very large but absurdly impressionistic.

By the time we had done this we were dead-tired so we
took the Intermural Railway and went back for lunch.
We do not enjoy our meals, first because they are not
good, second because the dining room has a glass top like
a greenhouse and is as hot as Tophet, and third because
our waiter is impossible. He trips around on his tiptoes
and when we have been waiting and fanning ourselves
for half-an-hour he brings a lot of things we haven't
ordered and insists on passing them around and helping
us himself. He is dirty and the plates and glasses are dirty
and he picks the tumblers up by the rim, leaving the
marks of his greasy fingers on them. Another pretty
trick of his is to wipe the perspiration from his face with
his dirty old napkin and then wipe our plates with the
same. Now I may be fastidious but my appetite was so
taken away, and what with walking so much and eating
and sleeping so little, I got so thin it was with difficulty
I could keep my skirts from slipping off me. Our beds
are fairly comfortable but I hate to sleep with anyone
and what with Julie bouncing all over the bed and the
lions at Hagenbeck's Circus next door roaring, and roost-
ers crowing and the sun blazing in the windows at 5:30,
my nights were not as peaceful as they might have been.

To go back to our first day—we went in the afternoon

to the Fisheries Building. The aquariums were very
extensive and the brooks and waterfalls pretty. There
were lots of sailboats and fishing boats from everywhere,
mostly Norway, and the walls and dome were hung and
draped with huge fish nets. We also went into the Iowa
Building next door, where the whole inside was lined
with corn cobs of different colors, making designs on the
walls in quite pretty colors.

Evening. Pa, Ma, Julie, Cousin Gus and the Hopkins
and I started out in wheelchairs to see the Electrical display. In the Electric Building they were testing the effect
of music on light or something, and there were orchestras
playing and lots of wheels of different colored incandescent
lights were whirling around all over the building. Up
the middle of the hall was a huge pillar of light revolving
slowly. It was a brilliant sight but in a minute or two
the music stopped and the pillar went out.

We wheeled through the long building and came out
in front of the beautiful Administration Building right
on the Grand Basin. It was a very wonderful panorama.
The great oval basin with the colossal golden statue of
the Republic at the far end, and behind that, dividing
the basin from Lake Michigan, the long Greek Peristyle:
a cloister of four rows of huge columns and at each end a
beautiful white classical temple, one used as the Hall of
Music and the other as the Casino. Along the top of the
long white Peristyle are about forty statues representing
the states. Twenty of these face the Basin and twenty
face the Lake and in the center of them is the finest
statuary group of the whole Fair which is saying a great
deal as the statuary is considered of a high order. The
basin is edged with electric lights so that every gondola
is visible and the grand white buildings along the sides
are also edged with light, bringing out the beauty of the

architectural lines. Imagine all this and a fine stirring
military band and the many brightly decorated gondolas
gliding around with the picturesque gondoliers bending
back and forth in their slow graceful motion! What a
happy thought to have brought them over from Venice!

As we stood gazing at this wonderful sight in silent
rapture, a bell began to ring wildly, a fire engine dashed
clanging through the crowd and the fireboat hissed by us
on the lagoon. There was a fire in the Electric Building
but it was put out immediately.

June 2. Mamma has found a nurse for Sally so she can
go about with us. Our hotel is right opposite the gate to
the Fair so we started out through the Plaisance to the
Woman's Building and went through this to the water.
Here we took a launch and went through the lagoons,
passing many pretty wooded islands, quite wild looking.
We went under very lovely little bridges scaring away
ducks and swans as we did so. We had vistas of the
beautiful white buildings and of the pleasant looking
houses of each country that edged our route and finally
reached the Peristyle, where we got out. Lake Michigan,
of course, looks just like the ocean only it looked greener
today than any ocean I ever saw.

After walking in the Peristyle admiring the beauty
and vastness of it, we walked out on the Pier which is
half a mile long. Then we went to the Krupp Gun
Building and saw the most tremendous guns; then by
contrast to the Convent of Rábida, an exact copy of the
old convent, and so peaceful and picturesque. The Pope
had lent some things from the Vatican and there was
also the anchor of one of Columbus's ships and many
portraits of Columbus but no two in the least alike. Most
interesting were the letters from Ferdinand and Isabella
to Columbus, and his to them, and also to his son. These

were lent by the Duke of Veragua, direct descendant of
Christopher Columbus. We liked the convent with the
old garden in the cloister and the cells around it immensely.

After this we took the Intermural Railway to the Plaisance. This is a wide macadamized road (no carriages
are allowed in the Fairgrounds at all) on which are always
crowds of people of all nations in their native costumes
walking up and down. Exhausted-looking Arabs are always scuttling by with their heavy sedan chairs and on
either side all the way along are side shows, each with a
hawker shouting about his particular attraction. We went
into a white building which said "World's Congress of
Beauty" with a Highlander in full regalia playing bagpipes
outside. Inside were some passably good-looking women
dressed in the costumes of their country waiting to be
looked at.

After lunch we set out again and went first to the
German Beer Garden. This leads off the German Village
and is a sea of little green tables under the trees. Large
blond men in uniform were at many of the tables and a
strong aroma of beer, sauerkraut and cheese pervaded
the smoky air. Everyone smokes and drinks while listening to a fine military band playing Wagner and Strauss.
It is a delightful way to get a rest.

After some time here we went to the Japanese Tea
Garden right on the edge of the lagoon and reached by a
fascinating Japanese bridge. We sat at little shiny tables
on rattan chairs and everything was very dainty and smelt
so good! Our tea was served by a jolly little Jap who gave
us little gifts and an extra package of tea.

On we went then, to the Massachusetts Building, where
suddenly we felt at home. It is a copy of the John Hancock house built one-third larger. Everything looked so

colonial and homelike. All our ancestors' portraits hung
on the walls and in fact anyone who ever did anything in
Massachusetts seemed to be there. Every table and chair
belonged to some Pilgrim father and the Adams cradle,
which had rocked two Presidents, was prominent. Of
course, we signed our names and quite hated to leave. It
was by far the best of the State Buildings and the contrast
to New York which we "did" next was great. Theirs
was pretentious, dreary, gorgeous, empty and hideous. In
the evening a lot of us went to *Buffalo Bill.* We had adjoining boxes and had great fun. It was like Bedlam with
Indians and Cossacks screaming and yelling, horses scampering, guns crackling and "an occasional quiet moment"
as Mr. Davis said.

June 3. Pa, Ma, Lizzie Beach, Cousin Gus and I went to
the Liberal Arts Building, the one that is as large as
Boston Common—one mile around. It would take months
to see it all. The most gorgeous exhibit was the German
priceless china and glass. The French exhibit was also
very large—huge diamonds and precious jewels of every
kind, also fascinating furniture. The Geneva watches
in "Switzerland" were exquisite. We dragged each other
from case to case and room to room only to see something
more wonderful further on. We lunched at the Vienna
Restaurant—decorated by old Viennese gates with lanterns
on them—and enjoyed the delicious coffee and the fine
orchestra playing Viennese waltzes.

Evening. Another party of us took a gondola together and
glided around the lagoons. It was a beautiful evening and
a restful and pleasant thing to do—always distant music
but nearby the music of the frogs and crickets. Swans
glided by and other gondolas with gay colored lanterns,
slowly passed. At last, after a few swift strokes of our
graceful gondoliers, we slipped under a bridge with fine

statuary at either end and came out into a blaze of light
and music. Searchlights chased each other across the sky
and the basin was full of gondolas all hung with their
colored lanterns. A group of these gathered together
under the huge gold statue of the Republic and the
gondoliers all sang Italian songs. Our gondolier had a
really good voice and Miss Beach talked Italian very
prettily to him. Back again through the dark lagoons
where the colossal statues of horses, bears, deer and cowboys along the edge stared down at us, so white against a
dark blue-black sky.

June 4. It was a scorching hot day and I was very tired
but anything was better than our hot sunny room so I
decided to go into Chicago with Pa, Ma, the Paysons and
the Lawrences to church. The city looked filthy, with
narrow streets, and tall buildings. We jumped onto a
cable car which only stopped a second for our whole
crowd—found after a while we were going in the wrong
direction and all jumped off again. Finally, after a long
walk we arrived at the church, hot and exhausted, in
time for the last part of the sermon.

Afterwards we talked to some people who knew Pa and
then took four hansoms and drove to Lincoln Park, where
the statue of Lincoln is, which was very fine indeed. We
drove down the Lake Shore Drive. I didn't see any other
thing worth looking at in Chicago. The so-called better
houses on the Lake Shore were very ugly and pretentious
and Mrs. Potter Palmer's was among the worst.

In the evening I sat on the piazza and talked to Guy
Lowell who is very pleasant. He goes to Paris tomorrow
to study architecture.

June 5. Mr. Brown, Miss B. and I thought we would
"do up" the rest of the big buildings so we took two

wheelchairs and started for "Horticulture" and "Trans-
portation." The first was a huge, glorified conservatory
with life-size waterfalls and brooks and woods and gardens,
and in the second was the very first steam engine right
next to the one that went 102 miles an hour just the
other day. Also beautiful models of ships. One of the
battleship *Victoria* was fifteen feet long. [The *Victoria*
collided with another English ship just a week after this,
and sank immediately, carrying down four hundred
sailors and the Vice-Admiral].

We went on to the Mining Building and saw Negroes
washing, cutting and polishing diamonds, and on further
to the Machinery Building. Everything that can be done
by machinery is shown in this building and that is all
that I can say about it—it is so vast. We could not hear
ourselves think, the noise was terrific. Finally we went
to the Administration Building to take a last look at the
Dome. This is a neck-breaking feat but is worth it as the
decorations and color are so beautiful. I left the Browns
there and walked back alone, which I thought brave
among all those foreigners.

P.M. We started out again to do the Plaisance. We had
to pay a quarter for every side show on the Midway. First
we went to the Street in Cairo, a narrow paved street—
donkeys and camels clattering up and down it and little
shops along both sides. Against the brightest of blue skies
the tall white prayer tower stood out with an Arab on the
balcony calling people to come and worship Allah. As we
walked down the street, we had to step aside for a wedding
procession to pass. It was led by two big Negroes doing
tumbling acts. Then came the bridegroom in gorgeous
array but mighty little of it. He was on a tall camel and
shaking and squirming as if in a fit. He was very handsome and at first sight we took him for the bride. After

this walked three fat women shaking, groaning and squealing, then the band which consisted of tom-toms monotonously strummed and hideous noises from some kind of fife, then more camels with canopies on them filled with children, and finally the bride who was *walking,* but under a canopy carried by four veiled attendants. She was entirely and completely covered in turkey red, so we knew no more than nothing what she looked like and wondered if the groom did. The wedding takes place twice a day which I should think was demoralizing to the people of Cairo.

After this we went to see the "Savage Soudanese." Papa, Julie and I ventured in to the tiny wigwam while Mamma looked in the door and screamed to us to "come right out!" There was a man, woman and child in the hut. The woman and child crouched in a corner while the man, decked in a *very* short skirt, made of skulls, skipped untiringly about the hut, yelling a monotonous tune at the top of his powerful lungs while the skulls rattled in time to his singing and dancing. We were all shaking with laughter but were not very comfortable as it was quite scarey. The man was very short but he would come rushing at us and yell in our faces and then turn his back and shake his skulls at us.

We finally got out and went to the Dahomey Village. In the centre of a large village of huts about fifty savages, male and female, were dancing, shouting and grimacing to the noise of tom-toms while the King—a doleful looking old fellow—sat quietly and sewed. They were all tall and athletic looking and seemed thoroughly good-natured. Some were very funny, strutting about in gay and incongruous clothes and looking as vain as peacocks. One of our party heard a Negro woman saying to her friend as they stood watching the Dahomeys, "Oh! take me away

or I shall take off my clothes and go in there with them!"
Papa went another day and saw Mr. Fred Douglass sitting
in the midst of them, so different and yet removed only
by two generations!

Aunt Sue arrived today and we all passed a pleasant
evening together at the German Beer Garden. Some of
the people at the hotel now are the Danas; Thorpes;
Longfellows; William Goodwins and Milly; Ameses;
Thayers; and Thorndikes all of Cambridge—and the Shaws;
Homanses; Shepard Brookses; John Grays; Lorings;
Miss Emily Sears; Charles Loverings; Hunnewells; Sargents; Choates; J. M. Searses; Henry Howes; Lawrence
Lowells; Robert and Frank Peabodys; Storeys and Ladds
and Katharine Kimball and family from Boston. So we
have quite a sociable time as the only place to sit is the
huge "hall of 200 rocking chairs."

June 6. Sally seems to be all well again though still
somewhat swollen.

P.M. I intended to rest but the weather was so lovely
Miss Brown and I decided to go once more to the Plaisance. We went into the Venetian Glass Works which
was like any glass factory and where I bought a vase
which I immediately dropped and broke so our afternoon
was not much of a success. In the evening we started out
again in chairs and listened to Sousa and his band for a
while playing by the fountain. Colored lights show where
the bridges are so that the boats can find their way in and
out. It is a magnificent spectacle and I shall remember it
all my life. We stood on one of the bridges to watch the
procession of gondolas going under. They are larger than
the regular Venetian ones and painted red, blue, or yellow
and trimmed with silver or gold. Each one has two
gondoliers in the picturesque big hats, white shirts, and

gay sashes. On Sunday they are magnificent in silks and velvets. Silently they passed under the bridge, the Italians looked up at us as they pushed under and the only sound the distant music and the swish of oars. We hate to leave and feel that we can never see this enchanted white city again.

June 7. Beautiful day, but hot. Walked through the Woman's Building, looking at embroideries, lace, paintings, then took a round trip through the Fair in a gondola, stopping at the Wooded Island to see the Japanese Priests' House which no one is allowed to enter for fear they will harm the exquisite interior. Then to the East India House where Mamma bought a lot of spreads and table cloths, and then to the German House right on the Lake with lovely decorations and painting on the outside. I have forgotten what was inside as my mind was too tired to work.

Then to the French House. The most interesting thing here was their way of measuring and finding out who a criminal is. There were many photos of men after a first offence and then some years later and you would never know they were the same men. They were fearfully bad looking and altogether it was weird and horrible but interesting.

After this we took a last round trip in a steam launch and then back to the hotel and I never felt so tired in my life. I just fell on the bed and did not want to move or speak ever again.

June 8. We arrived at Niagara at 9:30. It was a perfect day for seeing the Falls as the sun was so bright there were lots of beautiful rainbows in them. The air was so fresh and bracing after the stuffy, cindery train that I felt fine.

I don't see why anyone attempts to paint Niagara as it is the motion and roar and the brilliancy of the sun on the drops of water and the power of the water and the clear freshness of the air which makes it all so wonderful.

We arrived at 101 Brattle on Friday A.M. at 7:45. It took me three months to recover from this trip but I think it was worth even that.

CHAPTER 5

THE BUD YEAR, 1893

ﻦﺞ

I N THOSE DAYS few girls went to college. I knew one or two
who did but none of my group of friends went. Everyone
was excited about "coming out" and most of them devoted the
entire year to it. Naturally my father thought this a great
waste of time and a very demoralizing thing to do.

In our year there happened to be so many debutantes and
so many well-to-do ones that there was a dance, or sometimes
two, practically every night from December 5th to February
7th, when Lent began. Before the dance there was always a
dinner to go to at some house, usually of twelve to sixteen;
and there were also lunches almost every day and a reception
or matinee or concert or picture opening in the late afternoon,
where I was apt to pour tea. This left only the mornings, and
while my friends all slept I went to art school from nine to
twelve-thirty.

A good many rules were applied to me which gradually
disappeared as my sisters came along and "came out". I was
limited to three dances a week and the *hardest* rule to obey
was to come home at 1:00 A.M.! Things went by rule much
more in those days. Dinners were at eight sharp, cocktails were
unheard of. The first half of dinner you talked to the gentleman on your right—the last half to the gentleman on your
left. After dinner to another gentleman, and between ten-

thirty and eleven all adjourned to the dance which might be a big ball in Pierce Hall or Copley Hall or in the big new Algonquin Club ballroom. The Somerset and Copley Plaza Hotels were not in existence then. At midnight there was a sit-down four-course supper, for which one was engaged to a partner beforehand and soon after supper there was usually a cotillon from one to three for which one also had to be engaged. So it can be imagined how difficult my problem was. I think I finally persuaded my father that the evening did not "degenerate into an orgy" before 2:00 A.M. He had at first pronounced that it would be an "orgy" after one.

Some years (and several daughters) later, Papa was heard to say, "Oh, well, young people can't be expected to keep rules and hours, especially if they are quite a belle."

There were many house parties and these I think were the pleasantest. People lived in big houses with two connecting parlors for dancing, or perhaps a ballroom—this more often in New York. These parties were more informal and one knew everyone else there, and they were of course less late, and so they were better for me. Very occasionally the hostess had not procured enough men and then they were "sticky," which was awful.

My coming-out party was a reception held in June before we went to Bar Harbor, just after returning from the World's Fair.

June 15. My "come out" reception, and to our great joy a lovely day. Mamma has been working hard on the list for this tea for a long time, and I think we asked about two thousand people but did not expect more than five hundred to come as so many have gone away for the summer. All my girl friends and most of the College boys have gone, but Tradja* came back from York Harbor

---

* Mabel Davis, who went to the same school with me.

and most of those I knew from the North Shore. The place
looked lovely. The long French windows were open and
red-carpeted steps led down from them to the lawn where
benches and chairs had been arranged in shady corners.
The house was full of roses which friends had sent. The
first hour was hard work! Besides the ushers and pourers,
who were outside enjoying themselves, there were in the
parlor two ministers (one deaf), two theologs, two old
ladies who wouldn't speak to each other, a most unhappy-
looking Harvard student, Emily Proctor and her brother,
and Uncle Jeff Coolidge and Cousin Mamie Sargent
looking very swell! They left before the stream of guests
began to arrive. The ushers worked valiantly. Two girls
poured tea in the dining room, and iced things were in
the oval room. The lawn with people going in and out
of the house all in their gay Class Day dresses made a
very pretty picture. Many people spoke of it so I finally
went out with Harry to enjoy it. Old George Becker was
at the front door and said there were 720. Mrs. Sturgis
and Maizie and Mr. Jim Scott happened to be on their
way to Bar Harbor so they came and Mr. Sigourney Butler came, and a lot of people I had not known before. It
was almost eight o'clock before they had all left and, as
I had had a headache all day, I went right to bed.

My first "out" party came the following week at Aunt
Minnie Sargent's house, Holm Lea:

There were only twenty girls and about twenty seniors
and a dozen older men. I seemed to be the only Bud there,
the rest were all older. After supper Freddy Dabney came
up right away for a dance and then Starling Childs (a
Yale man in Winthrop Hall and very attractive) then
Bert, Harley and Gordon Bell and the latter asked me to sit

out on the porch and was very entertaining. Some of the girls sat out there amongst the palms and flowers all the evening. Just as I was beginning to think Bell might be getting bored, Lawrence Haughton [an older cousin whom I had not known before] came up and introduced himself, and then someone introduced a married man. While I was with him Aunt Minnie went by and in a moment came back and seeing me still with the same married man introduced the man she was with—Mr. Kidder, who was rather patronizing and I suppose they both thought I was a pill. Soon Aunt Minnie came back and introduced Alfred Weld—to relieve Kidder I suppose. I hated to have her think she had to look after me and as soon as she was out of sight both Bob Bowler and Ned Weld came up so I had three then for a while. Except for this incident I had a pleasant evening and got along very well. It was a perfect house for a dance with the tiled terrace overlooking a pond and rolling fields like an English place and in the house four large rooms for dancing and adjoining conservatories. It was really like a ball in a novel by the Duchess.*

"The bud year" was what we called the first season "out." Parties fell off very much the second year when the next lot of debs came out, but a few of our year were still asked to the big dances and, knowing much better now how to behave, I think I found them even more fun.

Art school was hard work but I loved it. Everyone knows what a great change has come in what women should or should not do; in my day they had small choice. To do anything for *money* was wicked, as it "took bread out of the mouth of the working girl," so we were practically forced to be dilettantes. My friends went in for either music or "art," with a few filling

* A popular authoress of the day of very light literature.

up their time on charity committees. This was of course
after their "come out" year. Marion Mason and Gertrude
Parker joined me at art school in my second year. I can
think of two who attained sufficient skill on the piano to be
almost professional, and Bessie Chadwick, Lolotte Potter, and
Charlotte Houston were equally good on the violin. All of
these girls played in the orchestra for the Vincent Entertain-
ment and occasionally at charity benefits.

I don't think people got married so young then as it was
not considered honorable for a man to propose unless he had
enough to support a wife in comfort. Five thousand dollars a
year was considered enough for this. Only one debutante became engaged, and her husband had enough to sport a four-
in-hand. But they were the only couple I can think of who
later got divorced!

The high point of the fall of 1893 was Papa's Consecration
as Bishop of Massachusetts, on October 5th.

Trinity Church was crowded with our friends and relations and two-hundred-and-fifty clergymen. The most in-
teresting-looking person in the long procession of clergy
and theological students was the Archbishop of Zante—a
Greek. He was in purple velvet robes with high black
crepe headdress and the black crepe hung down behind
and trailed on the ground. This headdress and his cloak
were held on to him by beautiful jeweled clasps. He made
an address in English and a benediction in Greek. Bishop
Whipple preached the sermon—fine, but very long.
Ruthie and Baby got restless in it, but on the whole they
were good. Bishop Williams did the consecrating and Bishops Clark and Potter were the presenters. It was a very
long service but many people said it was the most impressive they had ever seen. The Governor and his aides in

uniform were in the front pew in front of us and served to
amuse Baby for a while.

My father had bought a house in town. It was a big house
—not on the swell side of Commonwealth Avenue where all
our friends lived, but on the "shady side." The interior was
all finished in black walnut which my mother intended to
paint white, but Uncle Peter Brooks told her that "would be
a sin." He said it was such handsome wood that, even though
it was so dark, she would "live to regret it." Halfway up the
long heavy staircase hung a stuffed peacock fastened to a
perch on one of the steps. His long superb tail was the first
thing you saw when the front door was opened to you. The
large parlor was on the right and a small room for my father's
secretary on the left. In the back where there was glorious
sun was the dining room and my father's study, and gentlemen
in long coats with top hats were continually passing the parlor
doors to go there when Papa was at home.

Nov. 30. Thanksgiving Day and an unusual one for me
this year, as I waked up in our new house for the first
time, and was off at 8:30 A.M. with Papa to the House of
Correction in South Boston. We were let through the
iron gates by one official in uniform and led across the
prison yard by another. It was quite a pretty, quiet spot
on the river with a lunatic asylum on the same grounds.
The prisoners were marching in squads to the hall in lock
step and of course in prison clothes and with their arms
folded on the shoulders of the man in front. Each squad
had an armed officer and from a distance looked like a long
grey worm.

The hall and gallery were filling up quickly with the
marching prisoners. I went to sit down on a bench on
the platform while the Chaplain took Papa to the center,

but he came over and took me to the benches on the other
side and introduced me to his family who later explained
that I had first taken my place among the lunatics.

At first I found it embarrassing to face six hundred of
the toughest-looking men I had ever seen but after one
good look I could only feel sorry for them as I wondered
what they had to be thankful for on this day. The sad
part was that almost all of them were young except for a
few pitiful, broken-down old men. Some looked, if they
hadn't been so pale and sad looking, as if they might be
normal boys and these were the eagerest and most attentive listeners. Papa's address was very good and quite
touching. There were about fifty women prisoners in the
gallery, one, a girl, was very pretty with red hair and
dimples. We waited for them all to file out and found
that they were in the yard, and when we came out some
had started playing football, but they made way for us to
pass very politely. We were shown the cells and the
kitchen, where the cooks were preparing Thanksgiving
dinner, which I was glad to see looked very good.

As soon as I got home I dressed and went to the football game—Harvard vs. Pennsylvania—and very exciting,
as it was an open game with much running and kicking.
Charlie Brewer made a long run but was kicked in the
head by a Penn man, which occasioned much hissing and
calls of "Disqualify him!" Bob Emmons was also injured
and dragged off the field protesting vigorously. Great
excitement at the end when Harvard beat and twice as
badly as Yale had beaten the same team. Harvard Square
was crowded with a shouting, singing, cheering mob and
there were some private coaches covered with excited
boys, blowing on the tally-ho horns. Going over the
bridge, however, was lovely with a new moon over the
water and the lights twinkling along the edge of the river

and steam cars running through Chester Park in a thin
line of red lights leaving a trail of pink smoke against
the sunset sky. I was almost too sleepy to enjoy the
Thanksgiving dinner at Aunt Sally's.

From then on my days were very crowded.

Dec. 4. To a pretty pink lunch at the Wilsons', with
lovely place cards and ice cream in the form of pink rose-
buds. Afterwards poured at the Crowninshields' tea.

Dec. 7. The first real ball was given by Mrs. Rollins
Morse for her niece Marion [Mason]. Nellie [Sargent]
had a dinner first of fourteen. I wore a white dress with
bright red velvet flowers and my hair had been done by a
hairdresser for the first time in my life. It was very becoming but expensive and not good for the hair being
curled with hot irons. After the dinner we six girls were
so excited and scared we could not keep still. I entered
the ballroom on the arm of Selden, who was an usher, and
curtsied to Mrs. Morse and Marion and then the ever
thoughtful and faithful S. van Rensselaer came up, as I
should have hated to have Selden wait even a *minute.*
Dick Saltonstall also came and joined us when we finished
dancing and we three surveyed the scene which was very
gorgeous indeed. Everybody was there in their best clothes
and many more older people than young. It was not
at all crowded even though four hundred people were
there. I had some fine dances and then explored the
sitting-out rooms.

I felt rather dazed and stared around too much instead
of paying attention to my partners. There were very few
buds and boys there, but it was real Boston Society and
I had never seen anything like it before—all ages up to
eighty in their best clothes and jewelry.

Dec. 8. The Lymans' house dance tonight. I wore a
French dress. It was a sort of shimmery blue gauze over
a light blue silk lining, and the shimmery stuff was
caught up in scallops with white flowers, and with it I
carried a blue gauze fan, very large, covered with silver
spangles. I had a wonderful time and hated to go home
at one.

Dec. 14. Didn't go to the Kimballs' as I am limited
to two nights in a row. Of course, the girls said it was the
best party yet.

Dec. 18. Aunt Sally had a dinner for me and I wore
the gorgeous dress she gave me.

Dec. 23. I went to Cambridge for the Sunday School
Christmas tree. It is always a lovely tree and nice service.
My class is the biggest except the Infant Class. I have
twelve boys ten years old and am very proud of them,
only one is troublesome. Sometimes I have another boys'
class added to mine, and that is pretty hard to manage.

After this my diary shows a party every night.

Jan. 3. Did not go to the Cheevers' ball as Elinor Meyer
had a theatre party for me. We saw Irving and Terry in
Thomas à Becket. It was splendid but I did not see anything so *very* remarkable in the acting. Afterwards we had
supper at the Somerset Club.

Jan. 15. The Duncans' ball in Pierce Hall. They hired
the whole building and it was all hung with pink cheese-
cloth with electric lights all through it hidden in evergreen. They had the Hungarian Band from N.Y. and also
Baldwin's Cadet Band so the music kept going all the
time.

Jan. 18. Went to an awfully nice dinner at the Homans' but could not go on to the dance so called a Kenny & Clark* to take me home. On the way home the cab horse fell down twice as he was not sharp shod. The second time he got all tangled up in the harness and couldn't get up so I got out and ran home.

Jan. 29. Aunt Minnie Sargent gave a dinner for me. It was a terrific night—a real blizzard and some of the roads were impassable. Afterwards we went to a very crowded dance at the Country Club but I was enjoying it until Leo Everett calmly left me after "cutting in" and I had to go and sit with Aunt Minnie, which was *awful.* He is so rude I don't like him at all and, of course, this had to happen at *her* party so the whole evening seemed like a nightmare. He must be rude because he couldn't be so ignorant.

Jan. 30. The night of Aunt Harriet's party for me at 273 Clarendon Street. It was awfully nice of her to give it and it was a lovely party. The house was beautifully decorated with smilax and vines and lovely roses and lilies. It was done by a decorator. The rooms were all cleared for dancing and at the back of the third room was a long counter with waiters behind it, serving sherbet and champagne all the evening. The big library upstairs was fixed for sitting out and they also sat on the stairs all the way up to it. There were chairs around the dancing rooms for the chaperones and older people to sit and watch. Aunt H. and I received in the hall. I wore a dress that Ma got in Paris when she came out. It was muslin, all shirred and ruffled with lace edging and insertion over pink taffeta so it was a very pretty light shade of pink. I had an aigrette in my hair, which had been done by a hairdresser, and I

* Horse cab.

wore my new necklace of twenty-three little diamonds
hanging on a chain, and my diamond star. We asked two
hundred and twenty people, many older ones and lots of
Collegians, but *not* as many of the buds as I would have
liked. I received with Aunt H. till suppertime, and then
danced as hard as I could till one thirty when Aunt H.
had them play "Home Sweet Home" until they took the
hint. I was awfully tired, but had a fine time, and think
everyone thought it a great success. They were all swept
out anyway.

Jan. 31. At about 3 P.M., to our surprise, the baby, a
girl*, was born. She is thin but doing well, and looked
awfully cunning when Mrs. Powell, the nurse, brought her
into my room, all rolled up tight on a lacy pillow.

March 8. Felt awfully, but was bound I would go to
the Opera to hear Calvé, as nothing else is talked of now
at every lunch party, but when we got to Mechanics Hall
we found Calvé had a cold and the ever-useful Bauer-
meister was taking her place. However, the music was
fine and I enjoyed it though I coughed steadily and had a
racking headache. Next morning Dr. Putnam came and
my temperature was 102. I lay listlessly doing nothing for
two or three days. Had tickets for *Faust* on Saturday and
was so disappointed not to go. Julie said Melba was wonderful and sang "Home Sweet Home" afterwards. Miss
Greiner came to take care of me, making the fifth trained
nurse in the house within the last ten days, as Grandma,
Mamma and the little baby had them, and Appleton had
been *very* sick with double abscesses in his ears, so *he* had
one too. Papa and the new coachman and two of the maids
had also been sick.

* Elsie, my youngest sister.

I had pneumonia and was in bed almost a month and it got around that I was very ill. The front door bell was muffled and I did not even see any of the family or know or care much about anything. When I began to feel better, I was very mad with Dr. Putnam, because he would not let me get up. I didn't know, of course, that I had pneumonia and much of the time I felt better and happier than when I am supposed to be well. My family and friends were wonderful to me, sending flowers and presents, and Miss G. was nice and quite giggly and read aloud well and it was delicious to have everything done for me. When at last I was told I could get up, I found I couldn't stand or step and it was funny to see little "Dr. Putty" moving my feet for me and teaching me to walk all over again. Finally I got onto the sofa and then was allowed to see some friends. When Miss G. had gone I was quite sad, but in three days she was back again for Grandma.

As soon as I was strong enough Pa, Ma, Julie and I went to Washington for a change. I was thrilled to cross the Harlem River on account of *Hefty Burke*. I had been reading everything Richard Harding Davis wrote while I was sick and admired him and Charles Dana Gibson tremendously. Grandma had been giving me *Life* every week and I, for some time, had been copying Gibson's illustrations at the request of my friends who wanted them.

Washington. Cousin Kate [Mrs. Robert Lawrence] did not think it dignified for Papa to go and shake hands with the President with "hoi polloi" so she told him to send his card and ask to pay his respects. The word came back that the President had appointments all afternoon but Mrs. Cleveland would be pleased to see us at 5:30. Before then, however, we went to the Supreme Court and had the good luck to hear Mr. Carter of New York make a speech before

the Justices who appeared not to be listening even to *him*.
We then drove to the White House and Mrs. Cleveland
received us in the Red Room which seemed to me an exceedingly dreary place. She was very handsome and attractive—an ideal President's wife. The call was not of the
easiest nature. Julie and I sat like dummies and the first
subject was the weather, which lasted quite some time.

Washington has such an unfinished look—some streets
are wide and smooth and others like village streets with
dirty little houses. Some buildings are large and handsome
and right next to them are Negroes' huts. I am afraid the
"White City" at Chicago rather spoilt me for everything
else.

In New York. The evening found Aunt Hetty and me
at the Opera seeing Calvé in *Cavalleria* and then Melba in
Pagliacci. It was a splendid house, the boxes were all full
and I never saw such gorgeous clothes and diamonds.
Young men were rushing about from box to box making
calls and it was a gay and interesting scene.

Next day, Cousin Sally Newbold took us to see the new
Tiffany Chapel which is now on exhibition. They have
created the most wonderful effects in opalescent glass. One
window had the first blue-eyed figure ever made in stained
glass. After this we lunched at Delmonico's and this was
very gay. Melba was chaperoning a lunch party right next
to us and on her left was a man I had played tennis with
at Bar Harbor several times. Mrs. Rhinelander Jones was
also there and Cousin Jim Lawrence, who came and spoke
to us. Aunt Harriet ordered a most sumptuous lunch
which we did not have time to eat before taking the three
o'clock train for Boston.

May 12, 1894. The baby was christened in church this
afternoon. I was godmother and never heard what her

name was to be! They only decided just as they got to the church and forgot to tell me. I knew it was between Hope and Elinor, and when Papa said "Name this child," I said Elinor, and *hoped* it was right!

Class Day. Ma, Julie and I went to the Sanders Theatre Exercises and found our seats were right next to President Eliot! Jack Oliver wrote the poem which was considered good. Henry Copley Greene did the Ode, which to me was quite incomprehensible. After this I went home and rested, skipping the Wadsworth House Spread but going back at 4 to the Tree. It was perfect Class Day weather so I wore a French muslin dress with blue sash and Leghorn hat. Everybody was there. Ethel Phelps sat right in front of us which was nice. She looked very pretty. The class came marching in in lock step, all in fearful-looking rough clothes, to the music of a fine band. They marched round and round the Tree and then came the cheering. First for the President and faculty and then, to our surprise, for "Bishop Lawrence"! Then for the Crew and the Teams. Finally came the scramble up the Tree for the flowers which were much higher up than usual so they stood on each other's shoulders and heads and it got pretty rough. At last one fellow climbed above the rest and shinnied up the Tree, braced his feet against it, and jerked out the '94 emblem bringing it and the wreath down and falling backwards himself onto the hollering crowd below. We went home and got a solid meal and then went back for the Beck spread.* This was *lovely*. Lawrie Stockton came and asked me to go over to the Yard and that was *very* nice. The Stocktons are cousins of ours and Lawrie is the nicest of the whole family. The yard was as light as day with the thousands of Chinese lanterns and fireworks. The Glee Club was singing and it was all very pleasant.

* The Beck Hall Spread was a most elaborate party given by a group of Seniors for their friends

Went with Ma to the Commencement Dinner in Memorial Hall. Cousin Frank Appleton was Chief Marshal
and sent us tickets to the Ladies Gallery which only holds
about 15 or 20 people. It is a most impressive sight to see
them all march in to a fine band—the President and Cor-
poration and Marshals leading all the grads, from the
oldest to the youngest. It is not quite so moving to see
them eat their dinner and light their cigars.

CHAPTER 6

ART SCHOOL

I WENT to Art School off and on from the time I was eighteen until I was married. I even worked at it the year I came out. I think I was the only debutante who worked—the others came and joined me at school in the following years.

Usually I went by the month as it was hard work, standing most of the time, and I was very liable to overdo and had many colds and sicknesses. The School was in the old Art Museum which stood in Copley Square where the Sheraton Plaza is now. I used to get in three or four months of work in a year, with short rest periods between.

Philip Hale was our teacher for the first year, when we drew charcoal drawings of the statues in the museum galleries. Mr. Hale was an excellent teacher, but alas, nobody wanted his pictures. He was always fine to me. After this first year, we graduated into the Life Class taught by Frank Benson. His etchings of natural subjects were particularly well known—everybody had to have a Benson print of ducks. After that we moved up to the Portrait Class where we did oil paintings of models under Edmund Tarbell. Tarbell was a portrait painter and also known for his pictures of horses of which he was very fond. He was a good painter, but one can see why he is not fashionable today:

Went to Tarbell's Exhibition. I am crazy about "The Venetian Blind" and also the "Blue Veil" and like "My Family"—"Jumping the Horses" and a little sketch belonging to Uncle Augustus, but I think it a pity that he works so much for effects of color and few are pictures you would like to buy and live with. What is the idea in painting a lady in evening dress carrying a large blue and white platter under her arm—or a girl in "garden party" attire embracing a prickly pine tree with both arms?

At the end of every term, a "concours" was held, something like an examination. Everyone made a drawing, and then there was an exhibit of the good ones.

Jan. 19, 1897. My concours drawing got hung which surprised me as I did not spend half the time on it that the others did on account of having strained my eyes drawing in a dark corner.

Jan. 22. Mr. Davis (Lincoln's father) came wandering in to the Museum and seemed very surprised and amused to see me on my high stool in my long apron hard at work. He was very curious about everything.

March 23. I had to go home from Art School and give up concours. Awful disappointment as Mr. Hale was so interested in my doing well and thought I might get up into the Life Class.

March 26. Went to Art School and slaved five hours on my high stool without pause, trying to finish drawing. Amos nobly stood by sharpening my charcoals and running off with my drawing board so that I might look at it from a distance. I never worked so hard but I did finish it in two mornings while the rest of the class worked all day on theirs all the week.

April 8. Got a bad crit. Mr. Hale did not like the way I had done the David's hair! I said, "I did not know you meant me to copy each curl, it takes so much time," and he turned to face me and said in his serious but gentle way, "If Michelangelo took the time to sculpt them I think you could take the time to copy them more carefully."

May 14. Miss Elinor Davis came out from the Museum to tell me I won the Concours for the Antique! It was very nice of her and of course I was tickled to death. Mrs. Monty Sears gives a $50. prize to each class at the end of the year. Notices were in all the papers and I got a lot of letters of congratulation.

This was my drawing of the Apoxyomenos, which gave me such a friendly feeling for him ever after. I was very pleased by the award, though I let the prize money go to the runner-up, after Papa suggested to me that I should.

I did manage to get into the Life Class, and started in February of 1898. This was held in the one-story Crowninshield Building behind the Museum, a most unhealthy place, heated by big stove, near which one roasted and far from which one froze. For lunch we could go down to a room in the basement:

You can bring and cook your own lunch, both girls and men. It is funny to see the exquisite Marion Mason in a long gingham apron walking around stirring dippers and things. We ate our lunch together on a very dirty table.

Feb. 24, 1898. Marion, Gertrude Parker and Miriam Hamlin are with me in the Life Class. It is hot, close, charcoally, dirty and very crowded. The most exciting happening was an initiation which took place in the boys' room next to ours but the door between is locked. We heard a great hullabaloo going on in there and suddenly the door opened; amid much scuffling and shouting a voice was saying, "Now, one, two, three, four—one, two, three, four." I was sitting with my back to the door and thought they were so fresh I wouldn't pay any attention, but I looked around when the noise became alarming just in time to see a red demoniacal vision tearing right at me knocking everything helter-skelter as he came! I had just time to jump from under a shower of easels and heavy drawing boards. The novitiate was dressed in long scarlet draperies with a red tam, a red demon mask and blindfolded over that. A crowd came in with him but he had got away from them and rushed wildly forward smashing everything he could reach. He said afterwards that he didn't know he was in the girls' room. Miriam Hamlin's drawing fell on top of mine and both were ruined and the room looked as if there had been an earthquake. The other men were much frightened, and caught and quieted the new boy and hustled him back. Only one stayed to pick up things amidst a dead silence. I was so mad to have a whole week's work rubbed out, and all the girls were indignant. I went to a luncheon party afterwards and told all about it, thrilling the company who thought it very Frenchy.

Later I wrote:

I did several bits of work this winter—a frontispiece for the new Church paper, *The Militant,* and the outside of the appeal for the Children's Aid Society, but after Christmas there was so much going on in the way of parties that I hardly got to Art School at all.

Mr. Benson was a very critical teacher, which was good for me of course.

March 14, 1899. Mr. Benson didn't come last crit. day so we had pinned all last week's work on a screen for him to judge *and* he sent mine 'down' and only mine! one of the most gleefully triumphant moments for me, as he never has sent mine down before when he *knew* it was mine. He was more surprised than I or anyone else.

Later, when I was in Portrait Class with Mr. Tarbell, I won a good criticism in an unexpected way:

When I got to Art School this morning and glanced at the model stand to see what model we had for this week— what was my horror and amazement to see Richardson, my esteemed skating teacher! It *was* embarrassing! and ridiculous too. I didn't know whether to bow or *not* to bow and I hastily arranged my things to do his back thinking this would be the more tactful place to take. But I soon found that in order to get off the stand for rest periods he had almost to jump over me so it was the worst place I could have chosen. After two days of struggling not to catch his eye I decided that it was more sensible to bow, which I did, and he said "Good morning, Miss Lawrence" with great dignity.

But the result was the best criticism I ever got. Mr. Tarbell said, "Very good" a dozen times and seemed enthusiastic for *him;* so now I am grateful to Richardson for posing!

June 21, 1904. Carrie and I went to a Ball Game between the Tavern Club and the St. Botolph Club. Charlie
Sturgis had told us that Mr. Tarbell was going to pitch
and we *had* to see that as we just couldn't imagine it. It
was worth seeing, because for once we felt superior to our
little teacher. Never have I seen such ball-playing! A team
of girls could have whitewashed them. Mr. Tarbell made
one sensational hit, and his little legs went twinkling
around the bases pretty quickly considering what they had
to carry. In the middle of the game we had a terrific thun-
dershower and the rain came down in white sheets but
the players showed the stuff they were made of by never
stopping for an instant, tho' some did use umbrellas. The
field got so slippery that one man fell down five times on
the way to first base, arriving there quite black and dripping with mud.

I had some other opportunities to study outside of Boston.
One summer in Bar Harbor I studied with Charles Hopkinson,
who became the leading portrait painter in Boston.

My first painting lesson at Mrs. Sears'. Charlie Hopkinson teaches Mrs. Sears, Mrs. Leverett Bradley and me the
Denman Ross method. We paint in the garden which is
gorgeous just now. The system is, I fear, rather over my
head but it is a pleasant and interesting way to pass an
afternoon.

I think Dr. Leighton Parks, our rector at Emmanuel Church,
was the first person to think of doing something for the influx
of young people from all over New England who were coming
in to Boston for an education. Boston University was in its
infancy but was growing apace and the Conservatory of Music
and Art Schools were all drawing the youth of the country.

Therefore, he asked Mrs. Robert Grant, Mrs. Edward J. Holmes and myself to be a Committee of Hostesses and have tea every afternoon in a room in the Parish House. We took turns—each being hostess once a week. I thought perhaps I could do something for the Art Students in the way of an exhibition of their work which would benefit them and advertise the Students Club (as we had named our infant organization). I knew they would rather get a free chance to show their work than anything. Again Dr. Parks agreed and gave us all the second story of the Parish House from Monday to Saturday. Great excitement prevailed!

Feb. 13, 1900. Hung pictures all day long with two remarkably clever men, and I worked on the catalogue all evening. Slept only in naps and dreamt that nobody came to the exhibition!

Feb. 14. Finished last things as the exhibition opens this afternoon. I was very nervous about it as all the responsibility rested on me whose idea it was, but I got Miss Townsend and Miss Heywood to lend their names, and they came and helped sort the pictures and other things. Mr. Yeames, Pa's secretary, did a lot of typing too but that was all the help I had. I was given *no* money so I was responsible also for that and I had had a picture moulding put up in the big hall and four or five more electric lights. All this was a great bother as we were not allowed to use any tacks. I had also had 500 invitations printed and mailed and that cost a lot, and the picture hangers were very expensive but well worth it as they were most ingenious. It was a poor place for a gallery as two of the rooms were lined with little cupboards, but they seemed to enjoy hanging pictures over doors, windows and anywhere and it was remarkable how well it looked when

done. You entered the big room where the walls were covered with oil paintings from wainscoting to ceiling—all
beautifully lighted with no glare. I sat at a picturesque
Gothic reading desk facing the entrance. (I was sitting on
a book rest on top of a camp stool and was very uncomfortable but the effect was good.) The top of the desk was
dark red velvet on which were spread the miniatures and
also the prizes. Mrs. Mumford had given a little red
enamel watch for the best picture by a member of the club
and I gave $25. and others small amounts for the water
colors. I had made Alice Parks and Marion Peabody responsible for the tea and they looked very pretty pouring
it at a most attractive long table set with candelabra, handsome silver and china and lovely flowers. In the next room
were the water colors through wide folding doors so it
looked like a continuation of the first room. They looked
lovely—really like a professional show. Beyond was yet
another room of drawings and etchings.

Against the wall, where there was room, were long tables
on which leather and brass work, trays, bowls and handsome book bindings were displayed, and these added much
to the richness and color of the show. We sold almost all
of these. Marion and I had made hunting lampshades and
Ethel Forbes candle shades and I had made some menu
cards with water color miniatures of actors and actresses.
Mrs. Eben D. Jordan bought the set of eight, and I had
orders for many more but stopped after taking four as they
are a lot of work. They always had a crowd around them
and I could have had dozens of orders at $25. Also had
many orders for the hunting lampshades but wouldn't do
another for love or money.

All the teachers of the Art School—Tarbell, Benson and
Hale—were the jury who chose the work and alas, dis-
carded quite a little. This was very kind of them as it
certainly was outside their line of duty.

Everybody seemed enthusiastic about the handsome show it made. They would come up to me and say, "My dear, I had *no* idea," "So glad you let me know about it," "I might not have got here, and it is wonderful." Alice and Marion made $11. selling tea at 10¢ a cup with cake—free to exhibitors! The rooms were full all the time and crowded at tea-time. We sold three pictures and quantities of smaller things. I talked as hard as I could all the afternoon and was so happy because it seemed so successful. The exhibition was really a "succès fou" and everybody was saying so. How wonderful! I drove home in Aunt Sally's carriage in time for dinner chuckling to myself I was so delighted. Aunt Sue said, "Do you mean to say this was all your idea?"

In the evening we had music. Two of the boys from my North Bennet Street boys club, Stephen Leveroni and John Baderaco, played mandolins. Those three children were too cunning (Louisa played too) and everybody was crazy about them. John Baderaco's mother and Steve's sister, Elvira, came and the latter offered to sing for us, which was a real treat as she belongs to the Boston Opera and is a charming girl.

Next day the tea made $11. again and with some checks that kind people gave me we shall pay all expenses easily.

After such a successful beginning the Students Club exhibition got to be a regular thing, and I was often responsible for one part or another. In 1904:

Feb. 23. At Students Club all day—sorting and hanging and cataloguing and oh! how many bleeding hearts there will be! The jury rejected more than half the pictures. The jury were Leslie P. Thompson, a Mr. Kingsley—both in 'Advanced Life'—and Mrs. Watson, and they were the nicest jury I have had, modest and kindly and attending to business quickly and pleasantly—making the best of all inconveniences and *thanking* me for asking them to do it! Very different from the girls from 'Advanced Life' last year. Mr. Hale and Mrs. Watson awarded the prizes, 1st to Leslie Thomson, 2nd to a Japanese for a water color, and there were 2 or 3 more and some "mentions." June Leland my helper and I were perfectly dead at the end of the day.

Feb. 24. After much hard work the exhibition opened but owing to the weather we did not have much of a crowd today. There were many disappointed ones looking for their pictures and finding them piled up in the Students Club room. I sold two or three posters and two out of my three lamp shades which relieved my mind as to finances.

Gertrude and I had done six posters apiece for the exhibition, each showing the back of a girl sitting on a high stool drawing on an easel. They wore different colored smocks, so each one was a little different, and they were quite picturesque. They proved to be entirely too popular. First off, going down stairs about tea time I noticed that all the posters which were on the walls of the stairs to point the way to the Exhibition had disappeared! I was provoked as they were a lot of work and were selling at two dollars apiece. During the evening a parcel was brought in to me and on the outside was printed, "Sorry! didn't know they were for sale"—inside were the posters!

Next day when I reached the Exhibition, the first thing I noticed was that my posters were gone again. This time the thieves were not so honest and I never saw them again.

My father, Bishop William
Lawrence

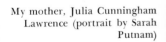

My mother, Julia Cunningham
Lawrence (portrait by Sarah
Putnam)

My great-grandmother Parker, her daughter Mrs. Frederic Cunningham, her daughter (my mother), and *her* daughter (myself)

Amos Adams Lawrence, my
grandfather (portrait by
Eastman Johnson)

Grandmother Sarah Appleton
Lawrence

Pa with his eldest son Appleton

My portrait of my father. now in the Episcopal Theological School
in Cambridge

Our house on Brattle Street in Cambridge

The Lawrences' house at Nahant. The three children are
M. L., my sister Julie and Cousin Amos.

M. L., aged 4

M. L. and Julie

CHAPTER 7

THE NINETIES,
GAY AND OTHERWISE

～§

I WAS GLAD that we were keeping our house on Brattle Street even after we had moved to Boston for the winters. One day when I took a girl out to lunch with me, in Cambridge, we found an interesting stranger seated at luncheon with the family. Papa introduced him to us as Mr. Turnour and he rose and bowed gravely. He had the rather stiff manners of an Englishman, but we were quite attracted to him nevertheless. In appearance he was very large and tall, light hair and light moustache, a little bald and very much sunburned which gave him the appearance of being rather florid. About thirty-five years of age. He was very gentlemanly, but had a great deal to say. He seemed very well-read and either knew or knew of all our friends in England.

Papa asked him about the Bishop of Derry and his palace, and he laughed and said, "Poor old Derry! You would be amused if you could see the palace. All tumble-down" etc., etc., which was very much what Papa had expected.

Mr. Turnour had been with Gordon in Egypt, and of course his account of that interested Papa very much. He had also been a guardsman and told us some funny stories about the Queen, not all to that lady's advantage. He seemed to have a keen sense of humor for an Englishman and laughed long and

loud at luncheon occasionally for very little cause as it seemed
to us.

After luncheon Mamma told me about him, while he went
into the study with Papa. She said Papa had received a letter
from the Bishop of Norwich in England about two weeks before
in which the Bishop said that a young friend of his and the
nephew of his friend, Lady Russell, lady-in-waiting to the
Queen, had left England suddenly "owing to the vagaries of a
young lady," and had gone to America about six months before.
Lady Russell had been much worried about him and had heard
nothing of him until quite lately when his old valet had told
her that he had heard from Mr. Turnour from Boston, Massachusetts, and that the young gentleman was very short of funds.
(He had quarrelled with his aunt about the young lady.) His
aunt felt badly that he did not come to her for money; so she
wrote to the Bishop of Norwich and told him to ask the Bishop
of Massachusetts to look up her nephew in Boston and try to
make him come home and she would be responsible for the
money Papa would lend him up to one hundred pounds. Papa
did not have time to look him up immediately, but one day
the telephone bell rang and a manly voice demanded, "if this
was the Lord Bishop of Massachusetts?" He said he was Gerard
Turnour and had received a letter from his aunt, Lady Russell,
asking him to come and see Papa on business.

Papa set a date for him to come; so he arrived one morning
and sent in his card. Papa was busy then; so Mr. Turnour sat
in the parlor waiting for an hour or two, and the maid, who
had occasion to pass through the hall several times, said he
seemed strangely nervous and started suddenly every time she
went by.

Well, then he told Papa his side of the story. He said he
had become engaged to an actress in London much against the
wishes of his friends and family. He said that the family seemed
unreasonable to him, especially his aunt, Lady Russell; the

actress came of good but poor people and, as she had a talent for acting, supported her family in this way. Lady Russell made a fuss and finally the actress with great firmness broke off the engagement, saying that she could never be happy if his family did not like her and she wouldn't make trouble between him and his people. He thought it was all Lady Russell's fault; so he skipped to America and lived on a friend's ranch in Colorado for six months. The actress, he said had married a lord immediately after breaking her engagement. Mr. Turnour had been on the ranch six months when his friend became quite ill; so he brought him to Boston and saw him safely off to England, and then found himself stranded in Boston without any money to get home with if he had wanted to.

After lunch Papa tried to persuade him to go back to England, told him of Lady Russell's generous offer, said he would advance him as much as he needed—how much did he want? Mr. Turnour thanked him for his offer and would leave it to him.

"Well!" said Papa. "Will a hundred dollars do it?"

Mr. Turnour said, "Could you make it $120? We English like to calculate in guineas."

So Papa said he would give it to him then. They would stop at the bank on the way to the College (he wanted to see Harvard).

Then they came into the parlor, where Mamma and I, Dodge and van Rensselaer were, and we introduced our English friend with great pride. Then we all went out and played golf on the lawn, which it amused Mr. Turnour to watch, and then Mamma took him to drive in the victoria to see Mrs. Burnett, James Russell Lowell's daughter, as his father and the poet had been great friends; so he was interested to see Elmwood, of course.

Later, Papa took him over the college and into the Union Club (putting him up there), and to the bank for the money;

Mr. Turnour insisting on giving Papa his note. Mr. Turnour said he would like to see Papa again before sailing; so Papa asked him to lunch with him two days later at the Club. He and Mamma had decided after some discussion not to ask him to stay with us.

Well, Mr. Turnour did not turn up at the Club for the lunch engagement; so Papa sent his secretary in to his lodgings to see what was the matter. The secretary said that no such person or no such lodgings had been heard of in that part of the town.

Then Papa wrote to the Bishop of Norwich saying that his young friend did not seem to want to go home and had escaped with $120 of Lady Russell's generous offer. The Bishop of Norwich wrote back, in a different handwriting with a different letterhead and different signature, that he knew no one of the name of Gerard Turnour and knew no Lady Russell, and he was afraid Papa had been the "victim of a hoax."

And that is the last we have heard to this day of the fascinating Gerard, though the police searched the country for him. Of course, it all came out in the papers, in a silly way, which made Papa very mad, as it sounded as if he had been so easily taken in; whereas our friend was a very expert confidence man, and Papa said he would have paid half the money to have seen it done, it was so clever.

Several other confidence men tried us during the year, as they thought we were so easily fooled, but we were sharp by then and they got left.

Spring and fall were lovely in Cambridge, and my room was my special joy.

Oct. 18, 1894. [Cambridge] This is a gorgeous afternoon and I have passed it sitting in my arm chair by the big open window looking across the lawn, and beyond to the river and the red marshes covered with haycocks. Way across in the dim distance are the houses, lawns, and trees of Coreys' Hill seen today because it is so clear. The sky and river are a bright deep blue, the trees gold, the ivy crimson, and I can see sunbeams silvery against the rich green and gold. I take a lot of pleasure in my lovely room. White paint, with blue, the color of the river today, on carved ornaments over the doors, two big windows, one looking towards the Longfellows, and a huge one in front, with a balcony and striped awning for hot weather. They have ruffled white muslin sash curtains and dark blue curtains, and the carpet is dark blue. The wallpaper is French and beautiful. Scrolls of blue and gold on white background. There is an open fireplace with white mantle, a big bureau, washstand, a big table with salmon pink cloth to match flowers in the wallpaper, a sofa covered in blue and salmon pink by the fireplace, nice pictures on the wall, and many photographs around.

A few years later I recounted:

After a sleepless night I was trying to doze in the morning when I heard a funny scattering sound like mice, which increased, and I thought it must be rain. I sat up in bed but it looked through the curtains as if the sun was out, yet the noise increased till—*crash, bang!* down came the ceiling making such a lot of lime dust I couldn't see, and it got in my eyes and mouth so I buried my head in the pillow until it settled. In a few minutes I looked out on a scene of devastation! There was a hole as big as the dining room table in the ceiling and my sofa, book-case, chairs and carpet were covered with slabs of plaster and such thick white dust over everything! If I had been on the sofa I might have been killed.

It seemed to take ages to get things put to rights and I remarked, "It has been horrid living in the entry since the ceiling
fell."

When one looks at this part of Cambridge today, it is hard
to remember how countrified it was even so short a time ago:

Lately the Harvard Hare and Hounds have quite frequently run across our place. First come the two hares
tearing across the orchard and lawn and vaulting over the
wall. They are in running pants with bags slung over their
shoulders from which they keep throwing out scraps of
paper. In a few minutes come the Hounds—30 or 40 of
them—after them. This performance always excites our
cow—tethered in the back of the place—and last time she
got so upset that she chased one hound who was lagging
behind, his legs being shorter than the others, and he made
for the stable and disappeared within. We had been watching all this from the windows and when the poor man
emerged, looking carefully in every direction, we saw that
it was our friend Arthur Train.*

The first year after I was out, we finally persuaded Mamma
to view a football game:

Oct. 20. Sally, Mamma and I went to the Williams game,
my first game on the new Soldiers Field and Mamma's first
game ever. She got quite excited and thought they were
killing each other. There are eight disabled men on the
team and I don't know what Bob Emmons is going to do
about Springfield. I drove home but Phantom was so
rampageous in the crowd that Ma got out and walked.

Oct. 30. Grandma roped me in to taking French lessons
with her at the Y.M.C.A. rooms of a man who guarantees

* Later the well-known novelist.

to have you talking French in five weeks so I have been going to town every day. He is an American, and his accent is atrocious but he is a good teacher and it is quite amusing. There are ninety women in the class and four men, two of them Negroes.

Nov. 25. Dr. Jekyll and Mr. Hyde. All we could get was a box and we were lucky to get that as the theatre was crowded and the standees were as jammed together as a Cambridge car in the rush hour. All Boston was down below us and Mansfield received an ovation when he first came on. How handsome and sad looking he was as Harry Jekyll and how *fiendish* as Hyde! Where he looks in the window and the girl shrieks and he springs in and murders her father, Florence and I thought we would go to the back of the box—but I was so fascinated by the stage I could not move. Where he turns from Hyde to Jekyll it is magnificent and in the last act, when he knows the next time he turns it will be final, pity is no word for what you feel for him. Afterwards I clapped till my hands were sore and Mansfield, after coming out eight or ten times and no one having left, finally had to make a little speech, but he seemed so tired he could hardly talk.

Christmas. We all went to Aunt Harriet's tree and party, where her children acted "Young Lochinvar." Hope was Y.L., who eloped with Hetty on the big rocking horse. This was most realistically accomplished by Uncle Augustus, unseen behind the parlor door, and the butler unseen out in the hall, each with a rope attached to the horse pulling it across the parlor so that it appeared to be galloping wildly.

Evening. Aunt Sue Loring had the dinner in her swell new house on Gloucester Street. Footmen to point the way up the stairs as well as opening the carriage door. We looked for presents all over the house, trying to avoid the mistletoe in the doorways and ending up with a lively game of "Going to Jerusalem."

April 29, 1895. Matinee of Vincent Club Show. Being so tall, I am always asked to take a man's part and as Mamma and Papa do not allow me to do that I am always an usher, wearing lavender dimity dress and white apron and cap. The play was very good—the Drill wonderfully done, the dances pretty and the audience enthusiastic. After the last performance Gertrude Whitwell gave a supper party in her house which got pretty gay. Of course, there were only girls there and Mrs. Gibson, Ethel's mother, but there was much dancing of the Café Chantant style and health drinking and one or two of the girls *smoked* though I would not mention this outside the club.

In 1895 I reached the great age of twenty, and noted on my birthday, "Feeling old!"

My friend Carrie pulled my waist in to nineteen inches, "but I can't say it was comfortable." We didn't insist so much on tiny waists as they did abroad.

June 1. Went to town to pass the night at Tradja's and go to the Pops. The Winsor Welds, Santayana and I were the party. It was a lovely hot night, too hot to go to bed, so we sat on the steps of 154 Beacon and ate oranges— Santayana is a great admirer of Tradja's brother Lincoln and considers him the best type of Harvard student.

One of the high spots of that year was visiting West Point. Julie and I both went with Papa (Julie had come out the year after me), and our first visit was commencement time in June.

. . . we found fine rooms reserved for us at the Government Hotel, overlooking the Parade Ground. Papa is an official visitor for Commencement Week. Cousin Fred introduced us to Miss Bessie Ernst, the daughter of the Superintendent, and we all went out and saw a splendid Cavalry Charge. We then had tea at the Superintendent's House and after it went out to see Dress Parade. In the evening a military band of forty pieces played in front of the hotel and we all sat on the piazza and enjoyed it . . .

June 4. Miss Ernst called before we were through breakfast. Then Papa, Julie and I went to hear the Engineering Examination. Col. Mercur and a fine-looking young officer named Flagler were examining the Senior Class and the poor cadets looked pretty worried. After lunch Miss Ernst came again with two cadets who took us to see the seniors build a pontoon bridge across the river. One cadet's name was Connor and the other, who fell to me, was Doray—very big and well set up and such a nice face and manner. I was not surprised to learn later that he was not only one of the ranking men of the Academy but also one of the most popular. He asked me to go around the famous Flirtation Walk . . .

June 5. Mrs. Parker, wife of Col. Parker of the Cavalry, took us to see the Cavalry Circus. We sat with the Secretary of War Lamont, who had just arrived and was escorted around the Post by all the cadets and a band while seventeen guns went off. The Circus was thrilling from start to finish. Such riding I had never imagined! They cantered around with their arms folded and went over very high jumps often standing on their horses, sometimes driving three abreast. The horses seemed to be vicious little nags

and often bolted or bucked. Why fifty men, some off and
some on, did not get trampled and hurt by those crazy
horses I don't see. The boys would rush their horses at a
jump and then leap off and vault the horse as he went over
and keep on vaulting over him as he ran around the ring.
They rode backwards with arms folded and then would
turn to forward again and jump from one horse to another.
Some rode two horses abreast *standing* or rode abreast of
each other and held hands as they stood on their galloping horses and raced at a jump. I can't begin to tell of all
the feats of horsemanship and can only say it was most
exciting. Afterwards we all had tea at the Ernsts with six
cadets, one being Doray, who talked to me all the time.
Miss Ernst said I should be flattered as he stayed so long he
had to run all the way to quarters to be on time for Dress
Parade . . .

June 9. Doray and a friend of his named McCoy for
Julie took us all around Flirtation Walk, Doray telling me
all the traditions of the post and singing all the songs in
a nice bass voice, "Army Blue," "The Girl I Left Behind
Me," and "Benny Haven."

We put on our swellest clothes to see the Secretary of
War review the cadets. After the review we went to the
Ernsts' reception. This was a jam! The military band on
the lawn, the beautfiul views all around, a lot of gold lace
and a perfect day made quite a picture. Here too I met
Flagler. He was a gorgeous figure in his full dress uniform
and cocked hat, or rather one of those long pointed canoe-
shaped things with white ostrich feathers over the top,
very picturesque and becoming on a distinguished looking
man, which he is and very big and tall and broad . . . That
evening we dined at the Mercurs and there we met Flagler
again, but Julie sat next him.

June 7. Bluer than indigo at leaving. On the window of my room was cut in the glass by some other sad inmate of former years, "Fare thee well, and if forever, still forever fare thee well."

In November we went on another visit to the Point.

The Superintendent's carriage was waiting for Julie and me so we went off in style. After getting warm and dry at the Ernsts we went out to see the football game. As we walked behind the crowd of people watching the game, one tall cadet turned quickly and then hurried forward taking off his cap and holding out his hand. Of course, I knew him at once and my first thought was, "He is much bigger and handsomer even than I remembered." He took us to our seats which were, being the Supt's, in the centre of the front row. It was a thrilling game. Yale came in with a rush and pushed West Point almost down to the line where they held. Connor, whom we met last spring, had his head bandaged for a bad cut he got in last week's game but despite this he made a touchdown which caused great excitement. As the game went on sometimes one side scored and sometimes the other and at the intermission it was 10–8 in favor of Yale. Doray and McCoy came over and talked to us then and we suddenly realized that it was snowing hard and that we were gradually sinking into the ground. The second half was sad for West Point, and their captain, who had played so hard and well, was hurt and taken off the field. But, considering that there are only 300 cadets from which to pick a team and that they are allowed only 15 minutes before breakfast to practice for football, they certainly do well.

We went to the Ernsts for tea and Mrs. Ernst asked me to pour it, which I did with the assistance of Doray. Without his heavy caped overcoat he was a vision in grey and gold.

He and McCoy stayed after the other people had gone and though everything had been just as I had pictured it there was something lacking. When they had left, I was looking at the many photographs around the room with Miss Ernst, and came upon a group of cadets and girls and in the centre were Doray and a girl looking at each other and laughing. Miss Ernst said the girl was her cousin, Sally Amory, and added, "Mr. Doray is very devoted to her." I remarked that she was very pretty and she said, "Yes, she is a dear. Here is another picture of her. She came here at just the right age, eighteen." She was *not* very pretty and looked affected. Ugh! It is a bitter, bitter world, but it can be so nice for some people.

At the hop I had the honor of entering with the Commandant. My cadet was one named Landon who was waiting at the door of the ball-room. The rule is your partner has the first, second and last two dances so I had only two dances with Doray, who dances divinely. I did not keep strictly to my card as there were quite a lot of Yale men there who could cut in . . . Capt. Parker engaged me for a dance next spring but I shall never come back.

Sept. 1895, in Cambridge. I screwed up my courage and went to call on Mrs. Dave Morris, the run-away bride. They are living in Cambridge while he finished his college course and she goes to Radcliffe. I remembered her as a beautiful little girl at Bar Harbor about my age.

Later that year: I had a big lunch of girls to meet Mrs. Dave Morris, which was most successful. All the girls fell in love with her as I had done and all said they had a wonderful time. Olga Frothingham played to us and Isabel Lawrence told fortunes and I think Mrs. Morris enjoyed it as much as anybody.

Nov. 12, 1895. We all went to see *The Prisoner of Zenda*. It is the most exciting play I *ever* saw and I hardly slept all night. Sothern was fascinating in it. It is much the best part he has had.

1896. On Jan. 9 in getting into a cab to go to a Cinderella Dance I hit my shin against the edge of the step. It hurt but I got to Pierce Hall and after limping around the dressing room a while I went in and danced hard all the evening. The next day Dr. Richardson came and said there were germs in it from my black silk stocking, and I must bathe it with a disinfectant and not walk on it for a few days. I did go out to lunch and dinner, but kept it up the rest of the time but the pain became worse. I ended up by being in bed six weeks with the doctor coming every day and probing and burning it, and I just escaped having to have the bone scraped. It appears I broke the periosteum, the covering to the bone, and it got infected. The girls were all awfully good about coming to see me and sending flowers and books, but it was very tiresome as it would *not* improve.

May 16, 1896. My 21st birthday and a lovely day. I received my property, which Papa explained, and gave me a little Russian leather account book marked with my name and he also wrote me a very nice letter. I felt very important, and old (and young at the same time).

In the evening I *chaperoned* Sallie and Alice Parks to the Freshman Glee Club and afterwards danced mostly with Max Sargent who dances beautifully, so I had a really lovely birthday.

We had planned to go to Europe as soon as school was over, but it was Papa's Twenty-Fifth Anniversary at Harvard and his class asked him to be Chief Marshal. In fact, I wrote, "they *begged* him to because if he wouldn't they thought they would have to ask Cabot Lodge and most of the class didn't like him or his politics. So he decided to stay."

The last few days before we sailed were hectic indeed.

June 17. Commencement at the school. To pass the night with Ethel Purdon and to the Pops with her. The next day Ethel and I went out to Peggy Perkins's wedding on the special train which had an awning over the entrance, and the conductors and porters all wore white gloves and boutonnières. There was a huge crowd there and all the swells in their best. Harley Parker asked us to come to his table in the tent, where we found a lot of our friends. L. Haughton came over and asked me to go to the ball game in Cambridge with him, but later he came again and said Mrs. Jack Gardner had asked him to drive over with her!

As soon as we got home Amos and I were busy over his spread, which Papa let him have on our place. We decorated the huge tent, which was already up, and after fixing up my room for the girls to use as a dressing-room, I went out and was busy trying to get the party going by introducing, relieving, etc. After supper I sat on the oval room steps with Harry and rested from my labors and listened to the music which was fine with lots of drums. Then I went back to the tent and danced hard till twelve-thirty, when it was all over and a great success, I think.

Friday and Class Day and a lovely night for it.

June 22. Groton Prize Day and I went up to stay with E. Joy. Later I paddled on the river with a boy and learned how to steer a canoe.

June 24. Papa's 25th reunion [at Harvard], which we stayed over from Europe for because he was Chief Marshal.

At the morning exercises we all had front seats of course. Then Papa had to give a big breakfast to all his classmates, aides and all the important visitors. When this was over, the procession formed and began to march into Memorial Hall. We were all up in the Ladies' gallery and at the first strains of the band all rushed to the little balcony looking down into the hall below. The band, which is a big brass one, makes a tremendous din in the marble hall. A few aides all dressed up and with batons in hand, came in first, then Papa, then the Governor, Pres. Eliot, and the honorary degree guests, and finally the grads in classes from the oldest to the youngest, each class led by a handsome aide in silk hat, frock coat and boutonnière.

After lunch each speaker was introduced by the President of the Alumni and then Papa would jump up on his chair, wave his baton, and say "Three cheers for the Governor" or "President Eliot," or another, as the case might be. Cabot Lodge made a speech which received great applause and the cheers were given heartily. Fortunately he had just done something good in Washington so it happened to be the right moment.

Booker T. Washington received an honorary degree and made the finest speech of all, receiving tremendous applause. Quite an interesting incident happened to show what a great man Washington is. When they all left Sanders Theatre for lunch, Papa saw Mr. Washington turning to the left and hurrying off towards Harvard Square so he called after him and said, "This way, Mr. Washington—the lunch is over this way," but Mr. Washington just waved and said, "Yes, I know, I'll be there shortly." President Alderman of Tulane University had received a degree too and Mr. Washington had thought he and possibly other Southerners might not like being at the table with him so he got his lunch in Harvard Square somewhere, and came in quietly a little late, though he was to be the chief speaker of the day.

Afterwards we hurried home and got ready for a tea at our house for the class and their wives and sons. It began at five and lasted till about nine and people were straggling in and out all that time. It was, of course, an awful mixture but they all seemed to have a good time and they presented the Secretary, Mr. Barnes of Cambridge, who had worked awfully hard over it, with a silver tea set. He has a nice son who is in college now. Mrs. Lodge said her daughter Constance, who was class baby, was awfully disappointed not to come, but she was sick.

The Class Dinner was a great success, Papa said, with excellent speeches, some *very* funny indeed. He was very glad he had put off the European trip for a month and did not miss this Commencement, and his 25th, and being Chief Marshal, and I am glad now too, as it was well worth staying for, and if we had not waited we should not have met the nice crowd we went over with.

CHAPTER 8

FIRST EUROPEAN TRIP

❧

June 27, 1896. We got aboard the *Umbria* at eight, after spending the night at the Fifth Avenue Hotel. There was a huge crowd on board, rather awful-seeming people, but we were glad to see that many of them left before we sailed at nine, leaving us with about 475 saloon passengers.

About three hours out of New York we suddenly rolled and shook and stopped! We had run aground and there we stayed until ten that night. All the steamers that sailed after us passed by with jeers or offers of help and we were surrounded by tugs and reporters all day. With the help of a dozen little tugs we were finally set free at high tide. We had run onto a wrecked coal barge which had two buoys to mark it, so it was very stupid of the pilot. At ten o'clock we heard that a diver was going down to see if the bottom of the ship was in shape to continue our voyage. He was beneath us on a tug, all dressed up for his task, but we heard him say it was too rough to go down. So we started across the ocean! This made Mamma very nervous as she thought there must be a hole in the ship's bottom.

The first morning was warm and I got out of the stateroom as soon as I could to get some air. On deck one of

the awful Cook's tourists men came up and asked me
"if I hadn't thrown up yet," and related his experiences
before I could get away from him. Leaving him abruptly
I walked around the deck and saw at least six horrible
exhibitions which sent me scurrying below, where, though
I didn't eat much breakfast, I felt restored in spirit.

We heard that 100 Yale men were to be on board but
it turned out there were only forty-five, going over with
their crew to race at Henley. Knowing Redmond Cross,
who is on the Yale Crew, we quickly met others of the
Yale boys including Cheney, a friend of George Gray's,
and Thorne, captain of the football team. Another good
friend was B. Learned Hand.* He and his friend Davy
Vail had just graduated from Harvard Law School and
became our steady escorts. The family we saw most of
was Judge and Mrs. Howland and their daughter Fanny.
In the evening our particular group gathered in the
saloon—the Howlands, Brink Thorne, Cheney, Mr.
Amory Gardner, Cecil Baring and George Booth—and
had roast beef sandwiches and drinks, about 11 o'clock at
night.

A few days after we landed in England we went to
Henley to see the races. In Paddington Station, we found
an awful crowd who rushed at the trains as they came in,
and all the carriages either had a gentleman hanging to
the door handle or a card in the window saying "Retained." But we grabbed a carriage door and got in with
an Englishman and two ladies, and to our delight the
gentleman put his hand out of the window and pulled
off the "Retained" card. Arrived at Henley, we found
the town full of gay crowds in every sort of conveyance
from donkey carts to four-in-hands. We found our seats

---

* Later the distinguished Judge of the U.S. District Court in New York.

in a decorated grandstand opposite the finish flags, and directly in front of us were Brink Thorne, Cheney, and Mr. Gardner. We were all thrilled by the colorful scene around us. The river seemed already crowded with punts, rowboats and launches, and across the river were rows of large gaily-decorated houseboats and beyond them handsome houses, beautiful lawns and gardens.

Before each race a bell rang steadily for three minutes to clear the course and all the little boats rushed to the sides of the river leaving none too much space for the racing crews to row through. It was all very informal and it seemed to us Americans as if there was little applause and enthusiasm. Of course, the Yale-Leander race was the event of the day and we got more and more excited as the time drew near. When the gun went off Brink Thorne took out his watch. It was a long seven minutes to wait and then the crews came in sight and the Yale boys cheered wildly. Thorne got up and said, "Leander's ahead," and the cries of "Leander, Leander," became louder and the Yale boys fell silent as Leander swept over the mark 1¾ lengths ahead. It was hard luck to be beaten on the first heat, but, on the other hand, perhaps it was best to be beaten by the expected winner. Redmond Cross' very pink back was still erect in the boat, but some of the crew seemed in a state of collapse.

Later in London we went to St. Margaret's Church, to see the window to Phillips Brooks. The old sexton was much surprised to find that Papa was his successor. Nobody believes he is a Bishop as he doesn't wear apron or gaiters.

We also went to a convocation at Westminister Abbey and saw all the Deans, Archdeacons, etc., in their red gowns or black gowns with red hoods (Oxford) or black with white hoods (Cambridge). They talked so queerly and were so formal and important over such petty questions, it was funny to hear them. They had an argument on whether they should stop talking when a noisy cart went by. The chairman was a solemn old man who kept calling in a reproving tone, "Ordah! Ordah!" and they would stop whispering or whatever they had been doing, looking quite squelched.

Messrs. Hand and Vail took us to hear a case in the House of Lords—before the law lords; then we went to the Courts of Law and heard five or six cases in different courts before several celebrated judges. The formalities, robes, wigs, etc., were interesting. We saw them "sitting in chambers," and also a chancery case. Then we went through the Middle Temple very thoroughly and the places where Goldsmith, Johnson and Pendennis lived, and Goldsmith's tomb. The refectory was a beautiful place—lots of atmosphere and charm.

We did all the touristy things in England, went to Guard Mounting at St. James's Palace and signed our names at Shakespeare's house in Stratford, and were hustled through the Duke of Devonshire's beautiful Chatsworth with a rabble of tourists. I fell in love with Haddon Hall and wanted to build a house just like it in America.

Crossing to Europe, the first real excitement was the pictures in The Hague and Amsterdam, many of them familiar from my art courses, but more beautifully done than I had imagined.

A glorious trip up the Rhine brought us to Switzerland, where it was pouring rain and I had a heavy cold. I wrote:

I am bitterly disappointed in Switzerland. I had read
so much about the chalets, St. Bernard dogs, and picturesque people and places that I can hardly bear the reality.
We hear that the Spanish Infanta, the Spanish pretender,
the King of Serbia, the novelist Daudet, and the Castel-
lanes are all in this hotel but we do not see them.

I began to find my dream Switzerland once the weather
cleared. But Italy was the real revelation.

August 12, 1896. Waked to a bright blue Italian sky
out of my window so life seemed more bearable. We all
took the steamer trip around Lake Lugano. This was
much the most picturesque and foreign thing we had seen
and I was frenzied by all the wonderful views to paint.
It was like a scene from *Cavalleria Rusticana,* the shady
cafes full of Italian peasants all talking excitedly, the
lovely villages, the houses of delicate pastel shades, brilliant flowers on white walls, and dark straight Cypress
trees accenting the scene everywhere. Rich green vineyards covered the steep hills behind the village and in the
background always the blue mountainsides. On the hill-
tops were the monasteries and wherever we stopped their
bells seemed to be always ringing.

Da Vinci's "Last Supper" was the high spot of our visit
to Milan, and the Titians in Venice. But Venice itself was
the most wonderful:

We hated to leave and took in every bit of beauty that
we could on our long slow gondola ride to the station.
As they glided in their stealthy way around the corner
of one narrow street a handsome young Italian, quite
naked, dove off one of the little stone bridges with a

tremendous splash and kicked and yelled and puffed around right next to us in the very questionable looking water. Our gondoliers were furious with him for splashing us and a lively conversation ensued echoing loudly between the stone buildings. Probably it was as well that we did not understand it!

Returning to Geneva, we caught up with the American papers and I noted:

> Politics and trouble. The Democrats have nominated a man named Bryan and the stock market has gone away down as he is a silver man. The Republicans have put up McKinley, who is not much either.

The next exciting spot was Chamonix, and from there we set off on mule-back early one morning to climb the Montagne Vert and see the Mer de Glace (possibly even walk on it).

Until I got used to the motion of the mule I thought I should be seasick, but it got better the steeper it became and at last it was so steep and rough that we had no time to think of other discomforts. At the halfway house we dismounted to rest, as we were about dead, and met a young man named Brookfield who had been at Geneva and Lucerne with us, and he joined our party, walking with Papa who had declined to ride. It had begun to rain and soon was pouring so we got soaking wet and my stirrup foot was awfully cramped. The wind blew and sighed among the pines and we slithered and scrambled around precipitous corners and up precipitous paths. After two hours of it, we arrived at the top and hobbled into the hotel. The hotel sitting-room was very crude and full of drenched foreigners eating and talking. There was only one fireplace, which had a crowd around it, and no place to dry our things. We tried to get something to eat and Mr. Brookfield was a help. One girl had fallen off her mule. We had seen her right on the edge of a precipice.

When we started again, it was *snowing* and our saddles had a half-inch of wet snow on them in which we had to sit. My black silk dress looked like crackly tarpaulin and my low shoes, which were very thin, looked like rubbers. My hair hung in wet locks over my face, my golf-cape hood was dripping, and the driving snow seemed to cut my face and went into my mouth and down my neck. The path was so wet and slippery and so badly washed in places that it was a marvel the mules could stand on their feet at all. As it was, mine seemed to sit down and slide most of the way, which was difficult for him too on account of the loose boulders and the holes and slippery rocks in the path but finally we arrived at the hotel. Everybody laughed at us as we went through the town. I could hardly walk I was so cramped and one knee felt very queer. I recovered by evening but it felt like a hundred needles to sit down. Papa went right to bed as he had a cold and had had no overcoat. I forgot to say that we had gone up 3000 feet and had caught a glimpse of the Mer de Glace but what I saw made me wonder why anyone would go through so much to see it.

Next day we set out to drive across the Tête Noir Pass to Martigny, a drive made unnecessarily exciting by the fact that one of our coachmen was drunk, and the road was narrow and winding and ran all the way along the edge of a precipice, sometimes so deep you could hardly see the bottom.

As we came down into France we passed occasional chalets but the people seemed wretchedly poor. We passed a little ten-year-old girl carrying a big fat baby and driving six cows— a crazy-looking old man dressed in nothing but rags—and many old women, like witches, carrying loads of grass or wood on their backs. It was picturesque but horrible.

When near the bottom of the mountain the coachmen cracked their whips and we went tearing around hairpin curves, swaying perilously from side to side into Martigny. We clattered through the narrow streets by dirty cave-like homes, almost running over babies, meeting shrunken, drunken men and women staggering home, many with fearful goiters. Our coachmen shouted and cracked their whips and the drunken one began to kick the horses who shied into a mule coming toward us, the mule's driver got mad, our driver laughed, and then we all laughed hysterically and thus we arrived at the hotel as all the liveried porters rushed out to meet us.

At last we reached Paris, where we started right in shopping at Revillons and the Bon Marché, and met old friends at every turn. When Papa preached in the American Church, it was filled with people we knew, Mr. McKim the architect, Shaws, Hunnewells, Greers, Grays, Zabriskies, etc.

The Saltonstalls took us to *Faust* at the Opéra. We had the centre box and the Opera House was gorgeous and very full. There was a most elaborate ballet which I did not care for at all—neither did Papa. I had never seen a first-class French ballet and it seemed so idiotic that I was quite embarrassed. There was one huge woman who merely waved her arms and kissed her hands to us and tried on necklaces and looked at herself in hand mirrors. Hundreds of fluffy and leggy ballerinas were on the stage and it lasted a long time, but I was not edified.

We returned on the S.S. *Umbria*, the same ship we had come over on, with our friends the Howlands, and a number of Yale boys, but, I sadly noted, "not the right ones."

CHAPTER 9

HOLIDAY TIMES

❧

Bᴀʀ ʜᴀʀʙᴏʀ which had been such a paradise when we were children, went right on being idyllic as we grew up. There was riding and tennis and golf—dancing and balls and all kinds of parties. I was nineteen when I wrote:

> It is a clear cool night. I have been leaning out of my window way above the tops of the still pines and birches, so I have a bird's eye view of it all. A merry dance tune comes floating up from the Malvern Hotel way below, which seems to intensify the dignity and silence of the mountains and the stillness of the sea. A great full moon floats over graceful Newport Mountain casting a silvery light over the gorge and the sea and making the nearby trees blacker by contrast. Bar Harbor is the most heavenly beautiful place on earth.

We kept a number of horses, for riding, and to pull the big buckboard. The summer of 1894, I had a new horse named Phantom. He was brown and looked very smart with my little yellow buckboard, and I admired the way he held his head. He sometimes got his tail over the reins and then tried to run but that was his only fault.

Often the horses were busy or resting and then we would get about on bicycles. I remember the day when Papa and I decided to take a bicycle lesson from a little boy in Amory Lane:

> After one or two futile attempts to get a start, the boy let go of me and by going very fast I managed to go quite straight all by myself. Then I heard Papa hallooing behind me. I knew he couldn't turn out so I went faster and faster until I came a frightful cropper tearing my skirt and churning my ankles up in the pedals.

Papa never really took to the machine, but I used to go all about on mine, and often rode the three miles to Hull's Cove to see the Dave Morrises. They were my greatest friends at this time and I stayed with them a lot when our house was full or when the family had gone away. It was a beautiful ride all the way overlooking Frenchman's Bay to the little village of Hull's Cove.

In this same period a new bicycle path was built through the woods under Newport Mountain, where Ruthie and I used to ride. "It was *lovely*," I wrote the first time we explored it, "the path was heavenly smooth with pine needles and the sun just flickering through."

We always looked forward to the arrival of the yacht clubs and the naval squadrons:

> Cousin Frank took us all out on his launch to see the N.Y. Yacht Club come in—such a beautiful sight! Mt. Desert for a background on a perfect summer's day— a fleet of 30 yachts all sails set coming through the wooded islands to anchor up the Bay. The steam yachts were already in, and were all dressed, their rigging outlined with

gay colored flags. As each yacht anchored all its flags went up and there was so much saluting that Ruthie was obliged to keep her fingers in her ears all the time.

Once when the Eastern Yacht Club was in, we went for a sail on Amory Gardner's schooner, *Mayflower,* and it proved to be a very interesting party. On board we met the parents of Winston Churchill.

It was a perfect day for a sail, with a brisk breeze that sent us spinning along with the water swishing up almost over the gunwale. We found quite a party aboard, including Lord and Lady Randolph Churchill who are at the Malvern for the summer. They were both in white flannel from top to toe, with yachting caps. She looked handsome and bright but he was most pathetic. He spoke hardly at all today but tottered around the deck very shakily—Mr. Gardner at his heels looking worried for fear he would fall overboard. He always had protruding eyes and looked rather like a pug dog but now he was really ghastly* He was in this country on a trip hoping to regain his health. One cannot imagine him as being the forceful statesman of a few years ago.

Years after, I read what Lady Randolph Churchill said about this party in her autobiography:

One of our many expeditions was a sail in the *Mayflower,* the yacht which won the International Yacht Race against the *Galatea.* There was a Bishop on board who was described to me as a "bully Bishop" but we thought his appearance somewhat disreputable and did not cultivate him. Mr. C. commonly called the "Greek

* Lord Randolph Churchill died a few months later.

god"—a name which suited him admirably—was also
there. When I told Randolph his nickname he declared
he could have nothing to do with a Greek god but he
did and liked him.

I can see just what happened. She probably asked Grafton
Cushing who Pa was and was shocked at his appearance. Though
always immaculately turned out, Pa never wore clericals except
when on duty and even his clericals were not what English
bishops wore. Also at that time he had a moustache so that his
appearance that day was exactly like the other men of the party
—in white flannel trousers and a dark jacket. I imagine that
even on a yachting party an English bishop would have worn
his apron and short clothes. She probably showed her amazement and disgust to Grafton Cushing and he being an admirer
of Pa's, and a teacher at Groton School where my father was
President of Trustees, said, "But he's a bully Bishop," which is
the way he talked exactly.

Fire was always a threat at Bar Harbor, with the pine
forest covering so much of the island. We had a scare in '95.

July 27. Evening. The firebells rang furiously and we
rushed out to see flames shooting up to the sky right
across the road near the Jesups'! We flew for it. I never
ran so hard, and it was all I could do to keep up with Pa
and not sprain my ankles in my high-heeled slippers. We
were the first to arrive but others came immediately, on
bicycles, in cutunders, and every way. We all stood help-
lessly and watched the beautiful sight. It was in dense
woods, rushing up the trees with a 'shoop' about fifty
feet into the air, like fireworks with a loud crackling
noise. We were sure the Malvern, the Jesups' and the
Catholic Church would go. After what seemed an inter-

minable time there came a great shouting—"Clear the
way—back—back," and up the hill tore a cutunder
dragging a little two-wheeled thing with the hose around
it. Behind it came a crowd of men who rushed into the
front of the fire with it and with the help of a sudden
shower soon put it out.

The island was not so lucky a few years later.

Of course, we used to go visiting in the summers too. One
of the most memorable house parties took place at the Stones'
on Fisher's Island, when I was just out.

One day when everyone was on a long walk except
Jimmy and myself, I dressed Jimmy up as a girl and when
they came home and found us sitting in the parlor I
introduced him as an old friend of mine who had heard
I was there. Mrs. Stone came in first and shook hands
with him in the most gracious manner; so we were pretty
sure our plot would work, and it did. We fooled them all
but the best was Harry, who came last and found us all
out in the piazza. Rodman went to meet him and told
him Molly Lyall was there, and, as he had heard much
about her, he approached and shook hands in his best
society manner.

The last day the weather, which had been perfect,
changed and in the evening a sudden terrific squall came
up. We rushed out to see the fun and immediately
wished we were in again as the wind knocked Carrie
flat, while the rest of us clung to posts and railings of
the piazza and watched the heavy rocking chairs go dancing down the road so fast that Arthur, who holds the
interscholastic record for sprinting, could not catch them.
I never laughed so hard in my life. The sea and wind

and thunder were making such a noise we could not hear each other, though all were yelling with all their might. It began to pour and I found a nearby window which I opened and crawled in, as the dust was choking me. Poor Mrs. Stone was frantically trying to close windows but she couldn't open the doors to the rooms in which the windows were open, on account of the suction of the wind!

The only drawback to a wonderful week was the diphtheria scare. When we heard there had been forty cases and five deaths, it was pretty scarey and I found myself thinking about it most of the time. We found that all our milk, eggs, and butter were coming from a diphtheria house and Mrs. Stone had a panic and told us all to pack and be ready to leave the next morning at 8. Of course, we all had sore throats and thought we had the dread disease. Everyone else who wasn't sick had left the island and an exaggerated account got into the papers and frightened Papa and Mamma almost to death and they telegraphed us to leave at once—but we had just gone.

Bessie Chadwick was a good friend of those days who lived near to us in the Back Bay in winter, and in the autumn of 1895 I went to visit her in Chocorua, New Hampshire.

Bessie met me at the station with her hair flying through the brim of an enormous crownless hat tied under her chin. Both she and Gertrude Parker, who was also there, wore dresses up to their knees and Gertrude had on a pink sun bonnet and her hair in two pigtails. After the station master had controlled himself sufficiently to get me my trunk (he was laughing at the sight), we climbed into a farmer's cart, Bessie and I up front and Gertrude sitting on the floor in back with her legs hanging over. We went off in a succession of leaps and bounds made by the most extraordinary white horse named Diana. After a lovely drive over hill and dale we arrived at the Chadwicks' house on a hill overlooking the lake. The view was beautiful, especially just now because of the brilliant autumn color on the mountain and nearby hills. At sunset it was wonderful to be on the lake surrounded by the vivid color of the trees reflected in the still water.

One day six of us girls drove in the cart with Diana to the County Fair. When we arrived at the town where the Fair was to be held, we met all the farmers' carts and gigs going the other way to the trotting races, so we went too, got a good position on the roadside and hitched our horse. It was a half-mile stretch of country road with mountains at both ends and the lovely foliage all around. The trotting races were amusing but the people were more interesting to watch. They seemed very unsociable and forlorn to me, especially the women who looked thin and worried and stayed on their wagons surrounded by their children. There were a few pretty girls, all awkward in terrible Sunday clothes, lots of country bumpkins, some gay young sparks in sulkies and many old men characters. One was dancing rather shaky hornpipes to the Carroll County Band which in scarlet and gold braid was playing on the Meeting House Square. . . . I thought he might be an old sea captain from the way he danced but when he fell down and dazed himself I decided he was drunk, but the Chadwicks scouted the idea and said it was old Mr. So-and-so just trying to make things more lively. We went into the Town Hall and looked at the prize pigs and poultry, apples, vegetables, and patchwork quilts, which the crowd seemed to find absorbingly interesting. Then Diana took us home in double-quick time.

Carrie Dabney was one of the people I most enjoyed visiting. I wrote:

> It is always exciting at Carrie's. If we play cards she and Freddie (her brother) fight and yell at each other. If we sail we seem always to be in danger of our lives and Carrie screams at me to take in or let out the sheet, steer to right or left, and I feel our lives depend on my instant obedience. If we drive she makes the horses go so fast everyone runs out of our way and the horse finally arrives in a lather, panting so that it shakes the carriage. Charlie Winslow, sitting behind with me, would whisper nervously "If this horse should stumble we'd be gonners!"
>
> Going to drive one day the horse had not been out for two weeks, so when Carrie touched her off with the whip she kicked, broke the dasher, and got her foot caught over the whiffletree. Carrie threw down the reins and jumped out, calling to me to do the same, but I grabbed up the reins and pulled on *one* unfortunately which had the effect of turning the horse into the woods. I caught a glimpse of Carrie lying prone in the road with her eyes shut and then turned to see a low pine bough coming at me and I was sure I was going to be crushed between it and the wagon seat; but just then the wagon tipped entirely over, throwing me into the air and then down on to the dusty road. I felt the reins pulling tight around me as the horse plunged on, and my one idea was to free myself, so I kicked and rolled frantically in the dust. I think I should have been dragged indefinitely if Carrie had not recovered by now and caught the horse. I got up laughing at our sorry plight, but Carrie was leaning against the trembling horse looking green and saying she was killed. The horse was bleeding from three or four cuts she had got in the woods. The cart was lying on its side, the dasher bent

and broken. Debris was all over the road, and Jockey, the dog, was whining plaintively. I ran till I found a farm and two very slow men, who came and helped us, and finally led the horse home sitting on the back of the cart while Carrie drove the farmer's horse. Carrie had a bump as big as a salt cellar on the back of her head and might have fractured her skull except for her stiff sailor hat which was broken to bits. She was black and blue and sore all over. I was none the worse for the trip, but did not enjoy my next drive with her much as this lesson had not improved her driving at all.

Another time at Carrie's, I had an awful head cold, and caught a chill driving. When I excused myself from dinner, the men made me a hot Scotch and Carrie brought me a mustard leaf plaster. She called me "sandless" because I would not drink the nasty stuff or put the mustard plaster on raw, so she left in disgust. So I put the mustard leaf on raw and kept it on all night and nearly burnt a hole in me. The red square on my chest lasted for weeks.

Papa definitely disapproved of one of my escapades with Carrie.

August 10, 1897. Carrie and I went to the Domino Ball at the Kebo Valley Club. We were dressed exactly alike in light blue dominos, enormous blue sun bonnets trimmed with white ostrich feathers, long white gloves, black satin masks, and black silk stocking and slippers. We curtsied hand in hand to the Countess de Langiers Villars and *nobody* knew who we were.

As we entered the ballroom we heard Billy Woodward say, "Here they come," and George Newhall, who is *very* attractive, asked me to dance. He said he knew me im-

mediately from my dancing, but I had never danced with
him before! My next partner was *sure* I was a Philadel-
phian and when I said, "But I have a Boston accent,"
he said, "Oh! that's plainly put on. I've been in Boston,
so I know the real thing!" One man asked how we
thought of our costumes and said they reminded him of
something he had seen in Yucatan, upon which we said
we had thought his face was familiar and we must have
seen him there. He said, "But there were six of you
then" and we said, "The rest were married, alas!" to
which he replied that he "couldn't see how two such
charming girls could remain single!"

We were not going to stay for the unmasking at supper,
and we had a wonderful time. We had difficulty getting
away as we had quite a following of men, most of whom
we did not know. Freddy Gebhard, who is pretty tough,
pushed a chair in front of us as we were running down the
piazza. Carrie stooped and with one shove sent it flying
right at him and we heard some one say, "Why they must
be boys," but we got away to my great relief and managed
to elude everybody and get safely home without our
followers knowing where we had gone.

There were all kinds of delightful entertainments in the
nineties. One of these was the Kirmess, an all-day festival.

It was a gorgeous day and everyone said the afternoon
part at Devilstone was very pretty but I did not go as I
was saving up for the evening at Kebo. We peeked through
the stage curtains and, as one girl said, "The Metropolitan
Opera is nothing to our audience." The ballroom and
galleries were jammed and everyone was in evening dress,
of course, and much bejewelled. First there was a Fan
Drill while Mr. Apthorp read Steele's Essay. Then came

the minuet which was lovely. The girls were in marquise dresses with powdered hair, big velvet hats on the sides of their heads, and carried tall gold-headed canes. Then came an eastern dance which was rather awful and *lastly* our Spanish one. We danced onto the stage playing our castanets and tambourines to the music of *Carmen* and then did a sort of Spanish variation of the lancers. May Tolfree did it best. Mrs. Bowler had lent me a huge handsome mantilla and said I looked "une vraie Andaluse." I certainly liked my costume and thought it very becoming. (So after that I wore it to practically every event that was fancy dress.)

Clarence Wadsworth celebrated his twenty-third birthday with a dinner party which was a little too much, even for Bar Harbor.

It was held in a private room at the Louisburg. The whole room—ceiling and walls—had been lined with ferns and flowers—solid. There was an almost lifesize canoe down the middle of the table filled with roses and a large bunch of them was at each lady's plate. There were also orchids scattered all over the table and orchids and lilies of the valley among the flowers on the wall. There were sixteen guests and at least ten waiters and the dinner was delicious but much too long. I sat on C. Wadworth's right though I was the youngest girl there. He took us all to the Kebo dance afterwards in funeral hacks which must have been imported from the mainland.

One of the most memorable Bar Harbor entertainments was given in 1897 for the Village Improvement Society, a tableau called The Old Bachelor's Reverie.

Peter Marié was the old bachelor dreaming of his old girls. Susie Sturgis was *lovely* as the Society Girl in a white satin ball dress. Lucy Draper was a fascinating masquer; Mildred Morris was a picture as a milk maid but her sister Lulu as the Duchess of Devonshire was the most gorgeous thing I ever saw. She wore robins-egg blue mirror velvet lined with old rose satin. Her huge hat was covered with white ostrich feathers and she carried an ermine muff out of which peeped a tiny dog! In her other hand she held a long ebony staff with a diamond on top and on a narrow black velvet ribbon around her neck was a diamond as big as a cherry and she was loaded with diamonds, pearls and turquoises. With her perfect features (likened to Mrs. Langtry) and her lovely complexion she made a dazzling picture and when the curtain parted there was a long-drawn 'Oo-o-h!' followed by much applause.

Lulu Morris was so beautiful that she made a very convincing Duchess of Devonshire, in a costume copied from the Gainsborough painting of Georgiana, the wife of the fifth Duke. She had worn the costume first at a ball in New York given by the Bradley Martins. It was a bad time for people to entertain enormously, and this ball was so expensive it turned the tide of public opinion against the rich. The Bradley Martins had to go and live in England, though Mrs. Bradley Martin protested feebly that she didn't see but what it had been a very good thing to do, it gave so much work to people—the caterers and the jewelers and the dressmakers.

The canoe parade was unusually good that year too.

The most picturesque canoe was Loring's—the son of Big Thunder whose portrait I once did in charcoal. He

stood and paddled with what looked like a whole feather
duster on his head, a tunic glittering in the sunlight as it
was embroidered with colored glass, mocassins and a cape of
blue chamois flying out behind. He had, alas, a dead
deer in his canoe. When the parade was over there were
quadrilles and lancers on the lawn.

The horse shows were always beautiful occasions, and one
year I came near to taking part:

Dr. Stokes has asked and *asked* me to drive his beautiful
pair in the horse show but Papa doesn't want me to and
I am not too keen about it myself. So this afternoon I was
at the Show and he came up again and said he would not
enter it unless I drove it. He was evidently crazy to enter
it and it was much the most beautiful rig there so I
thought it should be entered. The big black horse stood
like a statue, his neck curved—self conscious from ear to
tail seeming to know that he was beautiful to look at. He
wore navy blue rosettes at his ears and the smart new
runabout had blue lines on it and the groom was in blue
and white livery and everything shone and glistened, horse,
harness, cart and groom's hat, and Dr. Stokes stood and
looked at it gloomily. There were ladies riding in the present class, among them Olivia Thorndike looking very trim,
and the idea occurred to me to ask her to drive it. It
worked beautifully. She was glad to do it, did it well, and
got the red. They should have had the blue, but Dr. Stokes
was satisfied.

After this packs of hounds were shown and it was very
pretty to see them come tearing out of the woods, the red
coats of the huntsmen twinkling in and out among the trees,
horns blowing, dogs baying. They tore across Robin Hood

Park, the scene of the Horse Show, a flat field under the mountains surrounded by a race track, all taking the jumps as they went.

The last event was the Coaching Class. Four coaches led by Col. Morrell, after being inspected carefully by the judges, went around the race track on the gallop. After the others had stopped, Col. Morrell whipped up his team and continued in a cloud of dust, the groom playing his horn steadily and another groom on a fifth horse galloping after at top speed. As he dashed by us, Col. Morrell stood up and with one sweep of his arm threw a lot of little white cards at the grandstand. These said that this coach would make a round trip each day of the 1903 season stopping at Seal Harbor and North East. It really was a picturesque event and the Colonel is so handsome and dashing he could carry it off. Taken altogether, the beautiful scenery, gay crowd, handsome horses, carriages, women and clothes and dashing Colonel in his grey topper, it was lively and quite unique.

There was a beautiful golf links at Bar Harbor, at the Kebo Valley Club, under the range of mountains with a brook running through. Golf was so much the fashion for a few years, it even took the place of tennis. I had learned to play at the Essex Country Club when staying with Nellie Sargent in Manchester. They had Jimmy Mackrel from Scotland, one of the first professionals over here, and I took lessons with Nellie and her brother. At Bar Harbor I may have been considered a golfer but I wouldn't have been at Manchester. Going up to Stockbridge, with Tradja Davis and her family, I enjoyed the links there which reminded me of Bar Harbor—mountains all around and a swiftly flowing river with willows hanging over it, their branches almost meeting at some places. It was a difficult course, having so much water hazard, and the first day I drove

into eleven pools and lost seven balls. At the end of the week I
wrote:

> Our last golf match. Mr. Davis and I came out even—
> four balls up. My caddie, whom Mr. Davis calls 'the
> Admiral' as his name is Dewey, was as pleased and excited
> as either of us. He is at least six-foot-two and has a nice
> broad grin. Mr. Davis says he always takes my side and
> wants me to beat. When my ball goes into "casual water"
> he walks right in after it in his shoes, and when it rushes
> off down the swift current, he gives me another.

Tennis was my best sport, however. Many of our friends had
courts, and then there was the Pool, where the big matches were
held at the turn of the century. Of course, we wore a long-
skirted tennis costume, but it was really perfectly comfortable
and not such a handicap as people think, because it was full.
I remember one day when my partner and I were beaten quite
badly:

> We were told we *looked* well on the court, however.
> Dyer is slender and graceful and let us hope I am too! We
> were both all in white with silk shirts and high lace stocks.
> I had on a floppy white chiffon hat which partly accounted
> for my *bad* playing.

Generally I played well enough to hold my own in mixed
doubles, and my cousin Hasket Derby and I were one year
champions of the State of Maine. Many were the matches at
the Fabbris' and the Morrises'—they all had their tournaments.
I had a lot of cups which were burnt up in the big fire of 1939
when the house went.
Being tall I played at the net; up to then no girls had tried
it but it was the latest way to play, and Pinchot and my other

partners encouraged it so I was more often asked to make a fourth with men than the other girls. My sister Julie who played a good game always played back court and served underhand, which up to that time was all that was expected of girls. But they had to be steady and quick or they were a handicap instead of a help. Many tournaments were handicapped in this way: best man got worst girl and vice versa. They were not the most popular tournaments.

One year Amos Pinchot and I had a particularly exciting match:

Dyer and I went to Kebo to watch the tournament. Miss Jones was playing and she is what S. Gerard calls "the woman female champion of the U.S." Pinchot thinks we have the tournament pinched but I am not so sure. We played our first match and won 6–2, 6–3.

Next day Pinchot and I played Fanny McLean and Joe Alsop—a strong team—and for a few minutes I was quite scared but we beat them in two sets also. After this match I rushed home, changed my clothes, and drove out to the Pot and Kettle Club to a big luncheon for a yachtful of people from Islesboro. It is six miles out of Bar Harbor but the horse trotted right along and it was quite restful to be alone. The lunch was vastly more tiresome than the tennis and I ought not to have gone—or eaten so much good food. On my way home a thunder shower came up and I managed to take off my best hat with the $20 feather and put it under the seat. Then the sun came out and beat down on my head. I used to think my head was sunproof but after all my headaches this summer I begin to think it must have been a sunstroke I had in England.

At home I changed again to tennis clothes and was ready for the final match at the Club at four. This was, of course, against Miss Jones, the champion, and her partner, who had just cleaned up May Tolfree and Sumner Gerard. Of course we had a large audience and it was quite exciting. I played all right at first and got much applause and grateful commendation from my partner. We got the set 6–3 and started confidently on the second set, but alas! this was different. Miss Jones played better, Pinchot tried experiments, and I began to get rattled and lost my confidence and was too tired to recover again as I sometimes do. Miss Jones's partner, who I think had been scared of us, began to play *brilliantly* so we lost the set 6–3. The next set I felt completely *done*. I was so limp I could hardly move and my racket slipped around in my hand. Pinchot seeing I was used up tried to cover the whole court, which of course he couldn't do and this left me only the things he couldn't get, which naturally were very difficult for me. We had been leading by one game right along to 5 all. The audience was speechless and seemed to me to be breathless. To my great joy I redeemed myself at this critical juncture by getting a love game on my serve. I guess I surprised them as well as myself by sending a hard first ball into the far corner of each court and not one came back and in. Everybody clapped. But they got the next one, making 6 all, and thank goodness Pinchot lost that one and finally they won 8–6.

I was so sorry for Pinchot as he hates to be beaten and had thought we would win and it really was all my fault. He was *very* nice about it to me but he was furious with the linesman on Miss Jones's side who made three decisions against us, one of them in contradiction of the linesman on the other side, Dr. Stokes, and even in contradiction to the Umpire, Frank Sears! Miss Jones and her partner were good sports and everything would have been fine except for this one man who infuriated Pinchot to such a degree that the names he called him in an undertone which only I

could hear almost gave me hysterics. Of course, it is easier
to be nice when you have won and Miss Jones and partner
were very nice but Pinchot and I seemed to be very popular
too apparently. It was hard to hear from Frank Sears that
we made more points than they did and we only lost one
more game and he said one game was unjustly decided.
They each got a large silver cup and Pinchot and I small
pewter mugs, but it *was* fun all the same.

One summer, the Boston Symphony Orchestra (so called but
really only twenty of the lesser lights of it) played on the Club
House piazza and everyone used to go and sit there. I wrote: "It
is quite inspiring to play tennis to the Symphony Orchestra and
before such a large gallery of spectators. They played wonderful waltzes and Dyer and I could hardly refrain from dancing
over the court. I wrote Aunt Sue that people played tennis,
bathed and gossiped to the music of the Symphony. She will
think it sacrilegious."

The gay festivities that centered on the Kebo Valley Club
came to an end when 1899 brought us another fire.

July 1, 1899. Took a drive with Pa around the new road
and the Club. The golf links is much longer this year and
looked so pretty and well kept and the Club House so gay
and prosperous that in the evening, when I was reading
of all the entertainments scheduled there for the summer
and Reece came running into the parlor saying, "The
Kebo Valley Club is on fire!" it was a great shock to me.
We all rushed out intending to go to it but we were horrified to see burning cinders blowing towards us like a
shower of fire and lighting on the house and trees, so we
decided we had better stay and try to protect our own place.
It was most alarming on a dark night with a swishing,

howling 'souther.' It seemed like a dream I had had before as I heard the bell of the little hand hose cart ding dong and the men shouting as they pulled it up the hill. Then Julie and I were up in the third story handing pails of water up to Pa who was on the roof. Then Reece came running in again and said it was no use trying to save the house as the fire was coming through the woods as fast as he could run and he was going to take the horses out of the stable and down to the town somewhere. So Pa called out, "Everybody leave at once. Be sure not to come upstairs again and don't try to take anything except perhaps jewelry."

I rushed to my room and oh! there were so many things I wanted, but I grabbed only the two little boxes containing my diamond star and consecration pin and ran downstairs. Julie had already gone, with her best hat on, carrying Elsie, who had nothing on but a pair of drawers, which she dropped on the way. Elsie was fine. She was worried about her drawers and about Katy but she didn't cry at all. Let me hasten to say she was wrapped in a shawl and had her best hat on.

Ma and Ruth came running next, both quite hysterical; then Appie perfectly calm; then I carrying a wooden box of Walker-Gordon milk for the baby, which was so heavy I stopped at the bottom of the hill and sat on it to watch the excitement.

Lengths and lengths of hose pulled by cutunders and shouting men went incessantly by, amidst hurrying crowds going up to see the fun or to help. Going the other way were the few fugitives—Reece having a terrible time leading two prancing horses, terrified of the rain of sparks, on either side of him. A cutunder came down and in it Mrs. Powell half dressed and wholly worried. Across her lap was a clothes basket piled high with clothes and under them was the baby, who slept right through the whole excitement. I put the milk in the cutunder and jumped onto the step and the whole family arrived almost together at the Parker Cottage.

Grandma met us very much worried and excited. Mamma was just like the Vicar of Wakefield and kept saying in tragic tones, "Here we are—escaped with our lives but all our children gathered together here. Our beautiful home gone . . ." The sparks were flying even here and Capt. Parker was on the roof wetting it down. We heard later it had been on fire several times. All the old ladies were packing up and taking things out on the piazza. It looked at first as if the whole town might go. Big cinders were falling into the bay, but fortunately the wind began to die down and slowly but surely the flames did the same. I was wandering about the crowded streets wondering how all the firemen and apparatus had got there so soon from other parts of the island, and when the smoke and flames had cleared somewhat I suddenly saw the roof and chimneys of our house intact! I went to the Parker Cottage with this welcome news and we all moved back again. Papa, when we left, had paid three men who had come up, to keep wetting the roof as long as they could and they had done a good job and were still there.

When I got back to my beloved sky parlor with a most thankful heart I found one jewel box I had carried was empty—my consecration pin was gone! Early in the morning I telephoned Grandma to ask if she could see it anywhere around Parker Cottage and she found it underneath the plank walk. What luck!

Sunday. Lovely day. To Church. There were prayers about the narrow escape from fire. P.M. Walked up to Kebo. It was a sad scene of desolation with the poor headwaiter among the ruins, almost weeping, having lost his job and all his personal belongings, and "It promised to be such a paying year," he said. I was terribly sorry for him and could and did sympathize. What will Bar Harbor be without Kebo? No balls, no golf, no tennis, no bands, no races, no long rests on the pleasant piazza sipping cooling drinks. In short, no Kebo!

But in fact, things were almost gayer in the following years, if that were possible. September of 1900 when the British fleet was in was one of the gayest times:

Sept. 5, 1900. The town is so lively, especially near the wharves where boat loads of sailors and officers are continually embarking and disembarking. The streets are full of them too—the English walking six or eight abreast in the middle of the street as they do in English country towns. Overhead the red ensign and the stars and stripes float amicably next each other while smart little Union Jacks hang from many of the shops and houses and the air is full of music, bands, bugles and bells. Dark blue bronzed American sailors and red-jacketed Tommies swinging their little canes are in groups everywhere. The English look very young and pink cheeked and always natty.

I got home just in time to dress for Mr. Curley's big dinner of 30 at the Malvern. The Chief Engineer of the *Indefatigable* took me in to dinner. He was an older man and very big and I thought very attractive. On my other side was a jolly little Englishman named Horne—Champion lightweight boxer in England, and Lieutenant of Marines—in scarlet jacket. After speeches and drinking of health to the Queen and President, buckboards were waiting to take us to the ball at Kebo. Here we found ourselves in Fairyland as a special ballroom had been built on one

of the tennis courts and it looked like an Arcadian forest.
It was so enormous that it wasn't at all crowded and two
Navy bands, one American and one British, took turns so
we had music steadily for dancing. The Clubhouse and
piazza were beautifully decorated with flags where couples
were sitting out or promenading.

Mr. Wright started me off in a jolly lancers set and from
then on I had a *fine time*. The Englishmen put such a lot
of "go" into everything. They flew around with their long
slim legs and were really very graceful and seemed perfectly unselfconscious about it so that the Americans were
thrown rather into the shade with their soberer uniforms
and quieter ways. The English lancers were quite wild.
They are aptly named the "Kitchen Lancers." They sang
and stamped and flung their partners around and showed
off their "figgers" to great advantage. One Royal Artillery
man with a scarlet jacket was all over the place and the
Admiral's Aide, Lieut. Stratfield, in his skin-tight black
uniform with his short jacket covered with gold braid hanging in loops from his broad shoulders and a gold stripe
down his long slim trouser legs, was fascinating to watch.
They are so different from us in their way of talking too.
I got home at 1:30 A.M. after a very amusing evening.

Sept. 6. Helen Mahan and Lieut. Aylmer of the *Indefatigable* came to lunch. *P.M.* The Kennedys gave a
reception for the officers. They have a huge house and
place on the shore with beautiful formal gardens, and it
was a pretty sight today, the lawns all dotted over with gay
uniforms and light summer dresses and parasols. Gigs and
launches were continually going to and fro between the
party and the distant warships in the harbor. The heavy
English barges look so funny with their barefooted sailors
in large round straw hats, with broad elastic bands under

their chins. Both Navies' bands were on the lawn playing
in turn, and the Scotch piper off one of the ships strutted
up and down in full Highland regalia playing the pipes.
I met lots more officers and had a beautiful time.

That evening was the deGrasse Fox ball at the Malvern.
I had hardly got inside when two of my *Indefatigable*
friends rushed up and took five dances on my dance card,
and in ten minutes it was full up. I danced the first English
lancers with Lieut. Howard—tall, blond, pink cheeked
and very active. Such a romp as that lancers was. Sylvia led
it and all the American young men and the dowagers
looked on in obvious disapproval. I danced opposite the
Admiral's aide but when it was through my skirt was torn
to shreds and my hair almost down. At suppertime Lieut.
Berkler arrived and asked me for a dance so I divided all
my dances after that into fractions, until 2 A.M. when I
regretfully left as I thought the family might be worrying.

Sept. 11. Pelting, but we need rain very badly. Julie
and I went out to lunch on the *Indefatigable* in *open* boats,
very sloppy and not attractive, sailors in bare feet. The
Captain (Campbell) is extremely good looking and attractive as are many of the officers. After eight courses came
three desserts and they made us taste them all. Then we
seemed to begin all over again with egg salad and after a
few more courses we worked up to ice cream again! Duncan McCrea walked around and around the tables playing
the pipes steadily so that with the deafening noise, all the
food and the cold and the wet, it was rather a wearing occasion. Nothing would stop Duncan. We tried clapping and
gesticulating and finally one of the officers reached up and
got a pistol and pointed it at him.

That evening I went to the much heralded Domino Ball
at the Pierrepont Edwards' in Hull's Cove. I went with

Ethel Train who is about my height in yellow dominos and was much disappointed that Reggie Johnson knew me at once, but I puzzled many others, and I had a fine time with Capt. Campbell, who insisted that I had not been on his ship that day. Walter Damrosch was looking for Mrs. D. and said, "Are you my wife," to which I replied "No" rather abruptly and he said, "Oh! Don't you wish you were?"

There was another side to it, of course. In 1903, I wrote:

There are disadvantages in having Bar Harbor a Naval Base as it brings saloons and an undesirable element to town with which the town is really not prepared to deal. It is unpleasant to walk along the shore unless escorted by a man and many excursionists come to see the ships, all of which is undesirable in the extreme. The Y.M.C.A. put up a big tent on the Village Green but there was nothing for the sailors to do there except read magazines and 'write to mother' so it was little used though it was really the only *decent* place for the sailors to go and there were 10,000 sailors in the harbor. So, by dint of much persuasion and an enormous fee I got the music store to put a piano in the tent on a small platform and this was a wild success. It was an old "tin-panny" instrument but it was played on and danced to all day long and in the evenings the tent was jammed with an appreciative audience.

July 19, 1905. Papa had a most interesting afternoon. Mr. Peary* and his wife arrived by train to meet their ship —the *Roosevelt*—here and say goodbye to Mr. Jesup—our good neighbor who has been financing this trip to the Pole. Mr. Jesup took Papa over to the ferry on his yacht and met the train and brought the Pearys to Bar Harbor.

* Commodore Robert Peary—discoverer of the North Pole. [Ed.]

Meanwhile we, from our piazza, had been watching the strangest looking boat which had entered the harbor. It was large, ugly and strong looking—black with a white stripe around it. It had three masts and the middle one had a cross-piece. Mr. Jesup had not said a word about the Pearys coming here, so we all of us wondered what this extraordinary looking ship might be. Papa got back late in afternoon, full of his interesting experience. They had taken the Pearys to the *Roosevelt* and gone all over her. One item in their cargo which might seem unnecessary considering their economy of space, was 160 pounds of candy, but they will use it to cheer the crew at Xmas, and also to trade with the Eskimos who love it. As soon as they had finished coaling up, the *Roosevelt* sailed out of the harbor again for Cape Breton there to drop Mrs. Peary and take on more crew. Then on to the North Pole. They expect to reach the place where they leave the ship and take to sledges about next March—what pluck and fortitude that man has! So the *Roosevelt* and Peary were in Bar Harbor for an afternoon and nobody else knew about it!

CHAPTER 10

A MORE SERIOUS TURN

ৰ্৳

W HEN WE GOT BACK from Europe I was as busy as ever, but though the parties are fun to tell about, they didn't take up as much of my time as more useful things.

Spring, 1896. As I belong to the Hampton College Committee I was appointed one of a committee of three to run the exhibit. We got an empty shop on Boylston Street and fixed it up and then the things all came from Hampton Institute in the charge of a *very* attractive young man named Schofield, and he and I arranged them. Papa opened it on a *pelting* afternoon to a scattered few in Arlington Street Church. This was rather different from N.Y. where Chauncey Depew opened it in Madison Square Garden. After the opening everyone adjourned to the exhibit, where I was to receive. We had bad luck with the weather and probably not enough publicity, but more and more people came each day. On the last day, alas, our contribution box—by that time quite full and heavy—was stolen.

The next year I took on a particularly difficult job, going to the Children's Hospital to cheer up the little patients. I was more apt to depress myself.

Feb. 19, 1897. My afternoon at the Children's Hospital.
I am getting used to it. The first time I went I turned right
around and left, telling the nurse I had only come to find
out what was wanted of me. The poor suffering little tots,
one of whom was bandaged all over for burns, were more
than I could stand.

I wanted to be of use, but I found I had better do other
things that were helpful. The next year I noted:

I have seven charities going and should raise $7,000 for
the Deaconess Training School. Then Christmas is coming, and also Concours. The Vincent Fair took a lot of
time. Carrie and I had the lampshade table—again it did
well in spite of a blizzard. I pass every other Friday afternoon at the Students Clubroom at Emmanuel Church.

A few years later I was helping with the Infant's Hospital
Fair, which had its unexpected side:

With the aid of some scenery from Keith's they had made
a stable out of one of the rooms, and in it, besides stalls,
harnesses, rakes, pitchforks and other farm implements,
were 8 or 10 hens who insisted on laying eggs all around
and finally we gave up trying to distract their attention and
let them lay as many as they liked and we sold them for
25¢ apiece. Other colored eggs with presents in them were
hidden in the hay and of these we sold 30 dozen. It was
really great fun.

March 4, 1897. While working at Art School I heard
that the subway had blown up and many people were
killed. At lunch Papa told us about it. He was coming
from the Anniversary of the Inauguration of John Adams

and saw a large crowd at the corner of Tremont and Boylston Streets. The explosion had made a terrific noise like roaring cannon, and rocks and beams had flown way up in the air higher than the high buildings. The car that was passing over the spot flew up in the air and then down through the hole. This was a Mt. Auburn car but the one behind it was the little Back Bay one and that was wrecked and the old conductor, who used to take me to school every day from Aunt Sue's, was killed. The new Touraine Hotel was badly shaken and every window blown out. A jewelry store nearby lost a fortune as all the jewels were blown out the window and scattered on the street to be picked up by the gathering crowd. Fire engines and ambulances were on the scene in three minutes and all the city police. Nine people were killed and 70 injured. No one knew whether their families were there or not and crowds of anxious people added to the confusion. George Wells was frantically looking for his mother and found her in a hospital quite badly hurt, and Freddy Whitwell, looking for Gertrude, happened to find old Mrs. Bigelow, Carrie's grandmother, very badly injured.

May 30, 1897. Boston is all excitement over the Shaw Statue* and the 7th Regiment, who were all over town, walking five abreast down the Mall and driving, riding and biking in the Park.

May 31. Drove in town early to see the procession. The Governor rode through the lines and after him came Battery A on the dead run. Then Jake Peabody and Charlie Dabney on horseback. Others less fortunate were riding on the back of the heavy artillery wagons, clinging on for dear life and looking as if they were being shaken to a jelly. The

* This was the dedication of St. Gauden's famous monument to Robert Gould Shaw, Colonel of a Negro regiment of the Civil War. [Ed.]

N.Y. Seventh marched wonderfully and had a splendiferous band. Lorimer Worden towered above the crowd. The Veterans of the old 54th (Shaw's Regiment) came in for great applause, especially when the torn but still bright colors went by held up by a lame old Negro. The aides were very swell. Bob Walcott was one and looked extremely well on horseback. Papa went to the Music Hall and said it was a fine meeting. Booker Washington made the best speech.

June 1. Amos came in his swell turnout and drove me out to Aunt Minnie's reception for St. Gaudens who of course is being much feted. The Governor and staff were there and many officers from the warships, several of whom were introduced to me.

Fall 1897. I have decided to stop writing a diary. I think it makes me self-centred, wastes time, ruins my handwriting and does not help my composition. Since I have written one so far, however, I will not destroy it, and it will amuse me later on to read my rather one-sided and often ridiculous account of the ten years of my girlhood.

Not much later:

I meant to leave off my Diary but find it harder to do so than I thought. This fall I made visits at the Crowninshields' in Marblehead and at Chocorua, Waltham, Prides, Groton and the Hunnewells in Wellesley. I had my last two wisdom teeth out and cleared the decks in order to be in good shape for Art School as I am going to be in the Life Class.

During October the Lord Bishop of Rochester and his wife, the Hon. Mrs. Talbot visited us in Cambridge. We were expecting Canon Gore too but he was too ill to come.

The reporters got an idea that Anthony Hope was coming too and kept bothering us about that. The Talbots were most charming guests interested in everything and very appreciative. She is a niece of Gladstone and sister of Lady Frederick Cavendish. They were daughters of Lord Lyttleton and very attractive. She has very bright black eyes, and was brisk and energetic with a delightful English voice and pleasant smile. The Bishop was the plainest and most ungainly man I ever saw, six-feet-four and thin as a beanpole with bushy red beard and spectacles. He has one perfectly stiff leg and his moving around approaches the ridiculous as he hops along at a tremendous rate in his leggings and apron, his coat-tails flying.

In February 1898 we had the news of the *Maine** and in April the Spanish-American War came. I wrote:

April 19, war declared! Depressing and shameful the way it has been managed. It makes me very sad when I think of the *Maine* and our friends aboard it and of last summer when they were all at Bar Harbor. Now many of them are dead and the ship is gone.

Later we were enjoying the beautiful spring in Cambridge when I wrote:

Now it is a still, warm night in May. The air smells sweet with apple blossoms and the trees are still feathery. Some Winthrop Hallers are singing on their steps. Many windows are brightly lit, but enough are dark to remind us of the war. Sumner Gerard has gone, without his

* The U.S. battleship *Maine*, lying off Havana, was destroyed by two explosions. American jingoes blamed the sinking on the Spanish and this was one of the chief causes of the ensuing war, when the slogan "Remember the *Maine*" became battle cry. [Ed.]

family's consent, to join Teddy Roosevelt's "Rough Riders." Frank Crowninshield was among the first to enlist and he says that eighty men tried to join the battery in two days. Hundreds of Harvard students are drilling and the other evening we heard a "Tramp, tramp" and "Halt!" on our avenue and found a company of law students drilling under Mr. Delafield.

My sentiments about the war are first, that it is a great pity there has to be a war, and second, that it was brought on mainly for selfish reasons by crazy or wicked senators and congressmen and by vile newspapers, principally by Hearst's "Journal", which has attained an unheard of notoriety, even for a nasty paper. I think nothing is bad enough for whoever blew up the *Maine* but no one knows who did it. The Queen of Spain has behaved very handsomely about it and the U.S. Government has put that question aside, but still the war cry is, "Remember the *Maine*." I am sorry for the Queen and the young boy King and his people, and sympathise more with my enemies than with my patriotic countrymen, though I do not go as far as some, who hope Spain will win. It seems absurd to go to war "for human-ity's sake," which is the accepted cause, and then start off by killing three hundred brave sailors and wounding six hundred more. It is like giving a bull fight for the S.P.C.A., as I hear they do in Spain.

Everyone has nothing bad enough to say about Cabot Lodge. Papa was making a speech the other day in which he praised several people who had stood to their guns and tried to avert war, among them Secretary Long. He purposely omitted Cabot Lodge's name, but the paper quoted him wrong and he received a most grateful letter from Mr. Lodge, thanking him for his words of commenda-tion, so he had to write and tell him that he hadn't men-tioned his name, as he did not understand his position.

From the Art Museum steps we have seen every regiment that has gone off. When the first went off, we were out in front. Copley Square was packed. All the Tech. boys were on their steps* and gave some rousing cheers. Some of our girls wanted to cheer, but I discouraged that, as I think if there is anything foolish it is girls cheering. The soldiers looked splendid in their service uniforms, gaiters and sombreros, and the band was playing the latest Sousa march. To think that people should go to a real war with a Sousa march!

I suppose our friends on the ships are glad to go. The young officers last summer were crazy for it. Often I think of the *New York* and the *Maine* and the others lying in the sparkling waters of Frenchman's Bay with the blue hills around and little launches darting in and out of the Porcupine Islands and laughing sailors with nothing to do but applaud a boat race; all a scene of gaiety, beauty, prosperity and peace. In contrast to this, we hear that the ships are painted black and that a battle is imminent between Admiral Sampson's squadron and the Spanish fleet. My friends, Mustin, Castleman and Charlie Poor are all on his flagship. Julie's partner on the Monty Sears's picnic was killed the other day at Cienfuegos. Young Walter Gherardi is in charge of a torpedo boat.

Last Monday Katharine and I saw Frank [Crowninshield] off with the battery riding postillion before a cannon. Jake Peabody led the battery and Sam Parker, C. Cummings and many others were either riding or jolting along on a cannon. They looked very pleased and their uniforms were most becoming—gray-blue coats with big capes turned back, showing a bright red lining. They marched to Swampscott, where they drill on the beach, but Frank left them the next day to join "Teddy's Terrors," which

* The Massachusetts Institute of Technology was then on Copley Square.

is the popular regiment, though it is rather ridiculed by
Life as being "stagey." Garrison, my Yale steamer friend,
has joined it, and Dave Goodrich, Lorimer Worden and
other adventurous youths. Lt. Hobson's splendid act* is
much talked of and praised. First congratulations came
from the Spanish Admiral, Cervera! The papers said
every man in Sampson's squadron volunteered, which, if
true, is very fine and makes me think better of this war.

June, 1898. Teddy's Terrors have now gone from Cuba
to Tampa. Katharine says Frank writes most pathetic letters about their sufferings. They haven't had a bath for
two months and are allowed no brush or comb—simply a
sponge which is no good as there is no water — only one
faucet for 1000 men. On the way to Tampa Frank was
sick. The car was so crowded that only a few could lie
down on the floor, others sat in a cramped position. The
thermometer was 108 and no air filtered in from outside.
They have two meals a day and he writes he would "rather
have the pickings from the swill pail." The regulars are
much better cared for he says. General Miles has already
censured three Generals. In Cuba at first it wasn't so bad.
He was learning to ride and training his horse at the same
time. The horse's name is "Sweet Evening Breeze" and he
says it would be a good horse if it had a little sense. He
himself spent his first 24 hours with the regiment in the
guard house for impertinence, which much amused his
family and friends. June 25th was our first battle in Cuba.
We won but lost 13 men, among them Hamilton Fish, Jr.
I fear this is only the beginning.

* Naval Constructor Richmond Pearson Hobson, with seven men under his
command, on the early morning of June 3, 1898, took the naval collier, *Merrimack*,
into the mouth of Santiago harbor and under intense fire from the Spanish forts,
sank his ship in the channel to bottle up the Spanish in the harbor. All the
Americans survived. [Ed.]

We were in Bar Harbor when the news came that Admiral Cervera's fleet was destroyed and our troops were in Santiago. What a July 4th that made—"Papa and Appleton have been firing crackers and hurrahing all day."

By fall, we were begininng to learn the price. I lunched with the Crowninshields in Marblehead. "Frank looked sick and seemed feeble. His beard changes him. He had measles, sunstroke and yellow fever, and was also lost for some time."

Frank recovered, but my good friend Ward Cheney died in the Philippines the following spring. When I heard the news of his death I couldn't believe it. Later I wrote:

> I have done a life-size charcoal drawing of Ward Cheney and it is so like him it gives me both pain and pleasure to look at it. Stokes says if he had died in Cuba instead of the far-off Philippines he would have been famous. He had about a dozen men against a hundred Philippines and routed them but died afterwards of his wounds.

On October 28th, we were on Beacon Hill when the 6th Regiment came home. "Butler Ames, now Lieutenant-Colonel, was leading them on horseback and looked beaming. Even the Somerset Club men came out to cheer and the crowd was enthusiastic. The soldiers looked thin and rather scrubby, but straight and tanned and seemingly so happy. Several of them had little green parakeets on their khaki shoulders which gave quite a touch of foreign lands."

One day some of us went to tea on the *Enterprise* with Capt. Eaton whom I had not seen since he ran the *Massachusetts* aground off Mt. Desert on Egg Rock. Old Ironsides was next to us in dry dock and I don't see any use in keeping her unless she looks *something* like her old self, especially as they say that not a plank of the present ship

was in the old one. Her masts are down and she is all
boarded up and roofed over and painted pink! I am
thrilled by her history and all her brave commanders, especially Decatur and am the proud owner of a little snuff box
made of the original English oak from the old ship and
inside is written "To Amos Lawrence from his friend Capt.
Foote."

The next year at Bar Harbor we met one of the most famous
heroes of the war.

Papa preached on the *Massachusetts* and we all went
with him. (I sometimes wish the family was not so big.)
Victor Blue* met us at the gangplank. He is a real hero
of the Spanish War, second only to Hobson, and is to my
mind more attractive looking. The service was on the
quarter deck. Papa was in his robes and was escorted up
from below by the Captain. A sailor played the organ and
we all sang—a hundred sailors and marines were there,
such nice looking boys, and so attentive and interested.

In September, 1899 I went to New York for Dewey Day.

Was lucky to get one seat on a sofa on the 12:03, a very
slow train alas, and an hour late in arriving. The station
was pandemonium while from the noise outside one would
suppose there was an infuriated mob. I was quite scared
as I did not see the Morrises, but finally found them outside the gate, Angela beaming and loving the excitement.
Her "Man of Wrath" looked a bit gloomy. After escorting
us to the carriage, he went back and spent much time and
money trying to get my trunk.

* When the Spanish fleet had taken refuge in Santiago Bay, Victor Blue, then
lieutenant on the U.S.S. *Suwanee,* was twice sent on dangerous missions into
Cuba to spy out the presence and condition of Cervera's ships. [Ed.]

Sept. 29. Breakfasted with Dave in the new breakfast room and then we went to Harlem, where we got into a launch and went up the Hudson to see the floats of Victory and Peace. The streets and cars were crowded everywhere and there were pictures of Dewey in every shop window and wherever one looked. Staging and decorations were going up all around. The river we found very rough and Dave and the engineer tried to advise the launch owner how to steer it, and were a good deal worried I think. I was cowering in a corner in all the wraps I could find but in spite of this I was soaking wet. However, we saw the floats and very *few* did so, as that afternoon, even before the fleet got there, the wind smashed Victory and decapitated her down to the waist. She had been beautiful and reminded me of the statue at the head of the Court of Honor at Chicago. The figure of Peace survived and was also handsome and both stood up splendidly that morning in the river.

The afternoon was spent on our roof watching the Naval Parade. The *Olympia* led the procession of warships, the rest following in a double line in order of their size— then came Government ships and huge steamships. Then the steam yachts led by the *Corsair*. The *Olympia,* with Dewey aboard, stopped at the floats and all the rest filed by and the noise of the saluting guns and the many whistles from tugs and river craft was terrific, combined with the noise from the street and the crowds, it was Bedlam.

Sept. 30. Waked to a sparkling autumn day. The river was a deep blue and the shining white warships were fluttering with gay colored flags all up and down all their lines. Yachts in equal gala dress were all around and in the middle of everything an old black frigate, easily the most picturesque and graceful of them all, stood high, a beauti-

ful and dignified reminder of the past—flags flying from
every mast and up and down her rigging—all this set
against the rocky Palisades. The high cliffs themselves
topped with the bright autumn foliage. Down the middle
of the river came a procession of ferry boats laden down
with soldiers who cheered the ships as they passed and sang
the national anthems as the bands on the ships crashed
them out. These soldiers were going up to the start of the
procession.

Every house along the line had been decorated somehow, and at 7 A.M. all their steps were filled with people,
including our own, alas! Fortunately there was a small
balcony on the second story and we saw it from there. It
was a perfect place as we saw them come around the corner
from the Riverside Drive and then down the whole length
of 72nd Street. After five hours of clapping and cheering
and yelling until we were hoarse and dirty from chewing
dust, I couldn't help thinking how must the soldiers feel
who got up at 4:30 and were still marching at 7 P.M.

After the preliminary police officials came Sousa's Band,
150 strong, making a splendid crash of noise, but before it
had begun to die away it was drowned by cheering and
there was Dewey in a carriage drawn by six white horses
and bowing to right and left (and up to us). Next came
Sampson smiling benignly and Schley waving and kissing
his hand, then General Miles and Chauncey Depew and
boss Croker. Then the sailors of the *Olympia* and the
well-set-up Marines led by the one who drilled them this
summer. They were followed by more sailors, marines
and soldiers—an endless number and *then* the Rough
Riders led by Teddy on horseback and grinning to beat
the band. He got an ovation! The people in the next
house to us threw a giant firecracker which landed right
by his horse and made him jump wildly, entertaining the
crowd immensely. Then came the trim and natty West

Point boys marching so beautifully with their short quick parade step. Hennen Morris called them "little beauties" but they looked very tall and straight to me marching shoulder to shoulder.

The great and awful blot on the day was that the Seventh Regiment who came next (the beautiful soldierly 7th) was hissed all along the route. They marched better than any except the Cadets but oh! they looked so glum! I clapped as hard as I could but nothing drowned the horrible prolonged hisses and I did feel so sorry for them. It was such an unjust punishment for one official mistake.*

The 10th Pennsylvania just back from Manila came in for lots of applause. They were still in their worn uniforms, carrying flags so tattered and blackened there was almost nothing left of them. Troop A was the best looking Cavalry Regiment, in which were Pinchot, S. Gerard, R. Cross, Gus Shepard and Hickox who looked up and grinned at me. None of the procession was dull and the bands were the best I ever heard. When a company of old Confederate veterans went by to the strains of Dixie, old Mrs. Morris nearly fell off the balcony in her excitement. It was amusing to watch the crowds scatter at the end and people picking up the debris. West End Avenue was chock full of hansoms moving slowly towards us as far as we could see like a great wave.

Oct. 2. Fine still but cold. We drove down town in the brougham to see the Triumphal Dewey Arch. There are white and gold columns and hanging banners all up and down Fifth Avenue. A really handsome sight. The Arch is superb but awfully in the way where it is. It took

---

* The Seventh Regiment, a New York State National Guard Unit, had refused to volunteer to enlist in the Federal Army at the opening of the war. Actually, the troops hissed in the parade, through a mistake, were the Seventh United States Artillery, which the crowd mistook for the National Guard unit because of the numeral "7" on their knapsacks. [Ed.]

us a half an hour to drive the two blocks between 22nd
and 24th Streets. Souvenir cranks have picked the base of
the Arch so that there are great yawning black holes in it.
Now every corner of it is guarded by a policeman. The
groups of statuary are very fine.

Oct. 13. Dewey Day in Boston. We all drove in town to
see the fun. You wouldn't know quiet, sedate Boston.
Everything was decorated and the Common was a seething
mass of humanity and a cheering mob was in front of the
Touraine. We went to the Meyers' on Beacon Hill (the
William Appleton house where we always have seen processions from the curved balcony)*. This was so near the
fireworks that the children were frightened to death for
fear the fireworks would fall on them.

Oct. 14. A lovely warm day for the procession. We saw
it twice—once from Aunt Sally's on Arlington Street and
then we rushed across the Public Garden and saw it from
Mitchell the Tailor's right on the corner by the State
House, which was *beautifully* decorated. The people who
have been working so hard to save the Bulfinch front must
have been pleased with themselves, it looked so fine. The
crowd was tremendous and the mounted police had difficulty in keeping them back. A number fainted and had
to be carried off. We saw Gov. Wolcott point out his son
Roger to Dewey as he marched past straighter than anyone.
After the Procession was over we went to the Meyers' and
from there saw the presenting of the torn and tattered
battle flags back to the State. Then the 40 bands on the
Common joined together in "The Star Spangled Banner,"
a grand climax to the day.

* William Appleton, Mrs. Peabody's great-grandfather, built the house at 5
Beacon Street. [Ed.]

CHAPTER 11

THE BOYS' CLUB
ON NORTH BENNET STREET

ক্ষ

In 1898 I wrote:

The charity which I have enjoyed the most this winter has been the North Bennet Street Boys' Club. It is in an awful part of the city and hardly once have I been down there without meeting the patrol wagon, and often see an arrest or a fight. Once, alas, it was a fierce fight among our own boys, started by one of my pets, Dentoni, really the thuggiest looking boy I have ever seen. They were fighting like dogs and looked fierce and white. I was the only woman on the street except a wild-looking creature who poured water on them from an upper window, and as there were some rough-looking men in the crowd I didn't dare go in and try to stop the boys.

We play Crokinole and Parlor Pool and try to keep them happy and quiet. They mustn't get excited, chew gum, spit, swear, cheat or talk Italian. They are mostly perfect dears and so bright and funny. I asked some of them to go to the concert given by the crew of the *Canada*.

When I got in town, Aunt Sue sprang it on me that she had asked two Groton boys to go too. This rather annoyed me, as I didn't think they would mix at all well, and they

didn't. For interest and charm I much preferred the North
End boys.

There were forty or fifty youngsters, mostly Italian and Irish,
and about twelve years old—that is, when I first started with
them. Susan Shaw and I each had a boys' club at the North
Bennet Industrial School, and they were rivals in games and
other things.

A few years later, when their interests had shifted from
games to debating, they turned the club into a debating society.

March 6, 1900. The first night of my new Debating Club
for the North End boys. *Every one* came. First we elected
officers and I am president and Willie Mahoney secretary.
Then we debated the Transvaal question. James and I
were for the English and Willie and Mike for the Boers.
James opened the debate in a very professional manner
and then we all had our say. Nobody could decide who
won and we voted to have the same question next time
when we had all looked it up a little more. They were
much interested in our *London Illustrated News's* which
were down in the Billiard Room where the meeting was
held. They were clever talkers and knew much more about
debating than I did. They told me Miss Lovett [she was
in charge of all the clubs at the school] wanted to call it
the Century Debating Club but they said they would like
to call it the Lawrence Club "after a friend of ours" and
so the Lawrence Club started and went on for many years,
though I fear there was some bribery and corruption in
voting for the name.

The next time I went I discovered there seems to be some
trouble over naming the new Club after me though it was a
unanimous vote. The boys are excited about it but I begged
them to have no unpleasantness. I felt like Dewey when I

came out the door to get into my hack. The sidewalk was crowded—there was a rush to open the carriage door. Willie Mahoney thrust some tickets to the water color show into my hand (I don't know how he got them as they are complimentary) and I drove off to the cheers of the crowd. The Kenny and Clark driver was much amused.

As the boys grew up, we began to have socials, with dancing. I don't know how we managed to have so much fun and still keep from raising the roof, but perhaps it was easier in those days. After one dance I wrote: "It was the biggest dance they ever had there and hard work keeping the tough ones quiet and respectable, making the shy ones dance and be jolly, and making them all keep the rules of the building and yet have a good time. It was a great success and we drove home at 11:30 in a limp condition but happy."

About another dance I wrote:

Jan. 14. Our dance and play at North Bennet Street. Went off well, the audience enthusiastic. Malcolm Donald and I worked hard at it. We had all ages at the dance afterwards, Father and Mother O'Connell and Father and Mother Crowley, with at least six children each, and other families with less numerous progeny. I never saw so many big, jolly, red-round-faced Irishmen and they *did* have such a good time! I asked *everyone* to dance and some agreed "to stand up in a quadrille." This they arranged themselves and went through with much solemnity. Tommy Geary bawled out the figures and everyone whirled about and "turned partners" and chasséed back and forth. I was dancing with Steve Leveroni and Mr. Donald was opposite with Joe Laffy's sister. Our partners seemed to fall in love at first sight and Steve *would* not turn me but kept chasséeing over to Joe Laffy's sister and turning her every chance he got, and no matter what Tommy Geary was hollering. So Mr. D. had to turn me and as turning means waltzing, I must say I did not regret Steve's desertion and it finally ended in my having a fine long waltz with Mr. D. who dances beautifully. Then we had "buck and wing" dances from a spry young man and John Murphy "favored with a song." I started several tiny tots dancing together which much amused their papas and mamas. Mr. Donald made a great hit with them all and he was so kind and thoughtful too about saving me trouble all the time. We went home in a cab and I was simply exhausted by that time and even he said he "didn't feel much like moving though he didn't know why."

Another time we had some distinguished visitors.

Mr. Donald had brought George Marvin down, and his mother and his aunt were there. Senator John Fitzgerald came and I danced a quadrille with him in the same set with Mr. Donald and a little Irish girl. George Marvin sat and laughed at us as we were so stupid and our partners had such a hard time with us. Tom Connelly was there and he was also terribly nice and I had a fine talk with him. All the nicest boys were there. All the Temperance Club, and Mrs. Tilton [she headed prohibition work in Boston] told me it was "the best dance and the best behaved set of people they had ever had in the building." I was very proud of the Lawrence Club!

I didn't think so well of some of our other visitors.

I tried to make myself agreeable to the two members of the Legislature who put in an appearance. They were sleek, fat, prosperous, clean shaven and common—but also

smart, young and *meaning* to be gentlemanly, but oh! I
hope my boys won't turn out like that.

Spring, 1898. I couldn't stop going to North Bennet
Street when I moved to Cambridge, and would drive
in the open wagon, causing some excitement in Salem
Street. I always took the same table, where Mike and
Eugene and all my friends there would join me, and we
often had such uproarious good times that Miss Leavitt
would scold me as well as the boys. Once she delivered a
long lecture to the whole room in which she said, with an
awful glare, "I thought you were gentlemen but I have
decided that some of you are ruffians." Mike looked
around and smiled.

James Mitchell was no ruffian. Once in Twenty Questions, after asking "Male or female?" and being told
"Female," he then asked, "Nice?" to which Eugene replied, "Peach"! Then James, with a bow to me, said,
"Then it must be Miss Lawrence."

Susan Shaw invited forty of them on Saturday out to
Wellesley for the day. I met her and them at the station.
Of course, there were several in the station who were not
invited, among them poor Dentoni, and it was very hard
to leave them behind. One boy did manage to lose himself in the crowd and come, and wasn't discovered till all
were at the Shaws' house, where, after much discussion,
Susan gave him a sandwich and sent him home again.
Such a time as we had with them on the train and how
amused or scandalized the other passengers were! Even
before the train stopped they were piling out and into
Mr. Hunnewell's hay-rick, and those that couldn't get
into that hung on somehow to the cart, which took Susan
and me. All the Hunnewells and Shaws assembled to

see us arrive, which we did to the loud strains of "The Wabash."

Before lunch we had baseball and Steve Leveroni, with his brilliant smile and professional manner, won all hearts as captain and coach of his team. He is adorably attractive. Of course the game finally ended in a fight between Irish and Italians. Then we underwent a complicated process of washing in turns, and then came lunch. Some of the dirtiest boys would not come in to lunch, whether from shyness or because they didn't like it we didn't know, but it worried Mrs. Shaw a good deal.

Immediately after lunch they started in again with three-legged races, potato races, etc., and finally it got so hot Susan took the little ones off to see the chickens, while the big ones and I sat under a shady tree and sang. Then, with many cheers for all of us, they piled into the hay cart again and drove off, Susan and I driving along in the pony cart to see them safely on the train.

Baseball soon came to be one of their favorite activities and the Club had its own team.

May 22, 1904. Went over to North End Park to see a ball-game between the Lawrence Club and the Charter Oaks. A little Italian girl showed me the way to the Park, taking me down some narrow steep streets where everyone was yelling Italian and, as I looked down at the beach straight before me, I felt as if I was in Naples. The boys greeted me at the entrance to the Park, saw that I had a fine seat and John O'Connell introduced his father so that I should not have to be alone. Mr. O'Connell and I sat on a wall and he held an umbrella over me. A policeman who stood behind me was evidently very curious as to my business there. Mr. O'C. was very pleasant. He said he was a baseball "enthusiast" and he found much to admire and much to criticize in the game. He was much struck by the playing of one "clever little chap no bigger'n a pint o' peanuts." He talked all the time and is very proud of his sons. He runs watering carts for the city of Boston. I had to leave before the end of the game, but their new suits or something were too much for the Lawrence Club and they were being wiped off the field by the Charter Oaks.

In May 1904 the whole gang went up to Groton School to play their team.

May 28, 1904. After lunch I drove over to the School to the much anticipated game between Groton and the Lawrence Club. Harold Peabody had arranged this game and my boys had been practicing in all their spare time for weeks for it. Groton kept us waiting for an hour. Meanwhile Harold knocked up for the boys to practice and I sat in solitary grandeur on a bench. Suddenly Sumner Gerard*appeared and from that moment the day was a success. He brought Mr. and Mrs. Sturgis and Charlotte Barnes to sit with me and then he "jollied up" the boys. Finally he got into a baseball uniform and played himself —just as my boys were getting discouraged and Groton was feeling pretty confident. From then on we rolled up the runs and left Groton behind.

I was proud of the boys. They looked, played and behaved so well. In the 9th inning we were 5 runs ahead when Tom Connelly had his nail knocked off and had to stop. This left a bad hole in the team, and Groton beat in the last half inning.

* Sumner had kept up his interest in Groton more than most of the graduates, and was frequently there on weekends.

Just one incident marred the afternoon. Of course I had impressed upon the boys that the one essential thing, and the thing I expected of them, was to play a clean, sporty, gentlemanly game and to take a licking cheerfully and this they did to a really remarkable degree—which everyone remarked upon to my great pleasure. Imagine then their disgust and surprise when the Groton first baseman deliberately put out his foot and tripped up Tom McHugh, who was running very hard, having hit a home run. Tom fell heavily on his head and shoulder and my boys' faces instantly showed a general expression of, "So that's what you call gentlemanly playing!" Oh! how glad I was that Sumner Gerard was there in that crisis! He was furious—stopped the game, got the umpire to send the boy off the field and gave us all "a little oratory" as he called it. In fact he saved the afternoon for me and the boys and I were so grateful.

The Grotonians were very polite in coming out to see the game. Even the Rector came out for a little while. The boys were well satisfied in spite of the beating—but there was not time afterwards for them to see the river and the school for which I was sorry, but they were given supper and driven back to Ayer for the train.

The next year we managed to turn the tables on Groton.

Mr. and Mrs. Mark A. De Wolfe Howe are also passing the week-end here and they drove me to the school where I found a wheel-barrow under a tree and sat on it alone and watched the boys and Harold who was "knocking up" for them on the field. Mr. Gardner* informed me that Sumner Gerard had been and *gone,* tho' only last Sunday he had written me that he was going to play with us. But Groton had been horribly beaten by St. Mark's on Wednesday and he had apparently gone home in

* A Groton master.

disgust. As I expected our boys to get badly beaten I was rather relieved to hear the news but, to my utter astonishment and delight, the Lawrence Club wiped up the ground with Groton! Of course, without S. Gerard, we lacked a first base but Groton kindly lent us Richard Whitney and I don't believe they knew what a present they were giving us. He was just what we needed to steady our team and he didn't let a ball pass him—no matter how "wild" it was thrown. His mother, who came and sat with me—and who didn't know quite what to make of the fact that she wanted Groton beaten—was much worried because she said Richard was no batter, but I assured her that would not matter at all. Our boys could all bat like a streak and what we wanted was a steady man on first. I could hardly believe my eyes as the runs piled up because I feared, without Tom Connelly, we would not do as well as last year. But we kept ahead of Groton just enough to make it exciting until about the 7th inning when we made run after run till Groton got rattled and in the end we beat them 13 to 3! My gracious! I was excited and so was Mrs. Whitney. The Lawrence Club had certainly covered themselves with glory by playing a sporty and almost errorless game. Our battery was first class all thru'! Maurice at centerfield made many spectacular catches. McKenna at shortstop was marvelous. He had been working on a watering cart all the morning and hadn't had anything to eat since 6 A.M. but they were all given crackers and milk before leaving Groton for the train. I was immensely proud of them and they all cast proud, delighted and embarrassed glances at me as they ran by after the game to change their clothes.

Jan. 5, 1904. Evening went to North Bennet Street for the Social. Tom Connelly was there. I can hardly refrain from telling him he has the most attractive personality

I know, but I do refrain as I am afraid it would not be good for him. I told him about Willie Mahoney's fine "rise" and he told me Mike is doing well at the Navy Yard in the job I got for him there. Then he said, "All the fellows are doing well except one or two of us." But he is really trying now to get a job and regrets his wasted time. [He ended up a judge on the Massachusetts bench.]

Aug. 1, 1904. A telegram from one of my boys—Joe Laffy—saying, "Willie Mahoney killed. Elevator accident. Funeral Monday." He and Mike and Gene were my oldest friends in the Club and Willie was the smartest of all the boys and we were all so proud and fond of him. He and an underpartner in Brown-Durrell and Co. (just those two together) were sent to N.Y. this last year to start a branch there. He had enjoyed his work there but he was pretty homesick too and wrote me very often. I got a letter just a few days ago. His brother was killed in the Spanish war so it is awfully hard on his mother. She was so proud of him. This is the first death in the Lawrence Club and we shall miss him terribly. I seem to care all the more for Mike and the other boys and *hope nothing* will happen to them. I telegraphed Joe Laffy to send a wreath from the Club.

Later I heard that Sumner Gerard had offered to take the case if the Mahoneys decided to sue. I thought it was awfully nice of him—as he meant without pay, of course. I went to call on Willie's mother when I got back to town and on Mike's family too.

Jan. 22, 1905. Harold asked to accompany me on some calls I was going to make on the boys' families, so we went over to Charlestown and headed first for Mike's as I had been meaning to go there ever since his mother died. One of the girls was sitting in an upper window and ran down in the most cordial way to let us in. They have 4 rooms in a tenement one flight up and I immediately felt the greatest admiration for those two young girls when I saw how neat and attractive, not only the rooms but they themselves, were. They were about 18 and 16 and very pleasing looking, especially the youngest who had the most brilliant brunette coloring I have ever seen, like an Italian. They both looked as if they had been sitting up ready to receive callers, they were so fresh and neat looking in their black dresses. I was so delighted with them that I simply beamed upon them and wanted them to admire me as much as I admired them. Mike was out but Paul came into the room as soon as he heard who we were but *he* was the most awful shock to me. I had not seen him for several years and had never seen such a change in anyone. He peered thru' his glasses as if he could hardly see and he tottered when he walked like an old man and lay back in his chair and talked in a very weak voice. He still works half the day and half the night in the Western Union and won't give it up though he is obviously very sick. I tried to get him to go and see Gus Thorndike*—it made me feel so badly to see him like that.

After a nice call here we went to the Mahoneys' as I had not been there since Willie's death. Harold stayed outside here and it was lucky for him as I don't think he would have enjoyed it at all. The dirtiest scrap of a boy, with a slice of bread and molasses in his hand and all over his face, opened the door and then ran screaming to his mother that a lady was there to see her. Meanwhile I found my way into a cheerless room and seated myself on the strongest and cleanest looking plush chair. Mrs.

* A prominent doctor cousin of Mrs. Peabody's. [Ed.]

Mahoney came rushing in from the kitchen (where she had been "making some little cakes for the children's supper") beaming with cordiality and wiping her hands on *the* dirtiest apron I ever saw. Her gray hair was all awry, her figure shapeless and her hands constantly fluttering nervously. Her face was first smiles, then tears; whenever she spoke of "my boy Willie" she had recourse to the dirty apron and wept copiously, so that I quickly made some flattering remark about the ones she had left (several had followed her in from the kitchen) and more kept coming in the door every minute) and then her face was wreathed in smiles again. She had had 14 and now has 10 I think. Her oldest boy being killed in the war and then Willie's accident too were awful shocks; besides taking the two who were old enough to help financially. Poor woman! I was so sorry for her! What a life! and her only pleasures seemed to be telling about her sorrows, and relating how she "laid out" Mrs. O'Donnell and the beauties of that poor lady's funeral—apparently a keen pleasure that! She always referred to Mr. Mahoney as "him." When I left she asked me to be sure to come again and said she was *always* at home. Poor woman! work, work, work from morning till night from the time she was a child till she is dead or useless.

That Christmas the boys really astonished me.

Dec. 24, 1904. I had suggested to the boys that they all bring each other little presents, jokes, toys, etc. and hang them on the tree and this worked beautifully. They had dressed the tree last night with a box of stuff I had brought down and I put some finishing touches on this evening. The early part of the evening we all played pool —then we sat in a semi-circle around the tree which by that time was groaning under the weight of many myste-

rious bundles. Then John O'Brian acted as Santa Claus
and distributed the gifts with apt remarks. Mike was
showered with presents and John himself got all sorts of
useful things for a married man and Tom Foley, our big,
nice-looking new member, received a basket full of toys.
I asked what he could do with them all and he said he
was going to give them to the baby. I asked "what baby"
and then he explained that he had adopted an orphan
baby whose parents had been friends of his. It is now
nine months old, is learning to walk and is a jolly strong
little fellow and apparently the apple of his young foster
father's eye. His mother looks after it while he is at work
and he plays with it evenings. I immediately made the
baby an honorary member of the club and he is to be
brought over as soon as the weather gets warm enough.

About half way through the proceedings there was a
pause and when I looked around to see what was up I
found myself being presented with a very handsome
silver-handled umbrella. I was much touched and didn't
thank them half enough. It is remarkable what good
taste they have in picking out the right things to give and
tho' it is always something simple and useful it is the best
of its kind—nothing mean about them!

The following spring we had a memorable evening of a
different kind.

April 18, 1905. It was a beautiful night and before leaving I leaned out of one of the big windows looking down
on the roofs of the tenements and listening to the chimes
from Old North Church* when I saw the two lanterns
hanging out of the belfry above and was fired with a desire
to go up and live in the year 1775 for a little while—so,
after all the boys had gone out but two or three, we got the

* From the steeple of which hung the signal lanterns for Paul Revere. [Ed.]

janitor, Mr. Cleveland, and he led us around to the back
of the church and went to rouse the sexton—who I fear
had gone to bed. Soon we saw him returning with what
seemed to be an old witch, who held a candle high in her
hand and was preceded by a black cat. They came down
the outside staircase of the house next door and her
grandson, who was young and agile, led us thru' weird
places into the lovely old church which was hung with
flags and bunting. They were rather aghast at my wanting
to go up the spire, and Mr. Cleveland, after many remon-
strances, seemed to feel that, since I insisted, he would
have to come too. The steps were old rotten planks full
of holes and there were dangerous corners where there
were sometimes no steps at all! so that the ascent in almost pitch darkness was really exciting. There were five
men and myself and one candle which kept blowing out.
Poor Mr. Cleveland puffed and panted but I was enjoying
it, and the view from the top was well worth the trouble.

There was a full moon which cast weird shadows over
us through the old-fashioned small-paned windows. We
could just crowd into the little belfry and could look
all around and see the same prospect that the sexton saw a
hundred and thirty years ago at the same hour. There
was the harbor and Charlestown and Cambridge but it
was very different now and would have looked strange
to him. To us it all looked beautiful and prosperous but
I wondered what he would have thought of all the warships, the Bunker Hill Monument, and the tall buildings
nearer at hand. But the same old moon was shining on it
all. Harold tipped the old lady when we had made our
perilous descent and we thanked them all gratefully.

When I first started having a club at the North Bennet
Street Industrial School, the boys were little shavers and I

went down there almost every Thursday night until they had almost all of them acquired jobs and wives. With some I kept up for many years, and they would write or call up on Christmas or let me know of any happenings in their lives.

CHAPTER 12

CENTURY'S END

≈§

1898. MAMMA had an evening reception for Sallie's coming out. Papa planned a subway entrance, which amused people. It went over the grass plot and stone wall to the basement entrance through the billiard room and up two flights to the dressing rooms, after which the guests came down the *front* staircase to the party. Reese, the coachman and I with handsome screens borrowed from the aunts, and bay trees and evergreen and hangings had made this improvised passageway attractive and it prevented a crowd on the front stairs. We had asked our particular friends to come early so we got some fine dancing from 9 o'clock on. By eleven it was too crowded for dancing and Mr. Gott and his orchestra played Opera airs, so some couples went to the "sitting out" rooms when it filled up with older people. These rooms were in the front of the house and included my little room at the top of the stairs which I had fixed up very attractively. George Lee and Madeline got engaged there and never knew when the party was over! We saw them creeping down the back stairs after everyone else had left. Papa had to take the midnight train for Philadelphia and Julie and I left the next morning for New York so Mamma had to

clean up after the party and get a rest if she could. It was
so successful though that I think she felt repaid for all her
efforts.

There are Cinderellas again this year, (I wrote) and
they are nice because they are early. There were three
Pierce Hall parties and three Cheap and Hungries and
I went to all and there is no doubt about it, the more you
go the easier it is, and if you love to dance I think the
exercise is good for you.

October 29, 1898. Went to Wellesley to spend the
night with Mary Hunnewell for the Fancy Dress Dinner
at Margaret Hunnewell's. I wore my grandfather Cunningham's handsome Turkish costume of dark blue
broadcloth all embroidered, which he had made for him
in Turkey. My family allowed me to dress as a man
for the first time on account of its voluminous trousers.
With it I wore a red fez, a bright red sash, and dagger.
Mary Hunnewell was Joan of Arc, in blue flannel covered
with chain armour made of the things you clean pots and
pans with. Katharine Crowninshield was in a dress suit
of Benny's and went as Chauncey Depew. Susan Shaw
was a baby and acted the part to perfection. I did not
know she had so much sense of humor. Nancy Whiteside,
in fool's cap and bells, was the girl who kissed Hobson
. . . and there was a Lieutenant Hobson, and Teddy
Roosevelt, unshaven, grinning tremendously in khaki and
brown handkerchief.

The prettiest girl was my dinner partner, Gertrude
Hamlin, as the Empress Eugenie, allotted to me as I was
the only other royalty. She had on a beautiful dress which
had belonged to old Mrs. Hunnewell, of sky blue silk with
a crinoline skirt all done in puffs with the shoulders bare
and the dress so tight she couldn't lift an arm to reach

the salt. She wore a gorgeous aquamarine necklace that had belonged to the Marquise de Lafayette, and on her hair, which was parted, of course, and curled down over her ears, she had a gold fillet with a big blue jewel in front. She got the most votes for beauty and Dorothy Amory, who was a nun, was second. Jane Stockton, as a Quakeress, was the third.

There were clever dinner cards, each with a poem, and we had to stand and read them in turn. When we drank a health we stood on our chairs with one foot on the table. Never was anything funnier than the baby's big fat leg in sock and ankle tie! She recited a nursery rhyme and was covered with confusion afterwards. The beautiful nun danced a wonderful *pas seul* ballet. She kicked over her head and did splits and thoroughly electrified us until we discovered she had a third leg which she manipulated with her arm very skillfully amid much lace and lingerie. Old Mr. Hunnewell was the only man allowed, and he enjoyed it thoroughly.

We certainly had some lovely clothes in those days. I remember two ball dresses from this time, a black satin Princess style trimmed with big red roses on a winding stem with leaves, and a soft yellow satin with gold glass beads on the lace. And a more summery one was a French dress of sky blue moiré; the upper part of the waist was *all* rose petals and little bunches of the same velvet roses in the full sleeves and a small bunch in my hair pinned in with my diamond star.

I had a wonderful visit to the Morrises in New York in January, 1899.

I had a big sunny room, dressing-room and bath and I could ring for the most fascinating little French maid whenever I liked . . .

I was so scared when we were actually off for the ball that it was a great relief to find that the Morrises felt equally perturbed. Dave said he would know nobody and Angela thought everybody had forgotten her it was so long since she had gone about at all. As we drove down the avenue, there seemed to be an awning in front of every Vanderbilt house. In his new white castle on the corner of 59th Street "Uncle Willie" was having a dinner for little Willie and his fiancée. The Sloanes', where we were going, were living in one of the two huge square brownstone houses which took up the whole block between 51st and 52nd Streets. The entrance was palatial with immovable flunkies in lines. . . . After keeping Dave waiting quite a while we took the desperate plunge— our names were yelled out and we shook hands with Mrs. Sloane, Emily and her pretty "bud" sister Leila. Happily Joe Choate, Jr., and Frank Harrison came up to me immediately . . .

Dinner at Mrs. F. I. Morris's. She is very attractive in her Southern way, with which I am never at home, and lives in Oriental and French magnificence on Madison Avenue . . .

Dave took us to drive in the little wagon with a pair of trotters . . . We dashed over and under all sorts of horrible steam and elevated railroads to Morningside Heights, Grant's Tomb, Columbia, Harlem, the Speedway, the Park and the Avenue. I think we covered all New York in our fast drive of 2½ hours and it was such fun rattling along . . .

Box at the Opera for the unique production of *Götterdämmerung* which was to last six hours. I was rather doubtful if I was going to like that. There was to be one rest period of half an hour between 6:45 and midnight. There was a splendid cast, the two de Reszkes, Bispham, Nordica, Schumann-Heink. The high spot of the evening was when Dr. Rainsford* walked into the box next to us and sat in the seat right next to me! Naturally there was no more thought of my being bored by the long performance. We were both in the front row and he seemed to think he was in my way and tried to move back saying it was "a pity the Lord made people as big as he." He did not seem to recognize me as he kept looking at me in a puzzled way and surely if he had placed me he would have asked about Papa. I was sorry when the opera was over as it was so nice sitting there in the dark and listening to the gorgeous music and feasting my eyes on Angela (lovely in pink velvet and a most becoming tiara), and Dr. Rainsford. It was disturbing to look at the stage and see Brunhilde's old barrel-hooped hack of which she seemed scared to death though she looked twice as strong as he . . . After the Opera we went to Sherry's and had a delicious supper of caviar, oysters, etc. . . .

Angela's huge black velvet hat blew off in the middle of Fifth Avenue. Several men gave chase and caught it fortunately before it was run over. . . . Angela and I tried bicycling but the wind was too strong for me and the wagons and cars scared me too. I had her wheel and she had Dave's and wore bloomers . . .

I was sorry to get home and lived for the New York mail.

A year later I made them another memorable visit:

Dave took me to drive in his locomobile. It was the first time I had ever been in a horseless carriage and it was almost too exciting on the crowded streets. It *can* go 40 miles an hour when there are no bicycle cops

---

* He was the rector of St. George's, the biggest Episcopal church in New York, and considered a great preacher. He was a great friend of my father's, and also a sportsman. He would fish in the Restigouchi and send Ma a salmon.

around and it dodges in and out among the wagons and carriages silently and quickly. The walkers jump when they hear our gong and *scoot* out of the way. Everything went beautifully until we were on the way home on the Riverside Drive when something gave out and Dave said he "would like to experiment with it." So I sat for ten minutes or so, the centre of an interested crowd, while he fiddled with the machinery. Then steam began to escape with a hissing sound and all the horses in sight began to prance and caper and the horse of the mounted police-man, who had been watching us, immediately dashed off in the opposite direction. Some of the men around helped Dave push the thing over to a house where there was a hose and I got out—fortunately, for as soon as Dave had put the water in, he lit the fire again and presto! flames sprang up inside and out, and six feet high, and it was a fear-some sight. The crowd stood aghast and the ladies look-ing out the windows screamed. Dave grabbed out the nice rugs to save them and we thought it was the end of the locomobile—but suddenly the flames went out as quickly as they had begun and only the paint and varnish had been burnt off. Then the heroine stepped into the machine, the hero returned the hose, and we moved off in a dead silence—the crowd seemed to be struck dumb.

And in March:

Ed Harding came for me at nine and we took the Elevated to go down and see the Stock Exchange. This was most amusing. There was "a little flurry on sugar" and if that scene of frantic hoarsely yelling wild animals meant only "a little flurry" I shouldn't want to see a "panic." How can gentlemen go into such a low sort of business! Mr. Harding then took me around the business

section, which was very interesting. He, himself, belongs
to the leading law firm in town, Carter & Ledyard, and I
fear he was very late in arriving there today.

Evening. We dined at the Schieffelins' new house. It
will be lovely when it is done but fear that will not be for
some time yet. They have placed all their children with
their relatives and are living there alone to try to hurry
the workmen out. In this house and the Sloanes' (also
building) the whole second floor front is a ballroom,
with long windows, beautifully designed but I would
think rather a waste of good space. There were signs
all around saying "Don't spit on the floor" and as we
entered the dining-room, across the hall from the ballroom and taking up the whole *back* of the house a sign
said, "Positively no admittance except on business." Our
small party tonight was their housewarming and Louise
S. said she felt very sentimental about it.

Friday, May 19, 1899 was Papa's and Mamma's Silver
Wedding Day. We children gave them a silver salver
which I bought. Aunt Sue got up a surprise party. She
delights in them but we were rather nervous as we knew
Papa and Mamma hate the thought of them and neither
had been very well lately. It was obvious to all that we
were to have an addition to the family but I did not know
when as such things were never mentioned and never had
been. I imagine this was usual in those days but it certainly was hard on the children and made for many em-
barrassments and misunderstandings and worries. Only one
person—a schoolmate—had ever spoken of such a personal
affair to me and I was so shocked I never spoke to her
again if I could help it. However, we had to cooperate—
"ours not to reason why" but to carry out orders as Aunt
Sue had it all planned. I told Mamma Aunt Sue was com-

ing to lunch so she would be suitably dressed. Then I had
a large banquet ready in the dining room, arranged for
thirty people, and this was an anxious time for fear that
one of them might go in there! Sally went over to the
Washington Elm to meet the guests and show them the
way through the back of the place. The party consisted
of all the aunts and uncles, Cousins Frank and Lucilla,
Alice and Gus Thorndike, Cousin Gus Amory, Grandma
and Aunt Minnie Sargent. They looked too funny coming stealthily across the grass, all carrying huge bundles
and boxes of presents, Vickers driving behind with more
boxes and bundles and an oil painting 6 ft. by 3 in his
wagon. They got right up to the front steps before they
were seen or heard, and then Mamma looked out the window and was amazed and I fear horrified! She rushed
towards the dining room and opened the door but there
was the banquet and Vickers ready to serve it. Aunt Sue
had brought a huge wedding cake with a little bride and
groom on it and Aunt Harriet brought some quotation
buns. Uncle Amory brought his old Madeira and Aunt
Sally much champagne, and they all brought beautiful
silver presents. I had found a butter knife in the safe
which they all had given to Grandpa and Grandma Lawrence on *their* silver wedding and they were interested
to see it again. Both Uncle Fred and Uncle Augustus
had written poems for the occasion which they read and
which were both very good. I think Ma and Pa did enjoy
it, especially the latter, and it was a great success in spite
of my fears and worry.

Monday, May 22. After a fine house party week-end at
the Crowninshields' I arrived home to find I had a baby
brother!* It is ridiculous to be 24 years old and be still

* Frederic Cunningham Lawrence, now Suffragan Bishop of Massachusetts.

living at home and getting a baby brother when most of your friends have children of their own. But one thing that made it easier to bear was the surprise to everyone. Aunt Sue didn't believe the telegram and called the office. Aunt Harriet said her knees shook when she took the telephone message, and Uncle Peter drove over from Medford to see for himself if it was true and had Mrs. Powell hold the baby up to the window for him to see. Phil Dodge and others called in the evening but I did not see them and never slept at all with the baby squalling in the next room.

May 30. I have been reading the journal of Marie Bashkirtsev lately and with the greatest interest as she was just my age when she wrote it and I think her picture looks like me too. She thinks just the way I do only she expresses herself much better. I don't write all my thoughts in my diary as she does but that is the difference I think between a European girl and a New England one. I am sure she doesn't feel any more. I have always been a bit worried that keeping a diary makes one self-centred but I also think it helps one to accomplish things, if only for the sake of writing them down!

June 5. I have suddenly realized that I am turning into an old maid of late, easily irritated, saying sharp things, and taking no pains to look well and be agreeable—also feeling it was a waste of time to be frivolous and that I was doing more important things, namely, Art School and North Bennet Street. Therefore, resolved to be charming to everyone—family included. Oh, how difficult to be really interested no matter how dull things may seem— to look my best always, even at home. Oh! how difficult! I had better read this over often as I don't want to be an

old maid—neither do I want to *settle down forever* with
anyone who has given me the opportunity as yet.

March 8, 1899. To the Opera to see Maurel in *Don
Giovanni.* Of course, he was magnificent and Edouard
de Reszke was a wonderful Leperello, but I cannot en-
thuse over any heroines as big and fat as Lilli Lehmann
and Sembrich. They made it ridiculous because how
could a man as fascinating as Don Juan fall in love with
either of them? When he tried to go through a rose
arbor with an arm around each he *stuck* and was obliged
to go sideways pushing one before and dragging the other
after him!

June 18 1900. At 11 the Theological School picnic
started and bore along with it Sally and me. It was a
perfect day for it and we went to Arlington Heights in
the open cars. Luncheon was good and later there was a
baseball game. Sally was Captain of one nine and I of the
other. I had my usual post at first base and made several
runs by stealing bases. Prof. Nash cheated horribly and
bullied the umpire. My pitcher was George Parker of
Yale and Mr. Moulton [later Bishop of Utah] was an
excellent second base. Prof. Drown was a first-class catcher
and coach. Prof. Drown's elderly sister, who I think may
never have seen a ball game before, was something to remember at bat. Sally's most valuable man (besides Prof.
Nash) was a big fat ex-Princeton catcher. It was great fun.
We shall miss this Senior Class *awfully.*

CHAPTER 13

ITALY, 1901

&

In 1901 we all made a second trip to Europe, sailing from New York.

Feb. 14 1901. After breakfast the whole family climbed into a bus to drive to the ferry. The river seemed to be solid ice but we plowed through it and arrived alongside the *Fürst Bismarck*. After looking at our staterooms and renewing our acquaintance with that cold, musty, seasick smell, we went up on deck. There was a big jam of people, as the ship is to be very full.

I watched the poor steerage people get on. They were weeping and hugging each other and the men were embracing and kissing each other on both cheeks; and they carried their possessions, if they had any, in their hands or on their backs.

Here I met Chilly Ayre, who was with an attractive-looking man in a smart long coat, Otho Cushing, the *Life* artist who draws the beautiful Greek gods and goddesses. He was the man who danced so well in the "Stroller" too. I never saw any one more graceful. So here at last was one interesting fellow-traveller! At last those going ashore went off and we slowly moved out of the dock. The wharf was black with yelling, waving people looking so cold, and the band was playing a snappy Sousa march, and it was quite exciting. The harbor was solid with ice, away out to Sandy Hook, but it didn't trouble our huge ship at all.

Feb. 15. Still cold. O. Cushing very amusing but always flying off after a few minutes, leaving us Chilly!

Feb. 16. We have discovered and met several interesting fellow passengers, among them "Mr. Dooley," who turns out to be a gentlemanly-appearing quiet young man named Finley Peter Dunne, and whose books are being laughed over just now in every country in the world.

Feb. 18. Another perfect summer's day. Hard to believe we were surrounded by ice three days ago. Otho came up on the hurricane deck where I was and drew wonderful pictures in my sketch book. It is so pretty to hear the watch in the fighting top call out "All's well" in German; the bow watch answers him and then the bells ring out. I try to hear this every evening after dark. Oh, I do love a life at sea!

Feb. 19. Still beautiful weather. After breakfast we passed between the Azores and it was a lovely sight on this balmy summer day. They were both bold and rocky, and green and tropical lying in the hot sun on the pale turquoise sea. We were due to see some other Azores later, and while Mr. Davis and I took our daily constitutional together, I saw the Captain looking through his binoculars on the bridge, and I thought it would be fun to pretend we saw land, so Mr. Davis got some glasses and we gazed out to sea. Pretty soon an eager crowd gathered around us and we left them all looking as hard as they could, and then went to the other side of the deck and did the same thing with the same result.

Feb. 20. Otho drew the Pope, Vittoria Colonna, and others in my sketch book, and at the same time argued with us all about Boston women and girls, compared to New York and others, and he irritated Margaret Bowditch and me so that after lunch when we went back to our chairs and found his pipe lying among our rugs and things, Margaret suggested putting some hair in it, which she said made a very nasty smoke. So we emptied it of ashes, put some hair on the bottom, and filled it again and left it where it was. Mr. Owen was going by and said it was "enough to make the poor fellow sick for a week" and he said he hoped he'd be around when Otho smoked it. Well, then, as it was Ash Wednesday we all went to church. Unfortunately at dinner, Margaret and I were so amused by our practical joke that with much giggling we told what we had done. Mr. Bowditch, being a pipe smoker too, felt the full horror of it and Papa was also shocked and disgusted, so that we had to go and undo all our work.

Feb. 22. Lovely day for Gibraltar. Sally and I weren't waked up until we were almost *in* the harbor. I *was* provoked! We ate a hasty breakfast on deck, so as not to miss any of the sights. We soon came to a standstill in front of the rock. On one side stretched the bold outlines of Spain and in the blue distance was the end of Africa, but Gibraltar! How can I describe it? It has left an impression of grandeur, life, gaiety and sunshine. The color was so much more light and delicate than I had supposed (from the "Prudential Life" advertisement) and it was so

interesting to see the fortifications and the wee dots of
soldiers on the tiptop. The harbor was full of ships and
yachts and little boats, and the town was larger and more
picturesque than I expected. We got away on the first
tender, which was jammed with people, and suddenly Papa
spied Admiral Cervera*, who had evidently come from
Spain to meet some friends on our ship. As Papa had met
him after the war, he went up and spoke to him and introduced me, but then alas! One of our most undesirable
fellow-passengers, a Cook's tourist, discovered who the
Admiral was and had everybody go up and shake hands
with him and led three cheers for him, and embarrassed
the poor old gentleman extremely.

Margaret and I were the first ashore at Gibraltar, where
we and the Bowditches took funny little carriages with
fringed awning tops, in which we sat facing each other,
and how we did "rubber" and exclaim! I don't think I
could imagine a better place for water-colors than Gibraltar. The lovely color of the rock and the pale greens of the
verdure with the pink, pale blue, and yellows of the stucco
houses, and against this delicate background the scarlet
uniforms and bright colors of the women's dresses stood
out vividly. There were facinating little narrow streets all
up and down sharp hills and brilliant vines and flowers on
the light-colored houses and high walls. Everywhere, of
course, were beautiful vistas of the Mediterranean, or the
harbor, surrounded by the bold blue mountains.

Guided by a Tommy Atkins, we all walked up the rock
as high as they would let us go; first around the outside,
between high walls covered with tropical flowering vines
of purple and scarlet, and then through steep tunnels cut
by the Moors. Some parts were inky black and very damp,

* Who had commanded the Spanish fleet in Cuba during the Spanish-American
War.

but every little while we came to a big gun in a huge port-
hole facing out, and from each was a superb view. At the
last opening we squatted on the ground at the edge and
looked way, way down to the neutral ground and the race
course at some tiny dots target shooting, so far below that
we couldn't hear the noise or see the smoke. After looking
further down than I ever had before, I looked *up* and
couldn't see the top of the cliff that stretched off beside
up. I never imagined anything so grand as that sheer rock
that seemed almost to reach the sky.

At last, with great regret, we had to leave the wharf
and were welcomed once more to the dear old *Fürst Bismarck,* by the smiling stewards and sailors. At six o'clock
we began to steam away between the coasts of Africa and
Spain.

Such a sunset as there was! The long line of purple
mountains of the Spanish coast, with here and there a snow
peak of the Sierra Nevadas, the Rock standing out dark
and sharp against the gorgeous yellows and reds of the
sky, and on the other side the misty blue of Africa. We
saw the sun set between the Pillars of Hercules, and it was
a wonderful sight! A Spanish square-rigged bark in the
distance added a finishing touch to the picture. We all
leaned over the rail for hours, watching it entranced. Suddenly Mr. Davis saw a stream of water shoot up into the air
right near us. Then we all saw it several times, and a big
black whale flashed in and out of the water playfully.

Feb. 24. The *last* day, oh, dear! oh, dear! Last night
was very rough and many succumbed, including Julie, who
was sick all night (though she said it was not the sea, but
something she ate). Mr. Dooley talked with me all the
morning and I had a delightful time. Then as I was leaning on the rail and watching Sardinia go by, Otho joined

me and he afterwards did some more drawings in my sketch
book. That evening the saloon was all decorated for the
"Captain's Dinner" which was a hilariously gay affair. At
the end the lights were put out while the waiters marched
in with the illuminated ice cream, and there were gifts for
everyone, and much tinsel and noise. People whose headdresses were becoming or ridiculous, were applauded. Otho
carried off the palm. Colored paper was wound around his
head like a turban, and in it were stuck, like candles in a
cake, little flags of all nations. From each ear hung a
Chinese lantern, and red eyeglasses added the finishing
touch. He certainly is a born actor, and has been the life
of the ship.

Feb. 25. Went up on deck to see the entrance into
Naples, but it was all very dim and dark, and bluish grey,
and *so* cold. Then we anchored and everybody came up
and hung over the rail and listened to some Italians in a
small boat, singing "Finiculi, Finicula" and soon the decks
were full of dirty Italians, wanting to sell you things or
courier for you; and coal barges came alongside, filled
with the filthiest, blackest bunches of rags in the shapes of
boys, all screaming and clamoring and fighting for *soldi.*

It was very interesting driving through Naples to the
Grand Hotel and we "rubbered" at the streets of steps
going up and down; and at the donkeys and the lovely
dark-haired women and cunning children. It seems to be
a *very* large city, so *full* of people, and *such* a noisy city!
The people all talk to themselves and their friends and
their donkeys and horses, and shout and make queer grunts
and harsh cries. There are lots of very swell carriages too,
and *very* handsome horses.

After lunch we and the Bowditches drove to San Martino,
up a long winding hill, from which we got a beautiful

"Marian, you *must* not argue with your Uncle Caleb!" M. L. at school
in Boston

Sets of these menu cards by M. L. were sold for various charities

A sketch of Margaret Bowditch while she plotted
to get even with Otho Cushing

Otho Cushing smoking the famous pipe

My valentine from Charles Hopkinson

The house we built at Bar Harbor

The stables at Bar Harbor—Henry, Thomas, and the coachman Reece
with the horses

The Archbishop of Canterbury and Mrs. Davidson and his chaplains, Mr. Ellison and Mr. Holden, on their visit to us in 1905

Stanton King, who ran
the Sailors' Haven

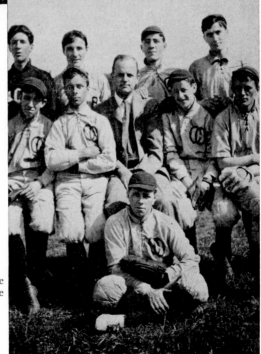

Harold Peabody and the
North Bennet Street nine

M. L. in Spanish costume for the Kirmess

view of Naples and Vesuvius, and on the other side a
stretch of *campagna* and a range of snow mountains. There
was a blue haze over everything and the sun was very
bright and hot; and the shade very cold and damp, and it
was all thoroughly Italian and delightful.

Feb. 26. Bowditches and Lawrences entrained for Pompeii. Arrived there, we found all the Fürst Bismarck
people again. Met Mr. Dooley in the newest excavated
house, and Otho in the public baths. It was a *heavenly*
day. I never imagined Pompeii to be lying in the sun on
a hilltop, commanding the most gorgeous view of snow-
capped mountains, and Vesuvius nearer and higher than
all. I had expected it to be a cellary sort of place, so it
was a delightful surprise, and the views between the pillars
and through doorways and down streets were perfectly exquisite—Vesuvius always towering above us, its white
smoke rolling off like a big thunder cloud in the otherwise
cloudless sky.

I was thrilled to see the ruts in the stone streets, made
by chariot wheels, and the worn places on the fountains,
where the people rested their hands when drawing water;
also the proclamation painted on the walls of one important street corner, announcing the result of an election.

Feb. 27. Took the train for Castellamore, where we took
two big carriages for our drive to Sorrento. At first we
were reminded of the Cornice drive at Bar Harbor, but
as it grew bolder and we went higher and higher, and
passed through endless groves of oranges and olives, and
clattered through picturesque towns, and began to see
snow-covered peaks above the bold high cliffs, the resemblance lessened! Bar Harbor is brilliant, clear-cut, wild,
rather cold and very beautiful; but this is far grander and

old, and crumbly-looking, with a blue mistiness over it all
which adds to the picturesqueness and romance.

Sorrento just suits me and would be absolutely perfect
for a honeymoon. Tonight when I was out on the balcony, looking at the sea and the gardens and the moonlit
terrace where couples were pacing up and down, the men
in dinner dress, smoking, the only sound their quiet talk
and footsteps on the tiled court, and the sweet scent of the
flowers and orange blossoms floated up to me, I felt very
sad and lonely.

Feb. 28. A perfect day for Capri. It was a beautiful sail,
of course; a lovely day in the Bay of Naples, drawing always
nearer to Capri's high, bold cliffs! The air was delicious.
The Italians sang and it was like a dream.

Of course we all went into the Blue Grotto, and this is
the only scary thing I have done yet. Inside, the water was
a very remarkable clear, light blue; but the roof was not
much colored, and after a moment we were ready to go out
again, but one after another the boats slipped in through
the hole until the Grotto was uncomfortably full, and still
they came. Finally we were jammed like sardines in a box,
with all the Italians screaming and yelling at each other
in the darkness. I began to think we should be crushed
against the sides of the rock and upset and drown like rats
in a trap. At last, when there wasn't an inch more room,
we shot out into the sunlight again and I never was so glad
to get anywhere.

March 2. Amalfi. The family find it very homesicky here
and don't like their little bare, damp rooms—but I love
mine. It has four casement windows looking out to sea—
in fact, the whole side of the room—and a little alcove
study, with a table and window seat, and all bare white

plaster walls, making it seem very pure and clean. I must say, however, that it *is* damp and the people look deadly. We seem to have done the wrong thing at the wrong time for meeting friends.

March 3. A terrific rain so that we are quite nervous about landslides. The huge rocks lying on the beach below, and the sweep of clay and stones on the other side of the monastery are a horrible sight when one considers that only last year there were more cloisters and gardens there instead of all this ruin.

A.M. Went to church service in the cellar of the monastery, after putting on all the clothes we had with us. A nice young English clergyman gave a good talk and got rather rattled and stuttery about praying for the King instead of the Queen.

After lunch it stopped raining and we drove to La Cava. The town of La Cava was real "Old Italy" with brigandish looking characters in long capes lounging around, and their families were milking cows and goats in the street, leaning over balconies, or playing pleasantly with pigs. The little children were sweet. All the church bells were ringing and the priests were actually quite hustling. At the Cava Hotel we met the Neddy Holmeses, Mrs. Fitz, Mrs. Dexter and Susie Dalton, and were very glad to see them.

March 4. The Neddy Holmes crowd and we went to Paestum together. Nothing has disappointed me yet but Paestum was *far* finer than I had expected, because of the beautiful color. The rich old yellow of the Temple of Neptune against the blue Italian sky was something wonderful! Here again we had not been led to expect any special *view,* and were again agreeably surprised.

Then we had a pretty walk to the station. The train was

deliberate, to say the least, and I thought Papa would go crazy. We accomplished the fifty-eight miles to Naples in about six hours. Within sight of the city a man tried to light the train. He ran along the top with a flaming torch, poking it down through into the little lamps, but it was rather windy and his torch and the lamps kept going out, so it occupied him fully half an hour. Four other officials stood outside on the platform of a station and encouraged him, and cheered him when he succeeded. I thought it was very funny, but Papa didn't. We were so glad to see Vesuvius and the lights of Napoli again that it seemed like home.

March 5. At about sunset we came to the Campagna, and I could not believe that I was *actually* on the Roman Campagna. It did look like the sea and at times it was hard to tell whether we saw sea or sky or land, it was so hazy and mysterious, and stretched off into such tremendous wavy violet distances. Finally came into Rome and drove to the Royal Hotel. Here we found the Bowditches again and many duchesses, countesses, etc., who seemed to look much like other people.

March 6. We voted to follow Neddy Holmes' itinerary which he had made out for us. A lovely day. The soft light colors of Rome are something quite different from anything I ever imagined. The grey misty light blues, like the dome of St. Peter's and the mellow golden yellows of old age that one sees in all the pillars, temples and ancient buildings are a dreamlike combination. Even the Tiber is exactly the color of the Vatican and looks older than other rivers.

March 7. Pouring day. We spent our whole morning with the statues in the Vatican and it was really thrilling.

I saw my old friend the Apoxyomenos in a commanding position at the end of a long corridor, and felt like embracing him. (He was the one that won me the $50 prize.)

Papa and I went to tea with the Meyers and Newbolds. They are still at the Grand Hotel and Cousin George is having a fine time being Ambassador. He hunts a lot on the Campagna and is now going to Sardinia to shoot.

Evening. We and the Bowditches went to see the Colosseum by moonlight. It was the first time I had seen it at all and the vastness, and feeling of age is almost overpowering. The moon was a little overcast so the light was dim and silvery, and the mistiness added to the hugeness and mystery.

March 8. Sistine Chapel this morning for a first impression. The Sybils and Adam were the finest part to me. We did a good morning's work on the Vatican, which seems to hold most of the treasures of Rome, and is beyond my wildest dreams. I had not known at all what to expect; but, from the big, handsome, boyish-looking Swiss Guards at the entrance till we drive away and look back at the peristyles and fountains, and St. Peter's dome, it is all perfect.

Evening. Mamma, Papa and I dressed in our best to dine with the Rev. Dr. Nevin. He is rector of the American church, and quite a swell; has a fascinating house full of rare and beautiful things. The other guests were Mrs. Waldo Storey and her daughter, and two young Englishmen from the Embassy. Mine had just returned from the war in South Africa and was very nice and tall, and most interesting. His name was Colonel Lamb and I had a fine time with him. When we said goodnight, he asked Papa if he might call.

March 11. We drove out to St. Paul's Without the Walls, a huge basilica which I liked better inside than

St. Peter's, and especially the little cloisters which are much
older than the church. The little courtyard was purple
with pansies and violets. The sun streamed in, making
shadows in the cloisters, of the varied twisty pillars, and
above was a square of the bluest Italian sky. It was so old
and peaceful and smelled so deliciously of violets that I
liked it better than almost anything yet.

March 12. A lovely day, though pouring at breakfast
time. Went to the Colonna Palace. This was the grandest
palace we had yet seen and the marble halls and huge
salons were really gorgeous. The Doria and Colonna families are still very rich. This Prince Colonna married
Clarence Mackay's sister, so the money here is American.
In the marble steps leading down into the great hall a
cannon ball had crashed and still lies where it fell—a
reminder of '48.

March 15. Tea at the Waldo Storeys'. They have a
beautiful apartment in the Barberini Palace, but to reach
it we had to walk up 123 steps! There were quite a lot of
ladies and about six men there. I met a shy, awkward Englishman, but nice; and a rather idiotic French count, a
connection of Napoleon. It was rather a painful and som-
bre occasion and we did not stay long. We went home by
the Via Gregoria, as I was going to tea with Ala Codman
and her brothers, who were all very nice and jolly.

March 16. The Pincian was very crowded—more so than
last Saturday. There was lots of style, and the military
band was playing. The weeping willows were just out,
delicate and bright against the dark cedars, and the almond
trees were blossoming below. Children were playing, and
swell nurses with red and yellow sashes trailing from their
caps to the ground were sitting in the shade and chatting.

March 18. We drove miles and miles out on the Appian Way in our barouche. We were going to the meet, and as far as we could see in front and behind us, there stretched a long procession of carriages. Such dust I never experienced, but it was great fun. We passed long processions of mounted orderlies leading their master's horses, and we passed the officers, too, in barges or in little rattly pony carts, and some very swell automobiles. Finally we arrived at the scene of the meet, and everybody got out of their carriages—a gay crowd talking in all languages. About sixty of the hunters were officers in uniform; there were only six ladies riding, and about thirty pink-coated men. We met the Merriam family and Abigail Adams, and Theresa and I ran after the hounds and the whipper-in for about a quarter of a mile. Then they out-distanced us and the hounds began to "find" so we drew up right beside a four-foot stone wall and watched the hunters take it. The officers always let the rest of the field go first, so we saw the ladies and the pink-coated gentlemen go over sedately. Cousin George Meyer took it very well and so did the young Italian at our hotel. When the rest were out of sight, we heard a thundering of hoofs and the officers came galloping down the field. The crowd separated and fell back, and *over* they came with a rush like a cavalry charge; and off they raced after the rest of the field. It was quite exciting. They rode *superbly* and had beautiful big mounts. We stayed to see the stragglers over, and a handsome young officer who remained to have his picture taken while taking the jump! This much disgusted Abigail A., who thought it typically Italian.

March 19. Cousin Sally Newbold got a cable saying Aunt Hetty Coolidge died. She is the fourth great-aunt we have lost in seven months!

March 20. Our last day in Rome, and so a day of good-byes. We did the Palatine Hill and from the top we looked our last on old Rome. It seemed strange that the Colosseum was empty and silent and that there was not a crowd of young ancient Romans walking over to the Cara-calla Baths—that there were no chariots dashing around the Circus Maximus, and no people on Hadrian's or Sep-timius Severus' balcony to watch them. I could almost see the Apoxyomenos taking part in the games in the Stadium and scraping himself while he rested; while a crowd of admirers gathered around to congratulate and stare at him, he towering above them and looking down with his lazy half-smile, but pleased and excited withal. Those were the good old times, but it is good even now to see the aged, dignified and mysterious remains of them in brilliant, sunny, misty Italy.

After we had driven home, Mamma and Papa went on with Cousin George to see the palace which they have just hired for the Embassy. It is very gorgeous and will take all of Cousin George's salary to pay the rent. It is the Brancaccio, built over the golden house of Nero, and the beautiful gardens go away down to the Colosseum.

March 21. On arriving at Florence we went right out to walk through the town. All I can say is, that it is more picturesque and fascinating than anything I ever saw. It is *all* like stage scenery and you feel as if you must be Romola or somebody. The streets were full of people walking, and one had to be quick to step aside when a carriage or a donkey cart, or one of their rickety old diligences with flapping curtains rattled by.

Whom should Papa and I meet in the hall of our hotel but Mr. Dooley! It will be fun if he is going to stay on here. Sir George and Lady Trevelyan are also at this hotel and in the evening Sir George came to our sitting-room

and read Browning aloud to us. He is fine—Sir George, I
mean. I do not always appreciate Browning.

March 22. Spent all morning in Uffizi Gallery, and of
course only got a passing glance. What can I say of miles
and miles of the world's masterpieces? All I can say is that
I like the oldest masters better and better every day. Fra
Angelico, Pinterruchio, Perugino, and Botticelli. They
are so beautifully delicate and decorative, and so sincere.
Titian's, Tintoretto's and Veronese's portraits are splendid!
I like them better than their other paintings.

For the first time in my life I was crazy to *copy,* and
looked with envy on the rather pathetic people at their
easels, working so hard over sometimes very bad copies of
the great pictures. But the galleries were freezing cold
and we got very tired. We met Mr. Dooley again in the
Tribuna. Alas! He is travelling now with a lady and her
daughter and evidently is quite absorbed in them and
very different from what he was on shipboard.

March 23. Pitti Palace. More interesting even than yesterday, as half the pictures were familiar to me and far
more gorgeous than I had supposed they would be. It was
so exciting to come across one old friend after another, and
many that I didn't know were there at all. The Guidos
looked very wishy-washy among the great masters.

March 24. Papa preached in the American church,
which was very full, with people sitting in the aisles and
chancel.

March 25. After lunch we drove up to Fiesole—such a
lovely drive, with beautiful extensive views—but I will
not describe another view!

Service was going on in the Cathedral, which was full

of peasants. There was beautiful singing, and a handsome
priest was dashing around the church, waving a brush and
sprinkling everything with holy water. After great prepara-
tion the big doors right by us were thrown open and some
gorgeously-clad young priests walked in backwards, bowing
low. Then they separated on either side, and in strutted
a fat old Cardinal, acolytes holding up his long purple
train, and others on either side of him—one to grab off his
hat when necessary. After much bowing and sprinkling
and chanting, he finally got settled in the chancel, and then
a brown monk went up into the pulpit and preached with
great eloquence and force.

When we got home the Motleys, Adamses, Merriams
and Trevelyans came to tea. Lady Trevelyan asked to see
my sketch book but it has nothing decent in it but Otho's
drawings. I poured the tea and had a most interesting talk
with Sir George about old Rome. He knows everything
about it, so I had a wonderful time.

March 26. Rainy again. Went to the Belle Arte and it
was by far the most interesting gallery yet, I thought. I
revelled in Michelangelo to my heart's content, for there
was his greatest of all—"David"—and innumerable drawings and casts and photographs of all his works. I was too
contented for words and had to be torn away to see the
pictures. These were also absorbing. All Botticelli's best,
so graceful and fascinating; fine Peruginos, Ghirlandajos,
Filippo Lippis, Bartolommeos and Giottos, and all arranged splendidly for study. After this we went over to
the Monastery of San Marco and went through the refectory, chapels, cloisters, etc., all with wonderful frescoes by
Fra Angelico and Ghirlandajo. In every one of the little
cells upstairs was a fresco of the Life of Christ by Fra
Angelico. He and Fra Bartolommeo were monks of this

order. We also saw Savonarola's cell and study. I sat at his desk and looked out of his little grated window into the cloister garden and handled his books and crucifix and rosary and it was all so real, it made me sad.

P.M. Shopped with Meyer, for more photos, and then back to dress for a reception given for us by a Mrs. Travers-Cox! There was quite a crowd there—about 200, I should think—and they seemed a very attractive and nice looking lot—mostly Americans, but some Italians and some English. I met Count Caccia, whom I used to know in Bar Harbor, and two other young Italian men who were very jolly. It was really very good fun and nice to see a crowd of English-speaking people again, who were on sociability bent, and not on Baedeker. Had a short talk with Mr. Dooley. He goes to Rome tonight (and the girl, too) but he left us two of his books as Papa wanted to show them to Sir George Trevelyan. I don't think he will understand them at all. (He didn't—but said Mr. Dunne was a very estimable young man.)

March 27. We took the loveliest drive yet, to the old Monastery of Certosa, and home by way of San Miniato. I am tempted to describe it but will only suggest it a little. Deep blue sky and bright sun; steep, rolling country with streams and rivers in the valleys; hillsides shimmering with silver olive groves, cultivated fields striped with vividest green and checkered with bright sun coming through twisted mulberry trees. High stucco walls and vines and flowers and spring foliage; picturesque peasants, pretty children and laden-down donkeys; lovely villas and gardens and shady walks and dark cypresses; and the towers of the old Monastery in the blue haze way above us.

From up there we got a glorious view all around Florence and its Campaniles in the distance, the valley of the

Arno and the Campagna stretching off like a sea; then blue hills and snow mountains. Way below us were some white-clad monks appearing and disappearing in a flickery, shady walk by the side of a blue stream. Vineyards covered the steep hillsides, because it is here that the delicious Chartreuse wine is made.

In the evening I went out on the balcony to look at the Arno in the moonlight, but was driven in again because some Italian men were singing and playing guitars right under our windows and thought I had come out to see them.

March 30. Took the noon train for Nice. I was quite sad about it. To think of spending only one month out of twenty-six years in Italy! Well, I am very thankful for that one month and shall enjoy art and history and life in general far more for it.

March 31. Nice. Rainy again! A.M. and P.M. Church. Papa preached.

April 1. Rainy again. Hard luck for our only three days on the Riviera. We started right after lunch by train for Monte Carlo. Such crowds as there were wandering around in the huge casino. Some awfully queer-looking ones, but on the whole not bad-looking. Lots of English people and some very smart looking women. There were about a dozen huge tables in the different halls and the people were standing three deep all around them, while others wandered about. We watched roulette first, and then rouge et noir, where it was all for gold and notes. No one looked in the least excited and some were yawning from the heat and closeness. It was all done very quietly and quickly, just like a business. In fact, it is managed in a more businesslike way than anything else we have seen in France or Italy. We saw people losing hundreds of francs and others raking in gold pieces in piles, but their expressions didn't seem to change at all.

Mamma wanted to go out after a short time, so we wandered into the gardens and out to the end of the terrace to look at the view. It is certainly an exquisitely beautiful spot. You can see Corsica lying opposite, on a clear day, and the scenery in all directions was a miracle of beauty. As contrast, just beneath the terrace they were shooting pigeons. They let the pigeon out of a little wooden box, and before it had flown more than a few feet it was shot and fell to the ground, usually only wounded. While it was fluttering on the ground a dog ran out and grabbed it in his mouth and took it back. Then another pigeon was let out, and it all happened again. This disgusted me with Monte Carlo, far more than the gambling. It seemed so mean and small and brutal.

April 2. Warmer and with more sunshine. The weather is considered remarkably bad this year, which is hard luck for us. There was an editorial about it in the London *Times.*

This morning we went by train to Cannes, and there at last we actually basked in the sun. The first time we have basked since Capri. The result was that I felt more cheerful than for some time and quite fell in love with Cannes, and envied Nellie her winters here, winning golf cups from the Prince of Wales, etc. The people were all much nicer-looking here than at Nice or Monte Carlo. There were lots of English and the atmosphere was much more respectable and swell. As a sign of this, we met Cousin Prescott Lawrence as soon as we went out!

To the station and, as usual, caught a much earlier train than we expected, as they are all so late.

April 4. Paris. Drove to the Hotel Liverpool, where we have a delightful apartment, quite by ourselves, with delicious food served in our rooms by two waiters! After cleaning up from the journey Julie and I went out to look at the shops, which were all too fascinating, and I bought two lovely hats in the first store I came to. Papa and I passed the whole afternoon in the Louvre and then walked home through the Tuileries gardens. The sculpture in the Louvre is not as attractively arranged as in the Italian museums, and the picture part is so vast that it is not so easy to see what you want as in Italy; but we had a most interesting afternoon and saw a bewildering amount.

April 5. Cold downpour. A.M. Church. Papa preached. Then I went to see about a book for my photographs. P.M. Drove to the Luxembourg and found it closed for repairs. Then to Notre Dame, and met two very elaborate funerals like the pictures in *Trilby*. Huge black coaches, and coachmen in cocked hats, and all the people walking led by some splendid officials. Notre Dame was grand and we appreciated the Gothic, after all the Italian churches. It really is far grander. The stained glass adds so much. Hordes of people were at a Communion service and there was a blaze of candles in certain spots, while the half-dark of the rest, with just a misty light coming through the colored glass, made a beautiful effect.

Later I had a very painful shampoo and came home very mad and exhausted, with only a wisp of hair left.

April 6. Pelting again. Pretty tough luck! Shopped all A.M. Papa took Ruth and me and we bought fascinating parasols, petticoats, stocks, and Frenchy knickknacks in gilt and glass. P.M. To the Louvre again and had a marvellous time, now that I really know my way about. Had to be dragged away from room after room.

April 7. Easter, and perfect weather for it. A warm spring day, horse-chestnut buds on the Champs Elysées just bursting. I have been out on my little balcony watching all Paris dashing by on its way to the races!—in automobiles, coaches and four-in-hands, and great, huge diligences. Our rooms are full of flowers. An Easter egg two feet high, of solid violets from Amos, two dozen American beauties from Mr. H. Burnham, a huge pink azalea from Mrs. Munroe, and two more big vases of white lilies and tulips from the proprietor. Papa preached at the American church and it seemed to be full of friends. Thayers, Burnhams, Van Burens, Gussie Jay with his family, John Saltonstall, the John Munroes, etc. Consuelo Vanderbilt, now Duchess of Marlborough, sat right behind us. She is taller than I, dresses beautifully, has a most piquant face and is the slenderest person I ever saw. Her waist can't be more than eighteen inches.

April 8. A holiday and another lovely soft spring day. Hired a landau for the day and drove out in the morning to the Bois to see the riders. It was very gay and a pretty sight. Smart-looking ladies and gentlemen were cantering up and down the row on beautiful horses and also scores of natty officers in different bright uniforms, while up and down the road dashed automobiles of all colors, barouches, victorias, dog carts and lots of little pony carts, and other smart traps driven by liveried grooms or beautifully-dressed women. Others walked on the paths with their pet dogs, or children with their *bonnes,* and sometimes through the trees we saw other riders, or officers hurdling their horses over practice jumps; and once, away in the woods, we saw a lot of deer scampering through the trees. P.M. Papa, Julie and I, and Miss Emily Sears drove out again through the Bois to the Cascade Restaurant, where

we had tea. I never saw so much style and fashion in my
life, or such exquisite clothes. Everyone at the Restaurant
was French. Of course there was lots of rouge and powder
and dye in the crowd, but also lots of lovely women.

April 10. We all and Abigail Adams went to the Théâtre
Français to see *Patrie,* which is the rage now. We had a
very good box and it was so interesting to see all the gay
and queer and swell people, and actually to be in this
celebrated theatre. It seemed very small to us at first, but
charmingly pretty, and the *gendarmes* with their lances and
big brass helmets, standing about the entrance and foyer,
added a very picturesque touch. The play was the most
harrowing I ever saw, but beautifully acted and staged.
Mounet Sully didn't seem to be to be as good as the rest of
the company. The leading lady was superb, very handsome
and a real tragedy queen. Altogether it was thrilling and
even Papa thought it was fine.

April 11. Papa and I had tea at Colombin's. It was
crowded just like Gibson's drawing of it. About a dozen
liveried grooms were waiting outside the door and a lot of
gay and swell-looking people were inside. Johnson, the
artist who has dogged our footsteps somewhat, and a nice-
looking friend of his came over immediately to speak to
me and I felt quite in the swim, but hoped no one knew
them and how stupid they really were. Amos came to say
goodbye and stayed to dinner.

April 12. Looked down on Paris for the last time from
my balcony. Then the Sargents, who had just arrived, came
in to call. Then the exquisite valet-de-chambre came and
said the carriages were there. Mr. Hippenheimer presented
us each with a bunch of roses and then we drove off, with

half a dozen people bowing like a row of wheat in the
wind. We had a very smooth crossing as it was a lovely
afternoon, thank heaven! It was nice to see English landscape again. Kent is the great sheep country and there were
quantities of the tiniest little white lambs skipping about,
and hedges and green fields and country churches—also a
beautiful gold and violet sunset. We arrived at Charing
Cross at eight, and everyone talked English with such an
English accent. At Claridge's Hotel we were met by some
very grand personages and powdered lackeys in white stockings and scarlet and gold, who showed us to our rooms.

April 13. This is the best hotel we have ever been in.
We have gentle music with our meals, which are exceedingly good and rich, and served to perfection. The powdered majordomos move quietly about the halls and everything is rich and swell and luxurious. Julie and I took
a hansom by the hour for shopping, but we thought things
very expensive and very English, and the shop girls were
extremely haughty and patronizing.

April 15. Papa, Mamma and I went to dinner with the
George Trevelyans. I wore my new light blue dress—the
turquoise chain I got in Florence, and a light blue gauze
jigger that Aunt Sally gave me, in my hair. The dinner
was thrilling from start to finish. The drive to Hyde Park
Corner, the line of footmen from the carriage door all the
way upstairs, and last but not least, the company! The
chief gun seemed to be Mr. Justice Wright, who is something very swell besides being a friendly little Scotchman
with a twinkle in his eye. Then there was Lord Knutsford,
a Privy Councillor and intimate friend of the King. He
was Colonial Secretary before Joe Chamberlain, and takes
after his father, Sir Charles Holland, in being the most

agreeable gentleman in England. He is very handsome and
his wife is very grand and stately and English. She was the
favorite niece of Macaulay. There was also Sidney Col-
ville, who has just edited Stevenson's letters; and there was
Charles Trevelyan, Sir George's oldest son and a very
handsome young man, with clear-cut English features and
the finest eyes I've seen on any human. There was also a
Girton girl who was the nicest English girl I have met yet,
but that is not saying much. Charles Trevelyan and I got
along so fluently that I was very stupid and did not notice
that the charming old Lord Knutsford, on my other side,
had no one to talk to for some time. I fear I was too much
excited and talked too much, and did not let my partners
talk enough, which goes to show that I am still a stupid,
unattractive bumpkin.

April 16. Sally, Ruth and I went to Guard Mounting at
St. James's. We happened to stand in the crowd next a very
polite Englishman who told us lots that was interesting.
Suddenly he began to beam and a group of Tommies
nearby stiffened up and saluted, as did two young officers
in civilian clothes, and I wondered what was happening,
when our English friend turned and said, "Should you care
to see Lord Roberts?" We almost said, "Well, I guess!"
in our enthusiasm, and he stepped back and pointed out a
little man who, with several other gentlemen in silk hats
and frock coats, was standing in the opposite corner of the
quad. After the guard had marched away, the crowd followed and we were blocked in a jam of hansoms and
people. Everyone wanted to see Lord Roberts and he was
so small he got rather lost in the crowd. We were standing
on the edge of the sidewalk when suddenly from across the
street came "Bobs" picking his way between the hansoms
and followed by his aide de camp, the Commander of the

home forces and others. They came right *at* us so we had to step back to let them pass. Everybody cheered and waved their hats, and Lord Roberts took off his hat and smiled, and it was really a thrilling moment.

P.M. I blew myself to a last hansom cab ride and drove around Hyde Park and Piccadilly. Later we all had tea with Lord and Lady Ashcombe at Prince's Gate. Lord Ashcombe said Mr. Morgan had just bought the newly-discovered lost "Duchess of Devonshire," by Gainsborough, for $124,000.

All our steamer trunks are lost somewhere between Rome and Paris, and all our steamer things are in them. We waited until today but had to get new ones, and shawls and rugs, etc., so it made us very busy and we were so tired we gave up going to see *The Second in Command.*

CHAPTER 14

THE WEST IN 1901

In 1901 the General Convention of the Episcopal Church was held in San Francisco, and we all made the trip west.

September 19. We left for California. Papa had to stay for a Memorial Service for President McKinley, but will join us at Niagara. Mamma, Ruth and Ap* go with us as far as Buffalo to see the [Pan American] Exposition. Ours is a special train—arranged for by Mr. [J. Pierpont] Morgan—and we have several "personal conductors" from Raymond & Whitcomb's who seem anxious to please us. When we get to the Canadian Pacific we shall only travel by day and be on a siding at night so as not to miss any of the wonderful scenery. I sat on the Platform at the back of the train all afternoon. It was dirty and cindery but the air and the scenery were worth it.

September 20. Niagara. We all took a barge and drove all around the American side, then the Horse-Shoe over to Goat Island and the Three Sisters Islands and home again. It would be silly to try to describe Niagara (I may have been foolish enough to do so in '93) but I can't help think-

* My brother.

ing how much more wonderful it must have been when
first discovered in the natural wilderness. I don't object
to the power house and railroads as much as to the cheap
rusticity and advertising signs, and most disturbing of all,
the tourists.

After lunch we took a train for the Pan-American Fair.
We took wheelchairs at the entrance in order to see all we
could. I expected this Exposition to seem very flat after
Chicago, which I still feel was the most wonderful and
beautiful thing ever accomplished by man. But to my great
surprise, it didn't at all! No attempt was made to rival
Chicago or to be even like it. The color scheme is wonderful. The buildings are quite ornate and all the different
colors are so delicate in tone and blend so beautifully that
the whole effect is very rich. It is daring, brilliant, new
and American.

It began to rain and I wished I was in a ginricksha as
they could, and did, put up their little buggy tops. We saw
the Philippine, African and Indian villages, passed one
barker who "would guess your weight within three pounds
or return your money" and another who "would tell you
your name though he had never met you." As we were
smoothly gliding along through all this noise—six bands
seeming to be playing all at once—I happened to look
around just in time to see a huge elephant bearing down
on me and within one foot of my chair. I *screamed* and
the chair-boy shot me off to one side. The elephant then
became interested in Papa and wheeled about and chased
him. Papa had to skip around lively to the great delight of
the crowd.

We stopped at the temple of Music to see where McKinley was shot*, but the place was so jammed with people

* President McKinley had been shot at the Exposition and mortally wounded
just two weeks before.

we could hardly move. There is a cross in the middle of the centre aisle, marked on the floor, and we could hardly imagine what the excitement must have been if the crowd was anything like today's.

Our Western train, alas, never started till 5 A.M. on account of some accident. It was a lovely day and we were glad of the ferry trip from Canada to Detroit when we got some fresh air and exercise. At one stop I asked a small boy standing by the observation car where I was sitting, "What place is this?" He grinned and said, "Kalamazoo." I thought he was sassing me and looked at him reprovingly, when Mr. Edward L. Davis went running by to post a letter and said it really was Kalamazoo. I didn't know that such a place existed.

September 24. Cold; and plains, plains, plainier than ever. The single track and the monotonous flat brown landscape depress Papa and make him nervous. We had occasional mirages today just like on the sea and for hours we saw no human habitation or any sign that man had ever been on this desolate stretch of prairie before, except the straight line of track behind us. In the afternoon the prairies began to be covered with snow and soon we were in a driving snowstorm which lasted until it was too dark to see anything. Of course it was bitter cold, but once or twice we caught a glimpse of a little shabby tent near the track with a woman or child peering through the canvas opening at the train coming through the driving snow. Near it might be a prairie wagon and huddled together the poor horses, so thin and cold. Or we might see a lonely cowboy—not at all picturesque—doubled over on his forlorn pony, fighting against the snow—the poor pony loping along, his tail tight between his legs. We had to go

slowly on the slippery rails and at times the engine seemed
to give it up and stop entirely to get its breath.

We got out once today at Moose Jaw where we saw our
first Indians and very interesting and picturesque they
were. We also stopped at Medicine Hat—just a muddy
street lined apparently with false-front wooden buildings,
saloons, barber shops, etc.

At about two we reached Banff—the place I had been
longing to see, and it was way beyond even my wildest
expectations. We got out at the tiny Log Station, and
looked all around at the bold mountains on all sides.
Three Indians were coming slowly down the road on their
ponies and I pointed my Kodak at them but they immediately stopped and seemed to hold a pow-wow. I turned
away and they came on again and when they were near
enough I turned and snapped them. My! they were mad,
and I was quite afraid of them but I snapped them again.
I thought they would shoot me but they contented themselves with sticking out their tongues and making faces.
I am afraid for once I descended to being that hateful
thing, a cheeky Kodak fiend.

September 26. Mr. Cook and Mr. Stuart [our Raymond
& Whitcomb guides] finally got us all onto the train again
and this was a day of such scenery as we had not seen since
the St. Gothard, but it was different and even bigger. I
never saw such gold and vivid green. We went across
trellis bridges and looked away down the sides of a cañon
to the rushing glacier streams below which varied from a
clear robin's-egg blue to emerald green but always rushing
and tearing along and all clear as crystal so that you
wanted to get some of the sparkling water to drink. All
through lunch we were rushing from one side of the car to
the other. Alice would scream, "Oooh! look at this!" and

over we would dash to see a mountain peak towering so high above us it was impossible to see the top without putting one's head down on the sill, and then Bishop McVickar would say, "That's nothing to my side," and back we would dash to look down into the dizzy depth of a cañon.

September 27. En route through the Selkirks in the rain. Alice and I rode on the engine while we went through the Kicking Horse Canyon to Revelstoke. This was fun but not unmixed joy as the quarters were rather a tight fit and my back was against a huge hot cylinder. The Engineer was good-natured and pleasant but he could only yell at us over the cylinder, but the fireman stood just behind us and was young and very chatty. We pulled the whistle and learned the meanings of the different signals and Alice fired the engine to the great amusement of the fireman—she was so huge in the small space there was!

The evening color was gorgeous. The hills became purple and there were big thunder heads billowing up right in the glow of the sunset and all outlined in gold— and while we were watching it a beautiful rainbow appeared spanning the river and standing out brilliant against the dark hills, and finally another one appeared above it—the colors fainter than the crimsons, lavender, nile greens and salmon pink of the lower.

Well, we thought we had had all the beauty that we could absorb, but the best was yet to come in the evening when we went down Glacier Canyon by the light of the full harvest moon. For three hours we were either in the Canyon rushing down it with the river or else way above it looking down a dizzy precipice at the shining river thousands of feet below and the dark mountain opposite. Finally I felt if I stayed a moment longer it would spoil the impression, as it had been growing all the time bolder and more wonderful and I knew nothing could be more superb than what I was seeing, so I rushed in and tumbled into my berth absolutely overwhelmed.

September 28. We came down to earth this morning by landing at Seattle very cross and hungry. Such a frightful city I never saw! Dirty and unfinished and hideous—muddy hubbledy streets and awful glaring advertisements. Then the perpendicular hills, when we all fell on top of each other in the cars rushing up at an angle of 45°. The Jameses' house was in a dreary neighborhood but had a wonderful view over Puget Sound, looking right down on the big steamships coming in from Japan and the East; and occasionally they see a large war canoe full of Indians who come from Alaska to get a drink!!!

One little incident we saw on the ferry to Tacoma; there was a young man dressed rather roughly in leggings, sombrero, flannel shirt and bandana. I took him for a cowboy or something of that sort. Old Mr. Nelson struck up an acquaintance with him and found he had been to Mt. Desert and was a friend of his son George! He was just returning home from the Klondike and had two savage-looking Esquimo dogs on a leash.

September 29. Arrived early in Portland, Oregon, and got up to the hotel in time for breakfast. A most attractive hotel built around a large open court which was full of palms and tropical plants! Portland struck us as the most homelike and pleasant place we had seen. It is older than most western cities so it looks more finished and its trees are good-sized. In Minneapolis we noticed that everyone was working on Sunday—builders and street laborers—baseball and theatres were going on, but here the streets were shady and clean and lots of nice-looking people were

going churchwards. We all went to Trinity Church and
heard the old Bishop of Montana. Papa was to have
preached this evening but, as the train was leaving earlier
than expected, he had to give out. This seemed to make
the rector mad as he gave us quite a tirade about travelling
on Sunday. Everyone condoled with Papa later about "his
scolding."

September 30. Stopped for breakfast in a funny place—
consisting of a field, one side of which was bordered with
false-fronted stores, an Inn, a colt, and lots of Alkali Ikes
lounging around, but I was able to get a toothbrush at
the store.

Our last day was a wonderful one as we circled Mt.
Shasta all the afternoon, finally coming to a stop within
fifteen miles of it, where we all got out and gazed our fill.
It was so beautiful as we came nearer and nearer it—sometimes seeing it glistening through the dark trees of a forest,
and sometimes reflected in a still small lake and finally
seeing its shining side in the sunset light.

Once when we were all on the observation car going
through a gorge in which were many turns and blind
curves, a brakeman suddenly came tearing through saying,
"Let me by! let me by!" and leaped over the back of the
train and ran up the track as hard as he could with a flag.
We knew a second section was right behind us so it was
quite exciting. We didn't wait a minute for the brakeman,
but went on very fast considering we were on a down grade
with a high wall of rock on one side and a cañon with a
rushing brook on the other. Just as soon as we had got
on the underside of the curve another train appeared on
the upper side, so it was a pretty close thing. We *left* a
brakeman a day or two ago! The poor man had run back
with a red flag and when he was nearly half a mile away

the train started. He signalled and signalled despairingly
and finally we, on the observation car, got hold of Mr.
Stuart and he stopped the train. It was very lonely country
and lucky for him we were watching him.

October 1. I was waked up by a bumping, seething
sound and looking out found the train was on a ferry.
As we came slowly into the dock we looked up at a clock
tower directly in front of us and the hands pointed to 7:30
exactly, and that was the time we were supposed to arrive
in San Francisco! After a twelve days' journey we weren't
ten seconds late! Everyone complimented Mr. Cook and
Mr. Stuart and they looked as pleased as Punch.

We went by cable car to the Palace Hotel—a vast place
of 1,400 rooms and apparently all full at the moment from
the complaints everyone seemed to be making about their
accommodations. After lunch we went out to walk about
the city and the first person we met was Harry Dibblee! He
showed us what to do and what to see, so we took in the
Cliff House, which was only a huge, dirty, smelly Pavilion,
and the surroundings and the crowds were like Coney
Island and depressed me—and the Presidio and Drake
Cross and Chinese Cemetery and the place where the *Rio
de Janeiro* went down last winter. As we went by the
Crocker house* on Nob Hill we saw Mr. Morgan, and he
and Bishop McVickar exchanged waves.

I thought San Francisco a lovely city. It is all hills,
even steeper than Seattle, and from their tops you get
beautiful views of the bay and ocean and Golden Gate.
All around too are the Sand Hills and they are so picturesque, especially when topped by a huge cross as so
many of them are, and you can see these crosses standing
against the sky from everywhere. There were lots of little

* Built by Charles Crocker, the builder of the Central Pacific Railroad. The
house was destroyed in the great fire of 1906. [Ed.]

gingerbread houses jammed together and very ugly, but
their front yards were a mass of color—fuchsias, geraniums
and even palm trees grew everywhere! The newsboys
were yelling out, "Extra! Morgan here!"

October 2. We went to the opening service of the
Convention in Trinity Church. It was very impressive and
also very long. We thought the Bishops who marched in
and filled the chancel a very big and handsome set of men.

October 5. Julie and I went shopping in Chinatown.
We met Bert Dibblee who was coming to call but he came
with us to Sing Fats, and told us not to go to any other
store. I think he was rather shocked that we were going
there at all! However, we met lots of people we knew and
found most fascinating things to buy so that I spent all my
money right off.

This was the day we were asked to tea at Miss Flood's.
She lives in the biggest and handsomest house on Nob
Hill,† but that does not describe it! There were two nice
old bachelors there for tea, and after it we all went over
the house with her. From the front door you looked
through a long hall and in the dim distance saw a handsome staircase going straight up and then branching off to
right and left and beyond it the whole back wall was a
superb stained-glass window. On one side of this hall was
the library, the huge banqueting hall and the dining room,
which seemed to us large and handsome enough for any
banquet. On the other side of the long hall was the living
room and *two* ballrooms both elaborately decorated with
frescoed ceilings, brocaded walls, satin upholstery; white
and gold and carved woodwork—long mirrors—all like a
French palace. There was a Sèvres vase in the centre of the
hall twice as tall as Sally! In the upstairs hall were the

† Now the Pacific Union Club. [Ed.]

pictures—two Corots, two Diaz, Daubignys, and other
celebrated artists (among them the two monks called "The
Funny Story"). The halls were wainscoted to the ceiling
and Miss Flood seemed to be especially proud of the wood
so I suppose it must be something special and it was beautifully carved. There were two bedrooms each 35 feet
square with four-poster beds, satin embroidered curtains
and quilts, etc. There was wonderful china and crystal
in cabinets and altogether we were quite overpowered.

October 6. Went to hear Papa preach in a church of an
ex-Theolog. Alice went with us and afterwards we all
went up to see the little Spanish Mission—a most fascinating old adobe church.

P.M. Papa took us three for a drive in the Golden Gate
Park. Twenty years ago it was all sand hills—dreary and
desolate in the extreme. Today there are long stretches
of velvety green and wide shady avenues bordered by
towering eucalyptus trees—lovely vistas over woods and
meadows of the bay and the ocean. There are lakes
covered with little boats and swans and ducks—there are
brooks and rushing waterfalls and attractive paths through
gardens *full* of flowers of every description—unbelievable
in their size and profusion. Everywhere were people enjoying it—whole families sprawling on the grass, and hundreds listening to the Band playing in a handsome stone
bandstand. It seemed a paradise for children and I wondered if any ever went to Sunday school. Everybody looked
happy—mothers and babies, 'arry and his girl, Major
Rathbone and his trotter, and a Chinese papa sailing a
toy launch with his cunning little moon-faced son.

October 7. Mr. Lewis, Cousin Arthur, Papa and we
three and a professional detective guide went to see Chinatown. It was really fascinating. Swarms of little Chinamen

and women in the streets and going in and out of the
houses—all so pleasant looking. They seemed like children, and the real children were the cunningest things I've
seen. Such cute babies who would say, "Hello!" or "Good-
night" with great pride as we passed. All the little houses
had high carved balconies usually painted some pretty
delicate shade and hung with big lanterns of paper. Some
of the balconies had pots of chrysanthemums along the
edge and the effect of the pale light from the lanterns,
the delicate colors of the background and the bright flowers
was quite lovely in the narrow streets. A curious feature
was the noise of slamming doors. We couldn't get used to
it at first—the incessant slam, slam, slam, and wondered
why it was.

We went first to the Joss House and saw their gods and
curious ways of worshipping them. Then we went to the
apothecary shops and the butchers and bakers and the
shops where they make gold jewelry and ornaments and
looked into the many barbers' shops and saw them having
their ears shaved!

Then we went to the theatre which was chock-full and
very hot. In the box next us were three cunning little
Chinese women, and in front of them two children, and
the mothers held on to their long red pigtails to prevent
their falling over into the pit. The pigtails of the little
children are wound with red tape if their hair isn't long
enough to make a decent-sized pigtail.

The play was most interesting and the costumes gorgeous. No women ever act, but men were dressed as
women and were wonderfully good representations. One
play will be continued for six months or a year every night
—the music was weird but rather fascinating and the actors
talked in a queer falsetto but kept perfect time and
rhythm.

The women in the audience do not sit with the men

but have a gallery to themselves. They told us the reason for this was because they wear such rich gold ornaments in their hair and ears they are afraid they will get stolen.

After a while we went through the green rooms and saw an actor rouging his cheeks and posing before his mirror preparatory to going on the stage. We then went upstairs and saw their living quarters which are the *worst* ever, and then we went out over the roof (you can go all over Chinatown on the roofs) and down dark outside stairways and through dark alleys to a place they call the Palace Hotel, which was an awful dingy hole. They call it this because it has a small place in the middle which is open to the sky like the beautiful court in the centre of the real Palace Hotel. In here around this unpleasant dark hole, were the opium dives and we saw Chinamen lying around on bunks, some asleep and some sucking their long pipes. The smell of the stale opium was most disagreeable and we were glad to get away and go to an attractive tea-house restaurant where we had good tea and preserved fruits before returning to the hotel and bed.

October 8. Lovely day but hot. Took the ferry and then train for Ross Valley. Pretty country of hills, meadowlands and marshes. There were houseboats on the bright blue water and long-legged storks were standing hunched up on the marshes. Arrived at Ross, we were met by Mrs. Bert Dibblee in a smart runabout looking very pretty in her light summery clothes. She drove me while another carriage took Julie and Sally. We drove through country roads and up a long shady avenue to the old Dibblee house where Mrs. Dibblee welcomed us and we spent an hour with her. She and Mr. D. came to that place when it was almost a desert and now it is thickly wooded, and they planted every tree! Now the eucalyptus towers a hundred feet high and there are arborvitae, madrona, bay trees, redwoods (sequoias) and even oaks shading the house and gardens. Virginia Creeper was hanging to the tall trunks like flames of red fire.

October 9. Went shopping with Mrs. Bert Dibblee and found the shops fascinating, especially the bookstore of Elder and Shepard on Post Street, which was the most artistic shop I ever saw.

Evening. Gave out of going to Bishop Nichols' reception. Papa went, but got so stuck in the crowd that he had to get out of a window. He is very busy at the convention all day and in the evenings always has a dinner and often a meeting again afterwards.

October 14. Harry took Julie and me on a trip up Mt. Tamalpais, in an open steam train up the mountain through a wonderful forest of redwoods. It was shady and cool, and the smell of the forest was delicious. Harry said it was the crookedest railway in the world, and the track seemed to tie into bowknots. At the summit, Harry pointed out the different towns with their attractive Spanish names and the peninsulas, bays, mountains, rivers, etc., and while he did it he *would* stand on a sharp ledge of rock balancing himself, with a drop of several thousand feet beneath him in every direction. I couldn't look at him but turned my eyes instead on some sure-footed goats that were browsing around clinging on the side of a precipice like flies on a wall.

October 16. Harold Blanchard gave a dinner for us at the University Club, which was awfully nice of him. The Bert Dibblees chaperoned and the other men were Jerry Rathbone and Harry Poet. It was a very swell dinner in a private dining room.

Everyone out here has such nice manners and seems so

cosmopolitan. I suppose it is because their families come
from all over and though they are thoroughly American
they have none of the faults and failings that come from
provincialism. Mr. Poet seems like the best kind of New
Yorker but his father was a 49'er and he was born here and
never has been to Europe. Mr. Rathbone is a Yale man
and H. Blanchard says he is a corker and H. B. himself
has bloomed out tremendously since he left Boston.

My father was tired after the convention, so he and Julie
remained while Sally and I set out on the southern part
of our trip with Mr. Stuart and Mr. Cook.

October 20. Los Angeles. Terrifically hot, and I am
suffering agonies with hives or fleas. I fear it is the latter
picked up on the ferry in 'Frisco, and I could have cried
with vexation.

The rest all went to church, but I balked at going three
times, and went out by myself. I took an electric train to
Westlake Park which Mr. Cook told me was a nice thing
to do, and it was—delicious. I watched the swans in the
lake and the children playing on the shore and smelt the
sweet scents of the wealth of glorious flowers all around
and listened to the soft splashing of a waterfall, and I really
think it did me as much good as listening to one of the
various bishops.

After an early lunch Mr. Davis, Bishop Johnson and
Sally and I took the car for Garvanza to go to the little
Church of the Angels. Papa was to have preached here
so a carriage met us where the car stopped and we drove
over a very dusty road to the Church. Years ago some
Englishman and his family settled on a big ranch here.
Their name was Campbell-Johnstone and soon various
friend of theirs, all English, came and joined them. As
they died off the younger branches of the family built a
memorial to them, and so it came about that this little

church away out in the wilderness was built. Every stone was brought from England and they got the architect, Street, to make the plans, and it is absolutely English from the top of the square tower to the porte cochere. They even built the little room in the tower looking down into the chancel for the Queen to sit in!

While we were at dinner in the evening a card was brought in to me on which was written in a shaking hand, "C. N. Wright, relation of Amos Lawrence," and out in the hall waiting to see me was a dear old man who said he was a friend and cousin of Great-Grandpa Lawrence. He had a prayerbook with his name in it which Amos Lawrence had given to this old man's mother, and he knew all about our ancestors, much more than I did, I am ashamed to say. He lived on Park Street when Great-Grandpa lived on Tremont Street, and the poor old man was so homesick that when Sally asked him if he wasn't coming East sometime, he began to cry, and then he was so mortified and apologetic! He saw in the paper that Papa was going to preach, and thinking he might be some connection of his old friend, he came in town to church and was much disappointed when he found Papa had not come —but he looked us up and came to see us on the chance. He got so excited talking about Boston that first he laughed and then he cried and finally left us with many blessings—as we had to go to the Missionary Meeting in St. Paul's Pro-Cathedral.

As we came out of the church a gray-whiskered gentleman spoke to me and said his name was Cunningham and he was a first cousin of Grandpa Cunningham's this time. He thought I must be I because I looked so much like Grandpa Cunningham!

October 21. Started at 8 A.M. for Santa Barbara. The beautiful Sierras kept right along beside us, and on the flat

plain between were orange, lemon and olive orchards—
but otherwise the country looked parched and brown.
Along the dusty road beside the track in dusty fields
grew weird-looking Indian figs and cactus all white with
dust, and dark-skinned Mexicans were driving big wagons
led by four or six mules, and all encircled in clouds of dust.
Cunning dark children were toddling around a group of
tents and on the sand dunes and beaches. The pitiless
sun scorched down out of a cloudless sky and there was not
a speck of shade except where some forlorn horses huddled
under a spreading live oak tree.

We went first to see the Mission. Of course it is Spanish,
but as I have not been to Spain it seemed like Italy to me—
the long white cloister, red-tiled tower, the brown-clad
monks, and finally the fascinating garden—all so foreign
and old looking.

After driving miles and miles along beside the ocean
and over hills and dales and ranches, we at last came to a
long winding uphill road bordered by a broad hedge of
pink geranium, and reached the beautiful Arcady Ranch.
This belongs to Miss McCall's brother who is an artist.
It was to me so perfect in every way that I wanted to
squeal with delight. The white house with blue shadows
flickering on its walls, the little terraced garden and the
grapery, the tall thin Italian cedars through which you got
vistas of vast distances and the winding paths with here
and there a little shrine or waterfall. We picked figs and
other fruits and flowers and the air was simply laden with
sweet scents. The inside of the villa was just as perfect
as the outside surroundings. The rooms were large and
square and with little steps leading to different levels which
I always like and the studio was a long beautiful room
opening out into the Amalfi cloister. Here were some fine
pictures and sculpture, also Rivera prints and books of

photographs—everything that I want and haven't got! I wondered about the Master and Mistress of this Palace of Delight. I imagined them to be paragons of beauty and grace and perhaps it is just as well that they were absent.

October 22. Got up at 5:30 and drove to the station with the McVickars and Mr. Cook just as the sun was rising over the mountains. We have seen much of Mr. Cook lately and he has been very nice. He seems to think Sally and I are his special charge so we get the best of everything. As Mr. Paine and the McVickars also think we are their special charge we have a pretty good time of it and haven't been allowed to pay for a single thing. They call us "the children" and thoroughly spoil us and either this or the fine air has put me in such a happy mood I giggle all the time.

As to Santa Barbara, that's where I am coming to live when my health gives out.

Today the train ran along the edge of a splendid sand beach with tremendous breakers rolling in and the wind blowing the spray off them as they broke, and I wished I could feel it as it was so hot in the train. When the sun got higher, it was almost unbearable. I longed to roll up my sleeves, and poor Bishop McVickar, whose collar had melted into a limp string, looked on the verge of tears.

Arrived at D'el Monte at last, we found Pa, Julie and Cousins Lena and Arthur waiting to welcome us on the piazza of the vastest hotel I ever saw. It is in a huge park laid out by Olmsted* and beautifully cared for. We were all very glad to sit quietly and feel cool again.

* Frederick Law Olmsted, the famous landscape architect who designed Central Park in New York, among many other brilliant parks and gardens. [Ed.]

October 23. We took the little horsecar over to Monterey village, a sketchable little sea-town, reminding me of Marblehead only the houses were of white or brown adobe instead of wood or brick. All the little fishing smacks with their three cornered sails were reflected in the harbor which was without a ripple on its light blue surface.

P.M. Some of us hired a mountain wagon and four horses and took the famous twenty-mile drive. I thought the California cedars, which are like cedars of Lebanon only crooked and windblown, were fascinating. They don't grow anywhere else in America and it is supposed that the seeds blew over from Japan.

October 24. Santa Cruz. We drove seven miles into the mountains to see the big trees. There was too much sideshow about it for me and it looked like a cheap picnic ground with little shanties, innumerable signs and even dancing platforms! Of course a lot of idiots had stuck their visiting cards up all over the "Giant" as high as they could reach and carved their names everywhere. But still they were wonderful, and when you think they are 4,000 years old, and nobody knows how much more, they are very impressive. Further in the forest I enjoyed them more, and it smelt pungent and delicious, and the foliage 300 feet above you looked so fresh and green and their trunks were so straight and tall that I was agreeably surprised even by the "great trees" although I had expected to be thrilled by them.

On the road we met many interesting things. First we heard a mysterious jingle like sleighbells in the distance, and pretty soon around a curve came a big wagon—or rather two big wagons tied together—both heavily loaded and dragged by eight horses, each with a sort of yoke of bells over his collar to warn teams coming the other way to stop in a broad part of the road in order to be able to pass. Another sight was a line of a dozen or more mules winding down the trail single file, and the whole procession led by a cowboyish person on a horse. We also met a heavy load of wood drawn by eight oxen, and all this added much to the interest of the big redwood forest.

October 25. Arrived at Palo Alto, we found Mr. Beylard was waiting for us having driven his coach up the day before in order to drive us back to San Mateo. One can imagine how superior I felt as I climbed up to the box seat next to Mr. Beylard. The groom let go the leaders' heads while they reared and pranced, but with one flip of the whip they came down to earth and we were off while all the rest of the crowd followed us in barges. We had Mr. Parsons on the coach with us who is the professor of Philosophy in the College and he took us all over the College and even into the new Chapel which will be superb when finished and far handsomer than other college chapels in America. We drove all around the buildings, in and out of the quadrangles and around the stock farm with our horn blowing all the time, and I imagine we were a lovely sight. Some of it was pretty tricky driving but Mr. Beylard is considered about the best whip in the country. I had driven with him before on the North Shore, and he used to drive a coach from the Vendome to the Wayside Inn, and he started to coach from Paris to Versailles. He is very attractive with the manners of a French gentleman, and good looks of an English sportsman and the sense of humor and companionableness of an American.

Back in San Francisco, we said some more good-byes, and Mr. Cook finally herded us on to our train.

October 26. Gave Mr. Cook my breakfast ticket and stayed in bed completely used up at last.

October 27. Salt Lake City. The hotel was the least attractive we have seen. It, and many of the houses, which had two, three and four doors for the use of the different wives, looked shabby and there seemed to be no really handsome buildings.

P.M. We all went to the Mormon Service in the tabernacle. Some fine music by a large choir accompanied by their glorious organ. Bishop McV. was very interested in it all and talked to several Mormons till his sister feared he might be converted.

We left Salt Lake City at 9 o'clock. It is always amusing to see Mr. Cook corralling us all in the hotel lobby and the place is usually full of people looking on. Of course we buy the evening papers and read all about ourselves.

October 29. I could walk over Pikes Peak and home to Boston in this air, I think. At 8:15 we started up the Mountain. The air was so clear and everything looked sparkling and fresh and the trees seemed to jump at you from the blue sky and it all smelt delicious but about halfway up I began to think I was "feeling the altitude." My head felt very full. My heart was thumpy and my hands and feet as cold as ice. I went back to the car and sat in the sun and did not take much interest in the panorama that we were beginning to see all around us. The summit still looked miles above us—and I almost got out at the next stop when I heard that we had 4,000 more feet to go up. But I stayed in and a *silly* stage set in. Julie, Sally, Ethel Cheney and I giggled hysterically over nothing at all till I felt so foolish and uncomfortable that I went and sat by myself and just felt dopy. And when we arrived at the Summit House and I attempted to get out of the car I found I could not walk straight. I clung to Ethel and staggered somehow through the snow and into the nice warm house where Cousin Arthur dosed me with

brandy and hot bouillon and in a few minutes I felt all
right and even wrote a pictorial postcard to Alice Morris.
Then I went out and looked at the view. The whole earth
seemed to be stretched out before me in a hazy brown plain
with stripes of darker color which we took to be forests.
This whole plain was surrounded by a snowy ridge of
mountains very bold and jagged, extending all around the
horizon. After having our pictures taken we were thankful to spring into the warm car for the descent. I was feeling fine again now, and the sun was so hot we opened the
windows, stuck our heads out, and took it all in, the wonderful air and view. We had been up 14,147 feet, almost as
high as Mont Blanc and higher than the Jungfrau.

We got home in time for lunch and right afterwards
started in a mountain wagon for the Garden of the Gods—
the gateway was very impressive but the absurd names
they have given to all the remarkable and interesting rock
formations take away all the romance and grandeur, and
make you laugh at them instead. When you think that this
splendid hollow was the Indians' Camping Ground hundreds, if not thousands of years ago, and that these curious
rocks were their gods, to have them called "The Washer-
woman," "The Kissing Camel" and "The Baggage Room"
is sad and horrible.

During dinner at the Brown Palace Hotel, Mr. Cook
came over to our table and very mysteriously gave Papa a
little note. Of course we all looked around immediately to
see "The Great Pinkerton." He was a big common-looking
man and he was dining with a very blonde lady who wore
eight huge diamonds on her fingers. Being such a great
detective he noticed our interest in him and was much
amused.

October 30. I breakfasted late alone and was noticing
how very sick my waiter looked as he went off, and another

waiter came and said, "That little feller can't hardly get around," and proceeded to tell me his sad story. It was the usual story out here as most of the waiters are consumptives, and it depressed me very much—it all seemed so hopeless. It made me feel better to give the other waiter something for "the little feller," though I know it couldn't do him any good.

October 31. Crossed the Missouri and said good-bye to the Wild and Woolly West. In Denver we saw our first and last real Remington cowboys. Two rode down the street on broncos with Mexican saddles and stirrups, sombreros tied with leather thongs, fringed leggings, handkerchiefs around their necks, etc.

November 2. A morning of goodbyes as the party was dropping off everywhere. Many got off at Albany, Cousins Lena and Arthur at Pittsfield, others at Worcester. We cheered everyone as they left and finally when we left at Back Bay there were only Mr. Sowden and the Allens to cheer us. Our last sight of the train was as it moved off with Mr. Cook standing on the back platform, hat in hand and smiling ruefully. He said he would never take another party "like this one."

Mamma and Baby met us and Baby looked awfully cunning and quite dazed by it all. Both carriages met us, and I went out in the open cart. It struck me that Boston is a very handsome, clean, swell-looking city, beautifully situated, with nice-looking people and smart equipages and handsome horses. I should feel very badly if I thought I would never see California and the West again, but on the whole I would rather live in the East near the centre of things.

CHAPTER 15

THE MISSED CORONATION, 1902

◦§

Aunt Sally and I arrived at the Berkeley Hotel, Piccadilly, on June 19, 1902, for the Coronation of Edward VII. Our rooms are on the corner looking down Piccadilly, which swarms with tanned soldiers from South Africa in the ugly new khaki and puttees, and jaunty sombreros turned up on one side with a feather.

After a couple of hours here we went on a search for tickets for the Coronation and were lucky enough to get two in the front row of a stand just going up in Green Park almost opposite our hotel. These were five guineas apiece. We shall have to cross Piccadilly before nine in the morning and sit in them all day, but we are fortunate to have them so near.

We were all sitting in the Coffee Room when the page entered, as in *Alice in Wonderland,* holding high a silver salver on which was an envelope about a foot square and in it an invitation printed in gold to view the Coronation Procession from the house of the Baroness Burdett-Coutts!* This was the wonderful result of a note of introduction from Papa which I left there yesterday. Hers is the big

---

* Angela Georgina Burdett-Coutts (1814–1906) was a famous philanthropist, created a peeress in her own right in 1871. It is said that King Edward called her, "after my mother, the most remarkable woman in The Kingdom." [Ed.]

house just the other side of the Duke of Devonshire's from
our hotel. The Duke of Devonshire's takes up the whole
block and hers is the corner of the next block. We wrote
an acceptance at once, Aunt Sally with a sigh of regret for
her wasted ten guineas.

Went to the last International Polo Match with Mr.
Endicott. Suddenly a hard shower came up, but it luckily
stopped as we reached the Club. Of course the grass was
sopping, but the English girls didn't seem to mind standing on it in their thin slippers or trailing around their
muslins. Then the sun came out hot and bright and it was
a lovely and very gay sight. We got fine places just in
front of the Royal box and among those in the box were
the whole Connaught family. Near us, too, were Lord and
Lady Roberts and sundry Indian princes wonderfully
dressed. One right near by had on a long tight frock coat
of pale blue brocade; in his turban were jewels as big as
eggs and around his neck, hanging below his waist, a string
of huge pearls. The game was more exciting than the
score, 7–1, sounds. The Americans did some brilliant playing but the English were steadier and their teamplay better and they also were more used to a soggy field. Afterwards it was very difficult to get away, there were so many
carriages and fully a quarter of a mile of grooms waiting
in line for their people. Some of them had powdered hair
or wigs and short clothes. There were also many huge
puffing, roaring, snorting, smelling automobiles.

Sunday, June 22. A handsome old man preached to us
on the coronation and then gave out several notices about
it, among them one requesting all the people, no matter
where they were, on the street, in the hotels, or anywhere,
to sing "God Save the King" at eight o'clock on Thursday
evening, a unique idea and interesting to see if it is carried out.

The crowd on Piccadilly was most amusing and a great
example to us of control and orderliness. The policemen
are so calm and decided, and the drivers so calm and good-
natured, and even the poor overstrained horses seemed
calm. The pace is a good sharp trot, and then a sudden
standstill for some minutes while the cross traffic goes by.
Then a quick start and another sharp trot. Nobody seems
hurried and nothing ever happens though there are a number of the biggest automobiles I ever saw right in the thick
of it! There are also lots of country people today and
costers in their little donkey carts staring at all the decorations. They are dressed in velveteens and uncurled
feathers, many bringing their children and babies and singing as they rattle past.

Monday, June 23. Aunt Sally has engaged a maid who is
very satisfactory—willing, untiring, knowing and young!—
name "Cochrane." I went shopping with her this morning
and searched in vain for the place I left my Kodak films.

The Khedive and family arrived at our hotel today, so
now we are under military guard and have a huge grenadier
standing immovable by the door. This afternoon we went
to tea at Claridge's, which also has a grenadier in front,
the sign of royalty staying there, and then we drove in the
Park. Carriages were six abreast and such gorgeous turn-
outs I never imagined, also many beautiful women and
girls, but others were too much frizzed and painted. The
soldiers in the Life Guards Barracks were hanging out of
the windows watching the show, and it was a gay but very
tiresome scene. Aunt Sally had to go to bed directly afterwards, she got so tired.

Tuesday, June 24. As I was coming up in the lift with
the silly-faced elevator boy he suddenly turned to me and
said in his hurried lisp, "I suppose you've 'eard the 'orrible

news, miss." I said, "No! What?" "There will be no Coronation; the King h'is very h'ill and 'as just been h'oper-
ated. The Coronation 'as been postponed quite two
months, miss. Yes, miss, very 'orrible. Oh! no! miss, of
course we 'ope 'e won't die."

I was so stunned I couldn't take in anything except the
dreadful fact—"No Coronation!" I told Aunt Sally, who
was immediately struck dumb, and then I rushed to see if
the Endicotts knew more. They hadn't heard it, so I told
them. Mr. Endicott gasped for a few moments and then
flew out for more particulars. Mrs. Endicott, senior, immediately began to pity the King, the Queen, all the Royal
Family, and all the English people—which was almost too
much for me. Young Mrs. Endicott began to giggle because
she thought my disappointment "funny," but I liked her
way of taking it better, so I giggled with her rather hysterically. Out in the street bulletins had sprung up and newsboys were waving them and shouting, and the people were
stopping and staring and talking. The workmen were stopping work on the stands and staring and I knew it was
too true. I went back to Aunt Sally and found her in a
curious state. She thought she had been out of her head
and dreamt it. So I had to assure her all over again and
she thought it was funny, too, and Cochrane thought it
was very funny and said all the servants found it a great
joke on all the Americans. Apparently there is not much
sorrow for the King in the lower circles of society. Cochrane was vastly amused when Aunt Sally audibly expressed
her wish for a funeral as better than nothing! This hotel
is insured for $70,000, so they are very calm here. It is so
crowded now, they are using the bathrooms to put the
valets in.

This afternoon I had to go alone to Lord Ashcombe's
reception because Aunt Sally was sick. It was really not

scarey because it was so hopeless. I didn't know anybody
and the English don't introduce. But it was so interesting
that I enjoyed it. There was a queue of swell carriages as I
arrived at 17 Prince's Gate. Several lackeys in plum-colored
liveries, silver buckles and pink silk stockings helped me
to alight, took my wraps and led me on through huge
rooms and finally to the old butler, who yelled me out, and
Lord and Lady Ashcombe nervously shook my hand and on
I went into the garden. It was pretty out there, but as I
found no friends I soon came in again. Lord Ashcombe
then kindly introduced me to several daughters and
daughters-in-law, and after being refreshed I left—with
these impressions: handsome, fine old house, splendid living, heavy, handsome good taste, deadly party, frumpy
dowagers, gauche girls with lovely complexions, and some
fine-looking old men. They were not allowed to have the
music which they had engaged, on account of the King.
No one talked of anything else and all wore very long faces.

Wednesday, June 25. King doing well. Apparently not
going to die. Amos telegraphed he was not coming over
from Paris and his lunch at Prince's Restaurant was off.
The telegraph wires are about twelve hours behindhand
which I think is doing pretty well. Mrs. Ashe took me,
with two very attractive English girls, to a reception at
Ranelagh Hunt Club for the Indian Princes. They were
having a gymkhana with races, pigsticking, and riding
stunts of every sort and it was most picturesque. They rode
beautifully and were lithe and agile in their smart riding
togs, gay-colored jeweled turbans and sashes, with their
dark faces and flashing white teeth. The beautiful old
country place, with its broad lawns and polo fields edged
with the dark thick foliage of great elms for a background
to the gay growds of beautifully dressed women in light
colors and parasols, the sleek looking men and beautifully

groomed horses, and all surrounded by lines of four-in-hands as far as one could see, made a colorful picture. There were hundreds of little tables under the trees where waiters served us tea and cake and the most huge and luscious strawberries, even better than Aunt Sally's.

Thursday, June 26. The King is better, but poor Aunt Sally is still in bed. The weather continues perfect and it is exasperating to think what we expected to be doing this lovely day. Instead of going to the Coronation I just went to tea at the Chamberlains* with old Peajobody† and some other Bostonians! In the evening Aunt Sally very kindly sent Aunt Hetty, Mrs. Ashe and me to the theater where we saw George Alexander in *Paola and Francesca*—splendid acting and beautifully staged. We enjoyed it immensely.

Friday, June 27. Another perfect day, but I felt more depressed than ever. I take care of Aunt Sally at night and she had a bad night and I was worried. She doesn't like any air in spite of the terrific heat, so I drag my bed over to the window, which is open only a crack, and lie with my face against this crack but not enough air comes in to stir the fringe on the shade. The only thing that comes in is smoke from the Duke of Devonshire's stable chimneys. In the morning after a few hours of broken sleep I am not much refreshed and my throat and head feel very queer indeed. The lights burn very late in Devonshire House as the Duke attends to his correspondence in the evening I am told. The story goes that one night he wrote later than usual and when he rang for someone to mail his letters no one answered and he found it was 2 A.M. He was in his dressing-gown, but he thought he would go

---

* Mrs. Joseph Chamberlain had been born Mary Endicott of Salem, Massachusetts. [Ed.]

† One of the Peabodys who lived abroad. [Ed.]

out and get a breath of air and mail them himself. He
crossed the courtyard, but the big gate was locked. However, the little postern wasn't and he slipped through;
mailed his letters and turned to go back but the little door
had shut and he could not open it from the outside. He
rang the bell but nothing happened except that a "bobby"
appeared. Seeing the strangely clad figure hanging about
Devonshire House ringing the bell, he naturally thought
he had to deal with a crazy man; so he gently persuaded
him to "move along." The Duke, who is very straight and
stiff and wooden-faced (as we know from our visit last year
with him at Trinity Lodge in Cambridge) said, "This is
my house and I want to get in." "Oh! yes," said the bobby,
"and I suppose you're the Dook of Devonshire, now ain't
yer?" "Yes," said the Duke, "I am." "Poor chap! Come
along with me," said the bobby as a small crowd of night
owls, very curious and amused, had gathered around. Fortunately it occurred to the Duke that, if he could get the
policeman to take him around the corner into Berkeley
Square he could get his brother, Lord Charles Cavendish,
to identify him; and this was done, the crowd of waifs and
strays following to see what happened when his lordship
was awakened in the middle of the night.

Well, there being nothing else to do this morning, I went
to Guard Mounting at St. James's, which I always love.
While we were watching the Grenadiers, the Horse Guards
suddenly went by, and then we saw the cunningest sight!
The three little children of the Prince of Wales* appeared
above the great high wall of Marlborough House and stood
there in a row saluting the Guards. Little Prince Edward†
knew all the technicalities, evidently, because when the
band began to play concert music he stopped saluting and

---

* Later George V. [Ed.]   † Later Edward VIII, now Duke of Windsor. [Ed.]

his brother* and sister† not noticing this, he grabbed their
hands down for them. The two little princes were dressed
in sailor suits and the little girl in pink with a big floppy
pink hat. The crowd were all watching them and on every
face was a smile, almost an affectionate smile. I waited to
see the Prince go over to inquire for the King, which he
does every morning at 11:30, but this morning, of course,
he didn't go. Lots of royal carriages keep driving in and
out of Buckingham Palace and one sees the scarlet and gold
liveries everywhere as all the visiting royalties use them
too. In this sunny hot weather they use open barouches
entirely, so it is easy to see them all.

In the afternoon Mrs. Ashe took Nina Hopkins and me
and a charming English girl named Iris Sopwith to a Horse
Show at Ranelagh. I never saw such a lovely dress as Miss
Sopwith's and she was very friendly and lively—different
from any English girl I have met before. The horse show
was very thrilling; the horses and the riding and driving
were all so fine. Lord Somebody drove his own coach with
a matched calico four-in-hand and a shabby old colored
man next him, who looked like an old slave but was probably a king of somewhere. The Duke of Cambridge‡ was
in the Royal Box, but he is such a good old sport that that
wasn't near enough to the horses for him, so he had a chair
put out right by one of the jumps and there he sat, two
gentlemen standing behind him, all in danger of their lives
it seemed. When he left the band played "God Save the
King," and he stood up in his carriage and bowed. He is
very popular.

Going home we met all the coaches coming in town on

* Later King George VI. [Ed.]   † Subsequently the Princess Royal, Countess
of Harewood. [Ed.]

‡ George William Frederick Charles, Duke of Cambridge (1819–1904), grandson
of George III and first cousin of Queen Victoria, was Commander-in-Chief of the
British Army from 1887 until 1895. [Ed.]

Piccadilly, a long procession of them from different parts, very lively with their tooting horns and bright-colored liveries. Hyde Park is turned into a huge camp, covered with tents, in which the Colonials are. The officers are always on Piccadilly, riding three in a hansom, smoking. We met also a lot of royal barouches, two men on the box of each in red liveries trimmed with gold, and in them gorgeously dressed royal visitors of every color, mostly black! These go dashing right through the traffic through a narrow lane kept open for that purpose. Why there are no accidents I know not. There are always some of these royal carriages outside the Berkeley while their strange looking occupants call on the Khedive.

People have been most polite about calling on us, too, in response to Papa's letters—Mrs. Whitelaw Reid (whose husband is Special Ambassador to the Coronation), the Dean of St. Paul's and daughter, Bishop of Rochester and wife (Lady Lavinia Talbot), and they have asked us to tea, but as London is so upset and Aunt Sally seems to get no better here she has decided to go to the Isle of Wight in a few days. The English are so absorbed in the King's illness that Americans can't help feeling *de trop* here.

Sunday, June 29. Very hot and muggy with showers. I went to the Intercessory Service at St. Paul's. I heard the preacher (the Bishop of London, I think) in the far distance, but could not see him. Afterwards everyone seemed to stop on the steps as if waiting for something, so I did too and was well rewarded. Around the Cathedral came one, two, three, about seven, real Cinderella coaches, all gilt and glass, on great C-springs, two men standing on the back of each, hanging to the straps and all dressed in gold with cocked hats, white wigs and pink stockings. The first coach, in which was the Lord Mayor in all his toggery, ermine

robe, gold chain, queer hat, etc., had six horses and postil-
lions and a regular old storybook huge coachman on the
box, with curly wig and big cape. It was a huge coach and
went rumbling around St. Paul's. The rest went down the
Strand followed by scores of royal carriages. It was the
Queen and Royal Family and visiting big-wigs leaving the
service by some other door evidently back of the Cathedral.
This was the best show I have seen yet and the first time
luck has been with me.

P.M. Aunt Hetty and I made calls, among them one upon
the old Baroness Burdett-Coutts. The door was opened by
an Adonis who must have been seven feet high and a gorgeous sight in blue and gold with white stockings. While
waiting for the Baroness to appear we looked our fill at
everything. It is a very handsome house—mostly in the
style of fifty years ago—and full of interesting things.
Many of these had brass labels on them, so I found Sir
Joshua Reynolds' painting chair! I almost gasped when the
Baroness at last came in. She looked like an old witch,
leaning bowed over on a cane,* wrinkled, mumbly, tooth-
less, ghastly, in a stiff lavender silk, trimmed with priceless
lace and a cap of the same. We went forward to meet her
and she mumbled something about taking my arm, so I
had to support her and place her on a sofa. She seemed
absolutely deaf at first and her mumblings were perfectly
unintelligible, but after a baffling five minutes we found
we were conversing with less difficulty and after fifteen
minutes I had forgotten how ugly she was and found her
an exceedingly bright, interesting and charming companion. She insisted on sending us to see the house in
charge of the old butler who showed us the great ballroom,
the wonderful pictures in the gallery, and out on to the
upper balcony to see the view over Green Park and up and

* She was 88 years old. [Ed.]

down Piccadilly. Here we had the agony of seeing where
we might have sat for the Coronation. The house was still
decorated with drapings of blue and white edged with
gold and caught up at the top of the house by a huge
golden crown. It was one of the most effectively decorated
houses of all! When we got back to the Baroness tea was
being served and a South African lady and daughter had
come in. They had come all that way for the Coronation
and were going back tomorrow quite mad. It was a relief
to me to have someone to sympathize with, the English take
things so calmly. The Baroness was almost affectionate
when we left and said Papa must always write her when
any of his family or friends were coming over. We thought
her a very wonderful old lady. She was one of Queen
Victoria's bridesmaids!

Tuesday, July 1. Aunt Sally and I went, by invitation
from Mr. Choate*, to see the Procession go by the Mall
from Carlton House Terrace, where they live. Today the
Queen, Prince of Wales and Lord Roberts review the Colonials on the Horse Guards Parade. There were splendid
bands and all the foreign representatives on horseback.
Then a pause and then cheering all down the lines of spectators, then horse guards and royal carriages. First, the
Queen [Alexandra] and Princess of Wales† bowing and
swaying and bobbing as they passed so that they almost
looked as if rocking in paroxysms of laughter. The Queen
looked slim and dignified in her usual lavender dress,
bonnet and boa, but she did look rather wiggy even at
that distance; such a quantity of red gold hair in front is a
mistake, I think. After them came several carriages of royal
ladies and then another pause. Then more cheering, grow-

---

* Mr. Joseph Choate, our Ambassador at the Court of St. James's.
† Later Queen Mary. [Ed.]

ing louder, and a company of cavalry appeared, then Lord
Roberts, riding alone on his gray charger, then the Prince
of Wales,* rather insignificant looking, and with him the
Duke of Connaught, handsome young Prince Arthur, and
other princes and dukes.

In the evening Aunt Sally and I dined in the restaurant
of the Berkeley. There it is gayer than the dining room
with a lot of amusing people and good music. Most of the
women smoke as well as the men. It is funny to see people
in evening clothes going by in hansoms out to dine as late
as nine o'clock and yet in bright sunlight. The weather is
so hot, too, that they don't even need evening wraps. I
saw young Winston Churchill go by in a hansom in dress-
suit and topper tonight.

Wednesday, July 2. The page brought me in a note at
breakfast and said, "From Mrs. Chamberlain," though I
don't know how he knew. It enclosed two tickets for the
Parade today, entitling us to two seats at the Horse Guards.
They are very hard to get and even Mr. Choate had not
been able to get any; so it was very nice of her. Aunt Sally
couldn't go, so I decided to go to the Choates' first and
ask someone there to go with me as they had asked us to
watch it again today from Carlton House Terrace. However, they informed me that if I once got into the Horse
Guards I couldn't get out till it was all over, and, as in that
case I should have missed our train for the Isle of Wight
this afternoon, I decided to stay at the Choates' and gave
my tickets to Mr. Choate who gave them to Mrs. Cowles
and Mrs. Robinson, President Roosevelt's two sisters, who
were there.

Today there were more people at the Choates' and it was
more fun—all the Bayard Cuttings and George Ward and

* Later King George V. [Ed.]

John Cross and Mr. John Ridgeley Carter, who said he used to know me in Cambridge, a Mrs. Stevens of New York, and, of course, Billy Woodward, John Saltonstall, and Joe and Mabel Choate. The procession was more interesting too. All the Indian princes rode with the Prince of Wales and wore all their jewels and medals, making a very gorgeous and colorful display, showing a little what the Coronation might have been like. The Queen looked prettier today, too (less wiggy and younger), and she and the Princess of Wales, both so slim and straight, looked their parts to perfection in their delicate colors and ruffs and veils. It was a much more splendid procession than yesterday's and a thoroughly satisfactory end-up to our London visit, disappointing though it was!

CHAPTER 16

A TRIP SOUTH, 1903

❧

"ONE O'CLOCK train to N.Y. for my southern trip on Mr. Ogden's special train with a lot of educators," I wrote on April 20, 1903.

This group was led by Mr. Robert Ogden, a rich and public-spirited New Yorker, and included a number of prominent people like Walter Hines Page and Bishop McVickar (Bishop of Rhode Island—"the biggest bishop of the smallest state"). Papa had been asked to go but wasn't able to, but since the Bryans of Richmond had invited us both to stay with them, I decided to go anyway.

The trip was supposed to interest people in what was then called "the colored question." "Civil Rights" lay in the undisclosed future. The party was going south to discuss the question with Southerners.

April 20. The clans gathered at the Twenty-third Street Ferry [in New York] and when I arrived I found Mrs. Russell, Mrs. Blake, and Mrs. Charles Russell Lowell and her daughter—sister and niece of Col. Robert Gould Shaw. Then came Professor Peabody with Gertrude, Lena Stevenson and Harriet Curtis—then the R. T. Paine party and I was

introduced to Mr. John Moors who is going to the Bryans'
too—then came William Jay Schieffelin and his mother—
his wife could not come. There were 120 in all so it was a
pretty long special train. We travelled in great luxury with
a most delicious diner. Mr. Shieffelin asked me to sit with
him and his mother and Bishop McVickar, which I was
delighted to do and we had a very jolly time. Except for
meals I had a rather intellectual time. First Rev. Percy
Grant* came and gave me a long discourse on Evolution.
Then he and Willie Schieffelin introduced a lot of men to
me: Dr. Crapsy, Dr. Shaw, Hamilton Mabie, Walter Hines
Page and an old man named Wheeler who talked about the
Civil War and explained what had happened at all the
places we were going through!

After Washington we seemed to step from spring into
summer—all the blossoms were out and the woods were
full of flowers. We saw more and more darkies and donkeys
and tumbled-down cabins and general shiftless picturesqueness. At Richmond a tall, red-haired young man in evening
dress boarded the train. He came into our car and asked
me if I knew where Miss Lawrence and Mr. Moors were.
He was a Bryan boy and he put Mr. M. and me into a carriage and said "Home" and off we went, but home seemed
to be a long way off upon a very bad road. When we met
another carriage I was sure we would tip over. I had rather
dreaded this long drive with my new acquaintance but
Mr. Moors turned out to be very chatty and much better
than he looks so I enjoyed it. We finally pulled up under
a porte cochere and ascended the steps of the Bryan Mansion. We had been feeling rather timorous at arriving to
pass a week with perfect strangers but we need not have
felt so, as Mrs. Bryan threw open the door herself and

* Pa's friend the Rev. Percy Stickney Grant, rector of the Church of the Ascen-
sion in New York, and regarded as being very radical.

greeted us as if we had been her long-lost children. Of course I recognized it immediately as Southern Hospitality.

At "Laburnam," Richmond, Va., April 22. Waked in my big, comfortable bedroom—bathroom attached—to find a perfect spring morning. There were lovely views from all my windows of shady lawns, fields with browsing cattle, avenues of flowering shrubs and lots of different beautiful birds. I laughed to see an old Negro—a typical picturesque old slave—who I afterwards learned was "Uncle Henry"—raking up leaves. He was in one spot the entire morning with a broom of twigs apparently turning over three leaves which lay upon the lawn. My black maid came in four times while I was dressing. I couldn't keep her out and such a chatty person I never met. She had, as each one of the family told me later, "no sense—not a mite of sense" but she told me I looked "beautiful" after I was dressed and asked, "How do you like our home, Miss Lawrence?"

I put on a white linen as it seemed so summery and warm and later I found that this amused the family who thought it was "right chilly out" and had a large fire lighted in my room. They all came wandering in to breakfast one by one. The Colonel is very tall, slight—always wears an open frock coat, has grey hair and a pointed beard. He has a handsome face with piercing eyes—in fact a typical Southern Colonel. He has cordial grand manners but gets much excited when he talks, especially about the war which is still his favorite subject. It really feels down here as if it had only finished yesterday. The older generation seem still to live in war times.

Stewart* was at breakfast when I came down. He rose and bowed low and was most attentive and polite. He is en-

---

* John Stewart Bryant became a distinguished newspaper publisher and President of the University of William and Mary.

gaged to the beauty of Richmond, Anne Tennant, and he reminded me that I had met her at the Coles' last summer at Bar Harbor. Mrs. Bryan was also at breakfast sitting behind the large silver tea set. She is not at all pretty but very pleasant and motherly and the greatest talker I ever heard and one of the most amusing. My fellow guest, Mr. Moors, was delighted with her quaint ideas and quick repartees. In fact, the whole family are great talkers and often all talk at once with the most curious but fascinating running together of their words. I couldn't understand more than half of what they said at first, and I must say it is ever so much like the Negro dialect. A pretty girl came into the room, kissed Mr. and Mrs. Bryan and was introduced as "Mis' St. George." After a moment I realized she must be the married one's wife. She asked me in a soft drawl if I was tired after my long journey and I found in her another representative type—my exact idea of the Southern girl. Soon after her came a most gorgeous individual, a Greek God in bronze with a haughty expression, a long tight-fitting coat and the jauntiest, best-fitting clothes I ever saw. He also bent double and showed me the part down the back of his head—sat down by the girl and began to talk harder than anybody. He was evidently St. George. Bob came in at last; he was on the St. George plan—not quite so handsome, but tallest of all—six-foot-four. I am afraid they pad their shoulders—such broad, square shoulders *couldn't* go with such small waists and hips! They were all so bright and amusing that I felt like a lump of gaucherie and stupidity.

After breakfast, "Mis' St. George" took me around the place. It is called Laburnam. The South is much more southern than I expected to find it. It is soft, sweet, slow and shiftless. The morning was lovely with a hazy blueness over everything.

Later we drove over to Brook Hill for lunch. Brook Hill

is where Mrs. Bryan lived as a girl and her mother and
sisters still live there. It is "the old place" and is two miles
further in the country than Laburnam. You drive over
a straight white road which is older than anyone knows and
is traced back to the "Three Notch Trail" of Indian days.
The stately old mansion stands far back from the road and
in front are lawns with fine magnolia and other trees and
the lawns slope back into meadows and woods. These
woods are full of paths and little gurgling brooks and ra-
vines and at the end of some of the paths are pretty "summer houses" which have seen much excitement and I
understand many broken hearts. At present the woods
were white with dogwood growing very high and the house
was full of great sprays of it—most decorative. I had never
seen any before (it was rare in New England until years
later). The old house was used as a hospital in the war
and Mrs. Bryan and her sisters used to play checkers with
the soldiers and let them beat them—much against their
will. Old Mrs. Stewart is treated as a sort of queen and
you are brought up to be introduced to her in her arm
chair when she holds out her hand and says with great dignity, "Welcome to Brook Hill!" The Paines are staying
here and are burbling with contentment, but I am so glad
to be at Laburnam.

It was a large lunch today. There were four bishops who
were awfully polite to me on account of Papa. I sat between the Bishop of Virginia and a youth named Pinckney
—a cousin of the Stewarts.

After dinner in the evening, Mrs. Bryan, Mr. Moors, Bob
Bryan and I drove into the opening of the Conference
which was in a theatre in Richmond. It was crowded and
there we met all our train party again and it really seemed
ages since we had seen them. After the meeting we adjourned to a reception given for us educators at "the Col-

lege," but I couldn't make out what college. It was not
very exciting and poor Dr. Bob was, I fear, extremely
bored, though he was very attractive and polite all the
evening.

April 23. Dr. Bob, "Mis' Saint" and I drove in to town
to sightsee. They took me first to the fine Lee Monument
and then we went to the Museums. First to the "Confederate" which was originally the Jeff Davis house and has a
fine commanding situation. It is rather pathetic inside as it
is full of poor old relics of the Confederacy from uniforms,
swords and letters, to the war doll that had run the block-
ade, in glass cases. Then we went to the Valentine Museum
and here at last I realized the grandeur of the Old Colonial
Virginia. It is a fine old house with huge, beautifully
shaped rooms, wonderful carving and gold decorations on
the white panels around the doors. The tapestries and the
beautiful hangings and brocades, the long windows and
mirrors and the exquisite mantlepieces were all a joy to
me. Then the fine pieces of furniture and the wonderful
china and glass that filled the handsome cabinets were so
tastefully arranged I could have stayed hours studying it all.
    After seeing this I appropriately went to lunch with Mr.
and Mrs. B. B. Valentine in their *present* home. They
were a charming couple and it was a pleasant lunch; Mr.
and Mrs. Thorp of Cambridge, Mr. Moors, Sally Fairchild,
Mr. and Mrs. Richard Watson Gilder (of the Century
Magazine) and Miss Mary Johnston of *To Have and To
Hold* fame. Of course I was thrilled to meet her as I had
read her book many times. She is quite young but patheti-
cally delicate looking—very small and slight and ashy
grey in color and she trembled so that she could hardly
help herself at lunch, and such a weak little voice as she
had! She seemed very sweet and natural and was quite
bright to talk to, but oh, so pathetic! She can only use

her eyes a few minutes at a time and gets about an hour's
work done in a day and yet this frail little woman supports
her whole family and made thousands of dollars out of *To
Have and To Hold.*

Mr. Valentine told me about the bust of the old colored
man in the Museum. He was Coachman in the family for
three generations and he drove Mr. V.'s grandfather to
Lafayette's Ball. When he died this Mr. V. and seven of
his brothers and first cousins were pallbearers at the funeral. I had a long, interesting talk with Mr. Valentine on
the Negro problem and it was interesting to hear an en-
lightened Southern gentleman's views and one who was so
in earnest on the question.

"Mis' Saint" called for me after lunch and drove me
around again and finally home. She is a charming com-
panionable little thing with lovely manners. I have lots to
learn from these Southern people and I try to keep my eyes
open all the time.

There are constant surprises—for one, I cannot get used
to the very ordinary-looking people I see all about being
such great swells as regards their family. In both museums
we went to I was introduced to the caretakers and in one
it was a very sweet ladylike person—but in the other it was
a common-looking woman with the most awful voice I ever
heard. She was descended from Pocohontas and the Boll-
ings and was a near cousin of the Bryans. Then in the
bank, "Mis' Saint" chaffs the young man in shirt sleeves
who leans through the window. She introduces him to me
and he nods to a rather seedy-looking young man who
joined us at the entrance. In answer to his question, as
to "what you all been doing"? I explained that Mrs. St.
George has been showing me the sights, to which he
replies, "Well, you certainly got a right good guide in
Mis' Bryan, but that's a mighty useless looking courier you

got along with you all." "Mis' Saint" tells me later that he
is young Montague Cavendish or something—the bluest of
the blue—while the seedy young man is the "sweetest dear"
and also a direct descendant of Pocahontas, not to mention
the Lee and Custis families. And so it goes. They may look
insignificant and even a little untidy (not the Bryans—they
are dandies) but they are all princes and princesses in dis-
guise. On our drive home we met two men who might
have been the plumber and the painter walking home from
work, to whom "Mis' Saint" bows sweetly and says, "That's
the Governor of Virginia and Colonel Robert E. Lee." I
don't wonder the English are confused about us!

The Paines and some of the Stewarts came to dinner
and an unknown man was also there whom nobody seemed
to be able to account for. The Colonel kept asking *me* all
through dinner who he was! It appeared that Saint met
him in town and asked him out to dine as he thought his
face looked familiar and then Saint didn't come himself!
However, everybody was as nice and cordial to him as possible though he certainly was no addition.

Meals at the Bryans' are so funny that it is a constant
temptation just to sit there and listen, they are all so bright
and lively and have such a lot of good-natured chaff with
each other. Everybody laughs when the Colonel gets excited as he often does, but he takes it most good-naturedly.
He has solemn stage asides with George, the colored butler,
and then he blurts out at him occasionally but George
seems delighted with either manner and grins broadly and
brilliantly. At *breakfast* the Colonel said, "Bring us some
of that whiskey. George, that ain't it, that ain't it! You
know perfectly well that ain't it, George. You've drank
enough o'that whiskey to know it mighty well!"

In spite of their well-ordered household and modern
conveniences, electric lights, etc., the Bryans are just as
"easygoing" as other Southerners. One day I went all over

the house to find a clock that was going. Finally I asked
Mrs. Bryan if she thought the dining-room clock was more
than half-an-hour slow and when we found it was she said,
"That clock does mighty well, though." And it *did* compared to the others. It didn't matter anyway as nobody did
anything at any particular time. So after dinner when we
all drove into the convention arriving about an hour late
there wasn't a seat in the house.

I was lucky as Mrs. Valentine beckoned me to come to
her box so I sat in great grandeur with Bishop McVickar,
the Gilders and Sally Fairchild. We had an hour's speech
from an ardent agriculturalist, all about babies and pota-
toes. Bishop McVickar kept taking pills to keep himself
awake. Then we had a very finished address from Rev.
Frank Peabody and then we all adjourned to a full dress
reception in the Masonic Temple. A band played all the
time so you had to scream to be heard but it was a much
more cheerful occasion than the other night and I had a
very good time. Billy Schieffelin joined me and then Dr.
Frissell came up and many of the Educators introduced
new people to me. Archie Coolidge* turned up and was
astonished to find all Boston apparently in Richmond. Of
course the Bryans brought him home for the night. The
nice-looking young Williams on the receiving committee—
who has been most kind and polite—introduced many new
young men to me and I in turn introduced them to Gertrude Peabody and Lena Stevenson. I am afraid *they* look
upon me as rather a backslider as they have been to all the
Conference Meetings but the Bryans are not particularly
interested in the Conference so it is hard for me to get to
all the meetings—I am glad to say!

April 24. Went to a luncheon given by Miss Ellen Glas-
gow, authoress of *The Voice of the People,* and found her

* Who was to become the distinguished Harvard professor of history. [Ed.]

another girl authoress even younger than Miss Johnston.
It was a lunch of fifty in a house too small for it and such
a gabbling and shrieking I never heard! My head was tired
in two minutes. I talked to Mary Johnston and a nice
gentleman I thought was a Richmond man but who really
was one of the Educators. Our table at lunch was the nicest
I thought. Bishop McVickar asked me to sit with him and
he and Mr. Ogden told a lot of very good stories so by the
end of lunch we had quite a crowd around us, including
Governor and Mrs. Montague, Hamilton Mabie, and others.

April 25. Mrs. Saint, Bob and I started bright and early
to go to the University of Virginia—on the special train.
Mrs. Saint met some men friends and for some unkown
reason we and they all went into the baggage car where
several other men joined us and they all had a rousing good
time. There is one curious and, I suppose, Southern trait
about Mrs. Saint and that is when men are around she completely ignores me—so much so that I feel very *de trop,*
and even feel as if she dislikes me. All the men are "sweetest dears" or "near cousins" or "great old friends of Saint's,"
and this I suppose is meant to explain her enthusiasm for
them. All I can say is I never knew any Northern cousins
or old friends treated so affectionately as everyone seemed
to feel toward each other today. I think they all thought
me amusingly cold and distant—but they were all extremely polite to me—except Mrs. Saint.

Arrived at the University of Virginia, we all gathered
in front of the Rotunda to get our orders—a session of the
conference would be held first, and afterward, sometime
between two and three, lunch would be served! I gasped as
I was more than ready for lunch *now,* having had a very
early breakfast—and kind Percy Grant* went and got me

* He was the Socialist who shocked everybody so in New York.

some crackers from somewhere and gave them to me at the Convention. The gay crowd I had come down with wasn't going to the meeting so I went with Stewart Bryan and we found it very interesting.

At the University of Virginia we were in the little theatre which is in the new building by McKim* made to harmonize with the inspired work of Thomas Jefferson. I had no idea I was to see anything so beautiful in coming to the University of Virginia, and was thrilled by the fine old buildings and their design and situation on a high plateau, directly overlooked by Monticello on a neighboring hill.

Sunday, April 26. Breakfast supposedly is nine but when I got down at 9:15 no one was there. It was a rainy day and we finished breakfast just in time to get to the little church by Brook Hill on time—at 11:30. Then we all dined at Brook Hill at two. This is the regular Sunday routine— unless there are more than 32 guests in which case some have to stay home. Today there were only 20.

Dinner that evening was great fun. Everybody was at home and feeling very jolly, perhaps because the Convention is over! John, Stewart and Bob have all offered to drive me into town at 7:00 A.M. They *clamor* for it, though of course they would rather die than get up at that hour.

April 27. A perfect dream of a day. It fell to Stewart to drive me in town. The Colonel and Mrs. and John and Stewart were all down at seven—but far more wonderful even than this, *Robert* appeared running just as I was leaving and this attention fairly tickled me—it was so funny. He looked so childishly pleased with himself and was so tall and handsome and immaculate!

Stewart saw me on to the boat and into the midst of the

* Charles Follen McKim. [Ed.]

educators, and I found a seat up in the bow of the steamer with the Schieffelins and the Peabody crowd but I felt really sad at leaving all the kind new friends at Laburnam. We were going up the James River and a man with a megaphone expounded to us all day long its history and the beautiful houses and places we were passing. He rubbed it in rather about our comparative youth in Massachusetts and also had a great deal to say about Ben Butler, so that we Yankees kept pretty quiet. The best part of the day was our visit of an hour at Brandon—one of the finest of the old Colonial places which has been in the Harrison family for over a hundred years. It is a long brick house with two wings at either side facing the river but set quite far back from it. The front hall goes right through the house—which I always like, so you look right through at the garden and view beyond. On either side are two large beautifully shaped and panelled rooms—Mrs. Harrison received us in one of these. There were fine portraits of the Byrd family on the walls—some by Sir Peter Lely and of course beautiful pieces of furniture and in the dining room handsome silver pieces. There was a big square lawn in front and around it attractively landscaped to set off the house, huge magnolia trees and clumps of flowering shrubs —I have never seen a place even in England that appealed to me so much and it was sad to see it falling into disrepair as the family at present in it cannot afford to keep it up. We were all entranced with it and could hardly tear ourselves away but after some despairing "toots" from our steamer we were all corralled and given a good lunch on deck.

After a short run we landed again, this time at Jamestown. A stone cross had been put up near the old church, in memory of the Bishop's visit five years ago. That was when Papa made a great hit with his speech and he heard often about it later from grateful Southerners. Miss Mary

Johnston told me that all the old Jamestown had been washed away in the flood, so she was perfectly safe in her descriptions in *To Have and To Hold*.

As we came in to Old Point Comfort we passed close to three or four warships and I recognized the *Massachusetts* shining in the sunset—her brass all gleaming and her white-clad sailors crowded to the rail watching us with some amusement. On the wharf as we stopped to chat with friends and I was about to pick up my valise, a very good-looking young man appeared and in the nicest voice said, "Won't you let me take this?" and calmly took it. I was completely nonplussed and did not know whether to walk with him, before him, or behind him—I finally decided on the latter and joined the Schieffelins who were right behind and had seen the little episode, I judged, from the amusement on Willie's face and the surprise on that of his mother who immediately remarked on my "very nice-looking friend." I was annoyed by my gaucheness and though I found my valise at the hotel desk my "friend" had disappeared for ever without any thanks on my part.

The hotel was huge, handsome and comfortable and at present full of nice-looking people, mostly officers and wives and all in evening dress ready for dinner and talking against a fine band from the ships. Bands always make my spirits rise, and I fell in love with the place at once. It seemed to be a sort of American Venice as the water seems to be all around the hotel and big ships come right alongside. In front is an Esplanade like Ryde and I went out on it at once and looked at the stars and the lights from the ships and listened to the bells, and the bugles from the nearby fort.

April 28. I began to rebel at passing this whole perfect day in intellectual pursuits at Hampton Institute, so at breakfast I told Mr. Paine (who is much more of an old sport than I had taken him for) that I was going to take a morning off. He thought it a sensible idea and asked to join me. We did not tell the other educators—they would have been so shocked! They were all eating their breakfast as fast as they could, intent on getting to Hampton as soon as possible.

Mr. Paine and I wandered out on the Esplanade and he found a very nice little steam launch which he immediately chartered and we shot off in it in search of adventure. We first circled the two old Ironsides—picturesque in the morning sun with their wash hung out to dry. Then we went to the Massachusetts. I had been in favor of going there first as she looked as if she was getting up steam, but Mr. Paine was a little shy about it. Alas! I was right! He sent up his card and the Captain spoke to us through a megaphone to the effect that he was "exceedingly sorry not to be able to receive us but they were just getting under way." We thought we would wait and see them get off and it was most interesting. They slowly started backwards, with much wig-wagging and bugling, and then they found they had a foul anchor, so we, in our impertinent little launch, dashed up to investigate that. They had three foul anchors, one after the other, and there was a terrible to-do. The Marines were drawn up on deck at salute and had to stand there for over half-an-hour motionless. Finally the anchor was up and the great thing began to move forward —we still following. The leadsmen began to throw in turn, the other ships signaled and wig-wagged goodbye and she went faster and faster till we were left far behind with the great battleship diminishing rapidly on the horizon. It is a never-failing wonder to me how the huge heavy things can float.

We landed at Hampton just as the battalion of students swung around the corner and marched up the greensward to the dining hall. It was a fine sight. After the huge jet-black drum major came the band and then company after company of straight slim boys in blue; after them, and walking just as well, with their light dresses fluttering in the breeze, came the girls, looking like a long carnation walk in a greenhouse.

After lunch we all went over to the Gymnasium where the speeches were to be made. Mr. Paine saved me a good front seat and we faced all the students who were on the stage. The singing of this huge chorus of students is one of the grandest things I ever heard, and indeed it is noted all over the world now.

At the Exercises we had a fine essay on Indians by a handsome Indian boy which almost made me weep. Finally Booker T. Washington made the oration of the day, and Mr. Moors said, "At *last,* I've heard a speech!"

I have agreed to take on an Indian girl for the next four years. Of course, I don't say so here but when I see fine-looking Indians getting civilized and ordinary I feel regret and I am sorry that wild Indians and cowboys and holdups and Alkali Ikes and buffaloes, etc., are disappearing. They say only one Indian in eighty in the school keeps his Indian name. They are all Smith or Jones when they might be Rain-in-the-Face or Wanawahkakcarra Saljo.

April 29. Today was commencement so we had many short addresses from the students and one cunning little Indian boy who read his father's paper (his father being an old grad. and unable to come) read it right through very fast and solemnly and when he came to anything in the least jocose his voice never changed but his big black eyes would look up over the paper with a twinkle in them.

Mr. Washington made the finest speech I think I ever heard. He started off with some of his good stories but he soon got worked up and finally gave us right out his thoughts and hopes about the Negro question. I felt that it was making history and everyone seemed to feel that it was an epoch and we were most fortunate to be where we were. Throngs of Negroes were standing in the back of the hall and tears were streaming down the face of an old man sitting near me. Afterwards Mr. Valentine, a southern gentleman of old family, told me that Mr. Washington had exactly expressed *his* views.

Evening. We were late to the meeting and Willie Schieffelin, who walked in with me, found himself being introduced to speak so he had to go right up on the stage and begin. He looked boyish and attractive and told some stories which he enjoyed so much himself that it added much to the telling of them. There was a small audience tonight (most of the crowd are exhausted) and it was more informal than usual and therefore pleasanter, I thought. The Englishman made a very amusing speech and kept saying "Heah 'Yah!" all through the others' remarks. George Foster Peabody undid what Lyman Abott did this afternoon (one man is always correcting the former man's mistakes on this convention it seems to me) but the hit of the evening was a truly remarkable speech made by a Negro woman—a graduate of Hampton who has a struggling girls' school up in the mountains somewhere. Dr. Frissell called her up from the floor and she was quite unprepared but she made one of the brightest and at the same time the most amusing and pathetic speech of the whole conference. Her voice and delivery were delightful too. Chapman was crazy about her. He kept wagging his head in wonder.

April 30. At 10:30 we stopped at Williamsburg and drove through the town, stopping to see the interesting old church and also William and Mary College. At the college

I found they were getting ready for more speechifying and as I couldn't have heard another speech without being left at Williamsburg in the Asylum, I escaped and sat out in the fine old yard. Bishop McVickar had the same inspiration and it was much nicer out there under the huge old trees with a solemn statue or two and a sundial. The whole of Williamsburg seemed pathetic! Everything was so gone to seed and hopeless—like a "decayed gentlewoman." The only cheerful things were the buttercups and I never saw such masses of them! The fields were literally covered with gold.

People began to drop off at Washington, Philadelphia, etc. At Richmond there was a great exodus and many sad goodbyes, especially mine with Mr. Valentine. He said he would send me his poem. Before they all left we had a meeting and Bishop McVickar thanked Mr. Ogden for all of us, in a very amusing speech. Mr. O. replied equally well and seemed quite affected by our gratitude and the enthusiasm of everyone over our delightful trip. We all separated at the ferry in New York and Mr. and Mrs. Thorp, Mrs. F. Peabody and I made a rush for the night train which we just caught by a minute.

May 1. Got off at Back Bay Station at 6:00 A.M. OOOOh! how cold it was! The Thorps kindly drove me home and I never was so chilly in my life. It was overcast, fearfully windy and dusty and I couldn't keep my hat on. *Never* had I such a disagreeable drive! The family were not up, of course, so I ate a hasty breakfast and went to bed and slept till noon!

CHAPTER 17

COUNTRY HOUSES AND
BISHOPS' PALACES

❧

O NLY THREE WEEKS after I got home from my Virginia trip,
Papa, Sally, and I again sailed for England.

Friday, May 22, 1903. Aboard the *Cedric.* The Misses
Loring brought Sally and me some flowers, which was very
nice of them. My friends did nobly, too, and I got far
more offerings than I expected, as this is the third year in
succession I have crossed. The Lawrence Club sent me a
huge bouquet, Bob Walcott sent flowers and books, and so
did S. Chase and Malcolm Donald, who sent Moody's
poems with an extra nice letter. There was also an exciting
anonymous box of flowers; but my offerings paled beside
those sent to the John R. McLeans,* for instance, who had
bushes of American Beauties. The saloon looked like a
flower show.

We got to Queenstown Saturday morning and immediately afterwards ran into a *dense* fog. The horn blew
incessantly and made a deafening noise. Everyone was told
to keep quiet, and was forbidden to go forward of the
centre of the ship. It was deathly still and we went very
slow. You couldn't see even the bow of the boat and only

* The parents-in-law of Mrs. McLean of Hope diamond fame. [Ed.]

occasionally the tarpaulin-clad sailor on the lookout. It was really exciting, and I enjoyed it. It lasted all night and we often stopped, and then I imagine everyone on board listened with all their ears. Sometimes we heard as many as three answering whistles or gurgling sirens. Some were quite loud and got *louder,* but most were faint and distant. Sunday morning everyone got up bright and early as we were to have landed at seven o'clock, but the fog was as thick as ever and no one knew where we were or when we should land. At 10:30 we were still *blowing* steadily, and apparently waltzing around in the Irish Sea without any definite plan. Papa suggested having church, and as the young Purser (who held a very good service last Sunday) was busy, Papa took it himself. After this we stopped and *anchored,* and a bell rang then incessantly. It was pretty provoking wasting all this time, so near and yet so far, and of course the passengers were impatient. Dr. Douglas, seeing the Captain in the Purser's office, stopped to ask in a peevish tone, "Well, Captain, do you know where we are?"—to which he received no answer at all, which I think served him just about right. The Captain had been thirty-six hours on the bridge and probably was more anxious to land than anyone. After lunch we heard a frequent and energetic little whistle, coming from different quarters but gradually getting louder, and suddenly from out of the fog came a hustling little tug which had been looking for us all the morning and which brought the morning papers. Finally, the fog lifting a little, we were able to land about 3. We scrabbled about collecting our luggage and caught the first train to London. Such a crowd as there was in Euston Station! The Pulitzers went off in a barouche, and left their servants to see to their saratogas. Mrs. Reggie Ronalds drove off in a bus with her "sixteen pieces" on top. The McCooks went by us,

three in a hansom—and finally *we* were off, and driving
through London streets once more. Arrived at the Berkeley, I tumbled into bed at once, in the very same room I
had last year. I felt as if I had never been away!

Wednesday, June 3. Papa and I went out to Slough to
stay with the Carr-Gomms.* Slough is the station used to
go to Windsor and Eton, and is only about a half to three-
quarters of an hour from London. We found a young giant
of a footman looking anxiously for us, who finally came up,
touched his hat and said, "Mr. Carr-Gomm?" I suppose he
couldn't believe that Papa was a bishop, and didn't know
how to address him anyway, so he got around it this way.
He showed us out to a smart-looking bus. The dignified
coachman touched his hat, and the footman and a porter
began to struggle with my trunk. Papa thought the footman was proud and haughty, but I thought Papa addressed
him too obsequiously—he does not enjoy footmen, etc.,
as much as I do.

After clattering through a quaint little town we skirted
a beautiful park with groups of deer lying under the trees;
then passed Stoke Poges Church; drove through a shady
lane and at last turned in at some high gates, opened for
us by a curtsying woman, surrounded by chubby children,
who all emerged from a typical English lodge. After this
beautiful beginning everything was typical. We drove on
up the avenue—a fine black breed of cattle pasturing on
one side, and a cricket field on the other—swept around a
corner and drew up at the porch of a picturesque Eliza-
bethan house. Conventional trees of gorgeous rhododen-
drons stood in rows edging the large court. The front door
stood open, showing through the porch a typical English
hall, and we caught glimpses of oak walls, heads, antlers,

* They were good friends of Dean Hodges of the Episcopal Theological School.

swords, whips, brushes and *everything* that should be there. Mr. Carr-Gomm appeared with outstretched hands, the best type of English squire.

Dinner was at eight and *very formal.* The ladies, Mrs. Carr-Gomm, Mrs. Parry, Miss Carr-Gomm (an uninteresting young thing) and her pretty friend, Miss Ross, were all in low neck, and I had been stupid enough to wear a high-necked gown! I sat next Mr. Parry who is very nice. He is in the Treasury now, but he *was* Mr. Balfour's secretary. I like him the best of all here, though the Carr-Gomm boys are both nice, too—the older one especially. Old Mr. Carr-Gomm took me in to dinner. He is a most cordial host and is great fun—sometimes when he means to be and sometimes when he doesn't. Three men servants waited on us, and we had delicious things to eat—all from off the place, of course.

After dinner I was asked if I was fond of music and foolishly answering "Yes," was obliged to listen all the evening to what I should not have included in the broadest meaning of the word. I might have known it would happen, as everything thus far had happened exactly as it does in an English novel. First Mrs. Parry sang, playing her own accompaniments. Then Miss Carr-Gomm gave us "Violets." She has studied in Germany. It was pathetic—but painful too. Then Mrs. Parry took to Grand Opera and the violin: but Hubert Carr-Gomm came over and asked me to look at some old miniatures and Indian paintings in another room—and I accepted with pleasure. At 10:30 *the men lighted our candles for us and we went up to bed.*

Thursday, June 4. Another perfect day. Rather sad to think we might have been at the Eton celebrations today! I seem to be a hoodoo in England. Last year the Coronation and everything given up, and this year one of the

three things we particularly came over for, and the first
one, has been cancelled, owing to a frightful tragedy—the
fire at Eton in which so many boys lost their lives. The
most terrible part is that they undoubtedly could have
saved themselves by jumping if it had not been for the
small windows and iron bars, behind which they were
caught like rats in a trap. Papa was to have made a speech
at the graduating exercises, and the King and other interesting people were to have been there. I shall never see
the *King!*

Instead, this morning I made a few little sketches around
the place, while the other ladies were practicing "Violets,"
etc., and in the afternoon went on one of the most beautiful and interesting drives of my life—Mr. Carr-Gomm,
Papa and I; with the respectable churchwarden coachman
and huge Thomas on the box. We went in an enormous,
rumbly barouche, with a big pair of bays who kept up a
steady trot up hill and down dale for twenty miles. *Of
course* we had to have our tea, so we drove into a lovely
country place, and stopped at an attractive house with long
French windows opening onto the lawn. All the windows
were open and awninged, and kittens were calmly walking
in and out. A gentleman—I believe it was the butler—
showed us into the drawing room, a delightful room of pale
green walls and gay chintz, fine mezzotints and engravings
and one lovely Romney over the mantel. The butler then
brought in a tea table (this is how I knew he was the butler)
and then our host came bustling in, and welcomed us
with some embarrassment but much cordiality. He was a
soldierly and eccentric old gentleman, a fellow magistrate
of Mr. Carr-Gomm's named Colonel Phipps. He had a
clean-shaven set mouth, bushy eyebrows over twinkling
blue eyes, and he talked in jerks, flicking his handkerchief
at the kittens in time to his remarks, and occasionally stop-

ping to eject the cat forcibly from the room. The lovely Romney was his mother when a girl.

Suddenly he stopped talking and glared out of the window, and looking we saw a truly wonderful sight coming down the driveway. It was a little old man skimming along on a bicycle, coattails flying, a huge white helmet on his head, white spats on his feet, black goggles on his eyes. Colonel Phipps got up muttering something about its being his friend Admiral —— and soon he returned bringing in the little Admiral —— and then what a time there was introducing him! At last it was done somehow or other, to the great relief of everyone, and especially of the old Admiral who was the shyest little man I ever saw. We all went out to see the garden and the Colonel's peaches, and then we came in to see his workshop, in other words, the room in which he is writing his great book on Napoleon's generals. He has been at it for twenty or thirty years, and I should think the room had not been rearranged in that time. I am sure that every book that ever mentioned Napoleon was in there; if not in the bookcases or on the desk or tables, then on the floor in piles or under the tables and chairs. It was a funny, messy place and I am afraid the poor Colonel will never finish his job.

Friday, June 5. I had a dreadful time at prayers this morning as the dog seemed to be having a sort of fit on my feet. Prayers are in the library, which is just off the long tiled gallery, in which the parrot is always jabbering. First we sing a hymn—Mrs. Parry at the organ; then Papa reads the Morning Prayer. Thomas, and a younger boy and the housekeeper and six or eight maids follow the lesson, all sitting in a row in morning clothes (not livery) and the old butler sits a little way from them and says the responses louder than anybody. He has been in the family all his life and has his Peerage at his fingers' ends. When Mrs. Parry, who is a cousin of the Carr-Gomms was engaged, and they asked the butler what he knew of her fiancé, he said, "Well, ma'am, he comes of a respectable but not a titled family." This makes it rather embarrassing for Mr. Parry to visit at Farnham Royal as he feels that he is only barely tolerated by the butler.

At breakfast, of course, everybody trots around and gets his own food—only the gentlemen are most polite about waiting on you, and I keep them pretty busy. Every day I cause a great deal of trouble by asking for a glass of water. They have to ring for Thomas and it takes him a long while to find it and they always ask if I would not prefer it hot. When we are getting through breakfast—fortunately—Mr. Carr-Gomm gets his horrid pet dove and fondles it, and the dove goes and grunts and hops about the table pecking at whatsoever and whomsoever it pleases. He lit on Mrs. Parry's head yesterday morning and she had a terrible time disentangling him.

About noon we began to fee and say goodbye, and then they sent us over to Eton in the "bus" again, very rumbly and swell with two stiff men on the box. We stopped for a few minutes at Stoke Poges Church. It was rather a blow to find that it was impossible to see "the lowing herd wind" over any "lea" from the quaint little graveyard. The church has a beautiful stumpy stone tower, upon which has been placed a frightful wooden extinguisher, which made me really sad.

At Eton we stayed with Stuart Donaldson, a housemaster, and his wife, Lady Albinia.

Sunday, June 7. Lady Albinia and I went to church in the Eton Upper Chapel and heard Mr. Lionel Ford preach about the school tragedy—a very good sermon. Afterwards Miss Dubois's brother, an Eton boy, showed us over the College. It was most interesting, and quite as old and picturesque and sketchable as anyone could wish, but oh! *so* uncomfortable and behind the times! Horrid, dark little rooms and narrow entry ways, and only tin basins to wash in. The dining halls and libraries are fine! We saw many distinguished names cut in the walls. The one cut in largest letters was Chas. James Fox. Any Eton boy is allowed to cut his name where he can find an ancestor who has cut his, but if he hasn't any ancestors he mustn't do it.

Lady Methuen and her son, Paul*, came to lunch. The Methuens are my ideal of an English family. Lady Methuen is tall, thin and aristocratic looking with a sweet face and pretty features. She dresses in black, has a charming low voice and lovely smile. Paul is quiet, tall and slight, with the pinkest and whitest of complexions—just as high-bred looking as his mother and has her smile. Lady Albinia asked if he "would be so kind as to change the plates for us and bring on the dessert!" He did it most cheerfully, but with a good deal of difficulty as he had to hunt about everywhere before he found the other plates and knives and forks. They all seemed to think it quite natural to be waited on by a future peer. At home we should think ourselves in a very bad way if we had to ask our guests to get up and wait on table, even if we only kept one maid. It passes me what all the servants do over here. Lady Albinia has two men to wait at dinner always, and yet there was no one to help at lunch today.

When we got home I sat down and read Mr. Arthur Benson's book as he was coming to dinner and I was quite excited at the prospect. It was rather a blow to find a caricature of him by "Spy" in a *Vanity Fair* that I chanced

* Paul in 1920 married a first cousin of Uncle Augustus Hemenway's—a young girl born and brought up in England.

to pick up off the table. I hoped he didn't look much like it. Mr. Alington* came to dinner, too, and I was talking to him when Mr. Benson was announced. He was better looking than the caricature—a great big Anglo-Saxon, very gentlemanly and pleasant looking. He sat next me at dinner and contrary to most Englishmen—and some Americans—he started right in to entertain me, instead of waiting for me to entertain him. He told some ridiculous stories of different embarrassing experiences he and his "DoDo" brother had had at country houses. They principally hinged on morning prayers, a funny subject for the son of an Archbishop to choose with which to amuse the daughter of a Bishop, but it succeeded beautifully.

Tuesday, June 9. Drove over to Lambeth Palace where we are to spend the next three days—the Archbishop and Mrs. Davidson having kindly asked Papa to set his own time to visit them. We found them at tea in an enormous, but pleasant and homelike drawing room. They were all in the bay window overlooking the terraces. We were introduced to Mrs. Davidson, who seemed very sweet and pretty with charming manners (Queen Victoria said her manners were so lovely she wished her granddaughters to model theirs on them). After tea we were shown our rooms, a lengthy proceeding covering a half-mile of ground, I should think. We had three rooms and a dressing room, all leading off the same hall, and we found our names already upon our doors. Papa's room was about the size of our Bar Harbor house, but everything was very plain indeed and there was nothing but a few candles to light it. We went down to dinner at eight and found everyone already in the drawing room. The Archbishop came forward to meet us with outstretched hands and I fell in love with him at once. He looked younger than I expected—he is

* Cyril Alington, later Headmaster of Eton and Dean of Durham. [Ed.]

so strongly built. His most distinguishing feature is his very deep-set eyes under heavy eyebrows. They can look piercing and severe, but they can also twinkle delightfully, and he has the friendliest smile imaginable. I had been rather dreading this evening, as I supposed he would take me in to dinner, but no sooner were we started on our long march to the dining room than I found what an easy, simple person he was, and felt at once as if we were old friends. On my other side was the tall chaplain, Mr. Conybeare, whom we had heard was quite a fascinator but who did not strike us as anything remarkable.

After dinner the Archbishop showed me some of the interesting pictures in the other rooms and the picture gallery, and then he went off to work and Mr. Banks played to us all. He plays most beautifully. The two requisites for a chaplain at Lambeth, they say, are that he can play the piano and play squash. The Archbishop has a new squash court and I hope to get a chance to play with him. He is also fond of riding. Years ago when out shooting with a friend the friend accidentally shot him in the back and he has suffered always from it until quite lately. The last year or two he has been all right, but I should think he would be afraid of breaking down as he works at such high pressure all the time.

At 9:30 we went into the chapel for prayers. My! it was cold in a low-necked dress! Mr. Banks played the organ and all the servants joined heartily in the hymns. I counted twenty maids, not including the housekeeper and her assistant, and there were six men, several of them in short clothes, white stockings, etc. Quite a congregation! Mr. Conybeare read the service and the Archbishop gave the blessing.

Wednesday, June 10. Was downstairs at 8:30 for prayers. When I see the Archbishop in his robes I cannot realize

that I am staying in his house and that I dare to chaff him
at meals, but it is so! He is a corker! and Papa told lots
of people that I said he was. It is a great relief being an
American because they don't expect much of you.

This morning we helped Mrs. Davidson and Miss Faithful address invitations for a big garden party they are
going to have. It is a complicated thing sending invitations
in England, partly because of all the different sorts of titles,
where of course a mistake is fatal, but besides these everyone seemed to have a country place with a name to it, and
then came the village with a name to *it,* and then you had
to look up the post town and finally the county. It seemed
exasperating but they took it very calmly, and we all ate
apples while we worked.

Thursday, June 11. Rainy again. In the morning I went
down to Woollands' to try on an evening dress. Mine are
all worn out as I have been wearing them every night.
This new one cost twenty-five guineas but it is a dream so
well worth it.

It is always a source of amusement to tell a hansom cab
driver to "go to Lambeth Palace." He usually peers through
the little hole on top and asks you to repeat the order.
Then when he gets to the Lodge at the outer wall he stops
in despair, but the porter urges him on and encourages him
inside the inner gate. This he peers through and drives
cautiously towards the Palace, stopping with great decision
at what looks most like the servants' entrance. At this I
cry out and urge him on and finally we draw up at the
great doors of the Palace to find a butler resignedly waiting there, the porter having rung a bell from the lodge to
the Palace which tells the men to open the doors.

Coming back from the House of Lords, the Archbishop
would hunt for the carriage himself, in the pouring rain
with no umbrella and when he got it I tore a big square

hole in my brand new bestest dress getting in. I had only
worn it because the Archbishop had said something about
our wearing our good clothes and seemed to want us to,
and now it was ruined; but I tried to be polite and take it
calmly, and had quite put it out of my mind ten minutes
later when suddenly he said, "I *am* so sorry about your
dress." In the evening also when he came up to take me
in to dinner he said, "How is the dress? I hope you found
Mrs. Davidson's maid could fix it." When I told him I
wasn't used to having Archbishops so worried about my
clothes he said he thought I had behaved very well about
it—which was nice.

Friday, June 12. Mr. White's* carriage called for Papa
and took him to the King's levée. He was gorgeous to
behold, rigged out from top to toe in the Archbishop's
clothes. Papa had asked him what he ought to wear and
the Archbishop said he would lend him everything he
needed and it would be all right. So his valet dressed Papa
and he was a work of art when done. He had on long,
bright scarlet robes over a purple silk cassock, silk stockings
and buckled shoes—and nobody knew that instead of small-
clothes he had his trousers rolled up above his knees.

Later we saw Mr. Morgan who said that Papa looked
gorgeous this morning. He himself, of course, was in black
velvet, short pants, etc., but he said he felt much more
comfortable in it this year than last, and did not trip over
his sword, as he had done last year.

In Clarges Street. In the evening we dressed in our best,
and *walked* over to Lansdowne House as it was just around
the corner in Berkeley Square. Our entrance was rather

* Mr. Henry White, then Chargé d'Affaires in our London Embassy, in the
absence of the Ambassador, Mr. Choate. [Ed.]

insignificant therefore, as we found a long queue of carriages, and we had to dodge between champing steeds in
the avenue to get to the broad stone porch, covered with
red carpets and a double row of huge, powdered and
white-stockinged footmen. Waved on by rows of these personages we reached the ladies' dressing room, and again
passing endlessly between them, we heard our names called
from man to man, until finally an ordinary butler got
them and yelled them out, and we found ourselves shaking
hands in the most democratic manner with the Marquis
and Marchioness of Lansdowne, who looked much like
thousands of other people. Though not striking in any
way except in the line of jewelry and orders, they were
cordial and pleasant in manner as they passed us on and
out of the queue. We found ourselves in a beautiful long
ballroom full of people, not one of whom we had ever
seen before. We tried to look interested in Papa's conversation, and meanwhile used our eyes to the utmost. As
Lansdowne House is one of the handsomest in London and
as this was our first London party we found plenty to interest us. Everything was very gorgeous and palatial—wonderful pictures, statuary, tapestries. Everything seemed to
be a masterpiece. We stood in the hall awhile and watched
the endless procession up and down the grand stairway—
then we stood in the long conservatory behind the room in
which the Lansdownes were receiving, and watched the
line of people who came in, and tried to catch their names.
I never saw such jewels in my life. There were endless
tiaras; crowns and necklaces of diamonds as big as black-
berries; ropes and ropes of pearls; and one lady was so
covered with huge uncut emeralds that she could hardly
move, they jiggled so and were so heavy. The men were
covered with orders and medals. The broad ribbons and
the little medals hanging in a row are very ornamental,

but not so the large spidery effects which they wore clasped on to any portion of their body.

Besides all this richness there was a great variety of people as Lord Lansdowne is now Secretary for Foreign Affairs in the Government. Some were jet black; there were little Japs, a gorgeously clad Chinaman and his wife, Indian princes, Egyptians and Fiji Islanders. We happened finally on one friend in the crowd, old Lord Kelvin, and he talked to us for some time adding distinction to our group at once, apparently. Then Mr. White appeared and introduced several people, and Mr. and Mrs. Phipps joined us, who were staying at the Butler Duncans' at Bar Harbor last summer, also Dr. Bilt, the Swedish minister, who thought we knew his son, at Bar Harbor—but I can't remember him—and Papa introduced some old lords he met at the levée but I couldn't catch any of their names. Mr. Carter joined us in the supper room, where I also caught a glimpse of the Rt. Hon. the Earl of Tankerville, with his lady on his arm, a typical Tacoma girl she looked, and by no means as beautiful as the pictures he used to show us of her. Mr. White had been so polite that when we were leaving I went up to say good-bye to him. He was standing with a lady and he looked a little distressed when I told him how amused I had been by it all, and when the lady asked me if I had had some supper, it occurred to me that she was our hostess! I had forgotten what she looked like and was leaving *without* saying good-night to her. I was so embarrassed by this incident that in my haste to get away I overlooked Lord Lansdowne too.

Saturday, June 13. This morning we all went up to Cambridge to stay with Dr. Butler, the master of Trinity, and apparently a wonderful person, as everyone has said, "Oh! are you going to stay there? You couldn't stay with

a more interesting man or in a more interesting place."
We also heard the Nat. Thayers say they had traveled way
up to Cambridge on a sightseeing trip just to see the house
he lives in, it is so historically interesting.

We found Mrs. Butler in the drawing room. She is
Dr. Butler's second wife, much younger than he, but almost
as learned, and, curiously enough, one of the leading
Christian Scientists in England. With her were a niece of
Dr. Butler and her husband, Mr. and Mrs. Fletcher; a very
pretty young sister of Mrs. Butler, named Pansy Ramsey;
and an old gentleman introduced as Mr. Galton, who was
very deaf but most interesting, and who, we heard later
from Mrs. Butler, had discovered the means of detecting
criminals by the impress of their thumbs. Shortly after our
arrival Dr. Butler came in, in his cap and gown, and with
him the Duke of Devonshire. Dr. Butler *greeted* us (he
is so very courtly and sweet and pious I can put it no other
way) and then he introduced the Duke. I don't know what
I should call it that *he* did. *He* is as stiff as a wooden image
and as interesting looking. He relaxed his mouth a little
and inclined his head about an inch. Then we went into
lunch. I sat on Dr. Butler's right next to Mr. Galton.
Dr. Butler talked with his eyes shut in a very weak voice
but incessantly and *very* precisely. I found afterwards that
he was tired and wasn't always quite so queer. I was so
busy trying to listen to him, and trying to talk so that
Mr. Galton could hear, and yet not so loud that the Duke
of Devonshire would put me down as a nasal, loud-voiced
Yankee, that I couldn't pay much attention to the other
end of the table, but even so it was evident that they were
in difficulty. Mrs. Butler was struggling with the Duke,
who ate his food stolidly, but otherwise seemed to be in a
comatose condition and did not once turn his head to right
or left, which was perhaps fortunate as Miss Ramsey, next

him, was exchanging winks and grins across the table at
Mrs. Fletcher and the Butler boys at his expense. Altogether there seemed a certain something about the whole
thing that everyone fought bravely against, but unsuccess-
fully. The spell lifted a little when the Duke took his
departure to catch a train, with a succession of unbending
bows. Poor man! Perhaps it is shyness! I believe he is
very clever in the House of Lords.

After lunch we were shown our rooms and here my
worst fears were realized! For the first time there was only
a double bed for Sally and me, and *such* a bed! It was a
feather bed built especially for Queen Victoria and was a
huge four poster, hung all around with crimson damask.
These curtains were lined with corn-colored silk, and hung
from a canopy which was lined with quilted satin and
which supported an enormous gilt crown. The bed was of
handsome mahogany with Victoria's and Albert's initials
inlaid in the headboard on either side of another crown.
There was a flight of steps on both sides with which to
mount the bed.

The room was a palatial apartment, and on the walls
were fine crayons of different members of the Royal family
at all ages. All the gilt frames had crowns on top, and
there were at least a dozen framed autograph pictures of
Victoria and Albert. It must have been so dull to see a lot
of pictures of yourself and your cousins whenever you went
to stay! You could never escape from yourself. You would
be forever turning up smiling!

Another beauty to the room is that it is haunted. They
told us so but would not say in what way.*

---

* I soon discovered though! In the middle of every night I was awakened by
horrible thumpings on the ceiling. They were so heavy and so loud that I
couldn't imagine what made them. I supposed it must be some wakeful and
very strenuous servant and it did not bother me much as it never lasted long.
It was several weeks afterwards that Miss Alexander, the daughter of the Arch-

Sunday, June 14. Still raining. I am rather homesick for
Lambeth, and feel as if the people here were "sorry we
came." Dr. Butler is extremely interesting but I find it
rather exhausting to live up to him at every meal. You
have to be so *very* attentive to what he says and so *very*
careful what you say. For otherwise he might be *pained*
by your ignorance or he may have to correct your English
as he did mine the other evening.

Monday, June 15. An Irish gentleman happened in to
lunch with a brogue and a gift of gab. I sat between him
and Dr. Butler, but, as they conversed most of the time in
Latin, I remained becomingly silent.

Tuesday, June 16. Before breakfast we went over to hear
the Senior Wrangler and other wranglers "read out," a
curious proceeding, neither exciting nor impressive. I was
surprised to find that the Senior Wrangler does not by any
means mean the brightest man in the class. It only means
a certain prize in mathematics, and some boy with a turn
that way might be Senior Wrangler and yet know nothing
of the classics, languages, history or literature. Later we
went to see the Latin and Greek prize winners get their
prizes. Only about a dozen people seemed to care about
this ceremony, and now that I have seen it I wonder that
there were so many. We were in a barn-like structure,
with a half a dozen old dons in caps and gowns sitting in
a semicircle near us. Half a dozen young men lounged
against the wall in the further corner. Enter three ordinary
men like pallbearers at a funeral, carrying each a large
mace, and behind them another ordinary looking man in

bishop of Armagh, asked me if I had heard anything in the haunted room, and
went on to say that she had a most disagreeable experience there, and then
described the same sounds I had heard, which had frightened her very much.
She said that no servants slept over that room, and there were no rooms above it!

cap and gown, who proved to be the Vice Chancellor, and who took a seat in front of the six dons. A much flustered master of ceremonies stood up in a corner and said, "Such and such a prize for the Greek essay by Mr. Smith," and one of the young men lounged forward a little, gabbled a paragraph or two of his essay, and was bunglingly led by the Master of Ceremonies over to the Vice Chancellor. The latter handed him a little parcel; they made awkward bows to each other, and the Master of Ceremonies drove him back to his corner with the big mace. This happened six times, fortunately taking only twenty minutes.

After lunch we said good-bye to the Butlers and were very sorry to leave them. It takes two or three days for English people to thaw out, but when they have got over their shyness, or whatever it is that makes them so stiff, they are delightfully friendly and unaffected. Dr. Butler presented us each with a book. Mine was a date book, because he was so horrified at my ignorance of exact dates. I told him frankly I only knew one date in English History and then when I proudly and glibly told him that Elizabeth died in 1616 he looked pained and I remembered that I had got her mixed up with Shakespeare. Hence my new book—an autograph copy by the author himself.

Between showers in the afternoon we moved over to Pembroke Lodge to visit our old friend, Canon Mason, who has married a wife and got a baby since we saw him. We met them all at tea. The wife was quite young and kittenish and the baby was sweet. Canon Mason is now Master of Pembroke College and they have just moved into the master's house which is charming, with many interesting things in it belonging to the college. He showed us the original of Gray's diary in which we found "The Elegy."

That evening we went to the ball at Pembroke with the
Masons. College dances are much prettier in England on
account of their setting, but that is their only advantage
over ours. We walked through the gardens into the Pembroke court. Here there were tents for refreshments and
covered passages with carpets under foot, from hall to hall.
There were Japanese lanterns everywhere and with the
fine old buildings and interesting surroundings it must
be quite ideal on a fine moonlight night. The dancing
was in the college Common Room, which was a picturesque
old hall with handsome wainscoting up to the ceiling and
fine pictures. It made a pretty setting for the girls' dresses
and needed no decorations.

No one seemed to think of introducing anyone to us.
Mrs. Mason was giggling excitedly over her partners, as
she filled out her own card but it did not occur to her that
I might like some partners, too, though I stood right next
to her. Finally I saw, by Canon Mason's sad and worried expression, that it *had* occurred to him, and in a few moments
he brought up a tall, handsome young man named Lancaster. Mr. L. whirled me round the room till I could
neither see nor breathe and hadn't even wits enough left
to ask to stop. I was so occupied in trying to keep up that
I hardly noticed the batterings I got, nor cared how my
poor skirt fared. When the music stopped we stopped—
not before. We sat out in the adjoining room to recover,
and Mr. L. was very pleasant and attractive—when he
wasn't dancing! Presently he asked if my card was full—
with a view to a repetition of our athletic feat, I suppose—
and I told him it was absolutely empty and there seemed
to be no prospect of its being otherwise, since he was the
only man I knew in the room. He was both surprised and
amused at this, and said it must be attended to at once,
and, though he was not a graduate himself and had nothing

whatever to do with the dance or me, he very kindly brought up several nice men, and throughout the evening kept coming up to see how I was getting along. I was very lucky to have met him, as he was so nice, and also so big and fine-looking, and his politeness changed the evening from what would have been a horror to a real pleasure.

I found that Mr. Lancaster danced far better than the average! I don't see *why* English girls go to dances. They are most exhausting affairs and there can't possibly be much excitement to them as you have to pass exactly so much time with each partner, and you can only have just so many partners and everyone must have just the same number, unless they are a *hopeless* pill. This particular dance began at 9 and was expected to last till 6 A.M., but we left at two. My supper partner was a nice young McDowell, a first cousin of Arthur Benson and evidently a great admirer of his. It was funny to find a mutual acquaintance when I felt like such a stranger in a strange land.

Wednesday, June 17. Pouring still. Desperately depressing weather. We have seen nothing of Cambridge, except an hour's walk around the "backs" one open-and-shut morning. Papa is sick in bed today with an awful cold. The Masons keep all the doors and windows open, regardless of weather, and it is a little chilly in a stone house after a week of rain. We are in a state of shivers all the time, and Papa had a chill last night after we had gone to the ball. So now he has decided that the only way to keep comfortably warm is to stay in bed. He has lighted the fire in his room, and got it up to a temperature which would probably give the Masons apoplexy, but no one knows about it, and he sends word to them by us that he is perfectly comfortable and happy. What with the weather outdoors, and the *excessive sweetness,* and *jocose playful-ness* indoors, I have to keep tight hold of myself not to scream. When we first arrived at Dr. Butler's, and saw his Brigham Young looks and heard his sweet precise voice, I did not know whether I could stand *much* rainy weather there, but *they* turned out all right; and perhaps this place would—but I should not like to stay and try it. I must go somewhere soon where I may be allowed to return to my natural character without the fear of shocking everybody. After such a dose of piety and sweetness I must let off some steam.

It didn't actually rain all day so Sally and I took a hansom by the hour and went out to see the sights. The insides of the colleges and the courts are lovely, and of course the "backs" are unique, but the trouble is there are *no "fronts"!*

June 20. Oxford. P.M. We stayed at home and had several stupid callers. Academic society is the same the world over, I expect, and when you leave off the usual American ease of manner a pretty poky person is left.

In the evening we felt we must have some cheer, so we decided to go and hear Sousa, whom we had seen widely advertised over Oxford. Sousa and Buffalo Bill seem to be the two features of Commemoration Week here, judging by the enormous bill posters everywhere. Sousa was great! The hall was jammed with visitors on theatre parties, scores of handsome college boys and then a lot of soldiers standing in the back. For once we saw English people enthusiastic. They howled and stamped and clapped, and even cheered and roared so loud, it almost drowned the music which is saying a good deal when the music is Sousa's. Mr. Sousa himself was really the best part of the whole show, and we laughed till we cried over his affecta-

tions in leading, his lackadaisical manner and his poses and
blasé attitudes and expression. After laughing till we shook
the bench, we yelled with the crowd over "Imperial Edward." After this we had the "Stars and Stripes Forever."
A dozen trumpeters came to the front of the stage, stood
in line, and almost blew the audience out of the hall, but
the blare of noise was fine, and the applause after this
patriotic combination almost raised the roof. To vary the
programme and save our eardrums two ladies sang and
played the violin—both showing marvellous gymnastic
ability. Perhaps there was more technical skill than real
musical feeling about the entire concert, but it was perfect
of its kind, and I would have paid my money twice over
just to hear one solo on the snare drum. I never imagined
such a roll. It seemed as if there must be a dozen drums at
it when it grew loud, but, by perfect graduations, it gradually died away into silence. The drummer had to repeat
it several times to satisfy the audience—while Mr. Sousa
looked as if he had fallen asleep standing.

Sunday, June 21. No street in the world can compare
with "The High," and the view from the curve in the
middle of it leaves nothing to be desired architecturally in
whichever direction you look. It is a lasting wonder to us
to have *everything* so picturesquely ancient, and when we
came out in a narrow lane between colleges, finding ourselves between the high walls of their gardens, and in this
narrow lane found a huge white and brass touring car
with coats of arms on its sides, puffing quietly away all to
itself, we felt some sense of incongruity. Also we cannot
imagine American youths, dressed in white and pale blue
flannels, lying back in lounging chairs piled high with
cushions, smoking and studying at the same time, with the
birds twittering in the motionless trailing purple beech

Tradja (Mabel Davis)

Angela (Alice Morris)

Bessie Chadwick

Nellie Sargent

Louise Crowninshield

Marion Mason (in Kirmess costume)

Carrie Dabney and Katharine Crowninshield

M. L. as bridesmaid

The bride

The groom

Marian Lawrence Peabody

nearby, and everywhere about bright flowers and velvet lawns. How different this from the hot room with the windows open to the June bugs, the green shade and the wet towel of our native town!

Most of our Oxford acquaintances strike me as distinctly dirty, or perhaps *dusty* would be a prettier word. Also there is a great lack of social tact and grace of manner among the average don's family. Here at Magdalen we found a pleasant change.

Today we were to lunch with the Spooners*—the Head of New College—and we reversed the order of Friday. We went to the college only to be told the lunch was at their house. The Spooners are a very nice family and made us feel quite at home. I found Mr. Spooner delightfully amusing and interesting but his looks are against him; he is a nervous little albino.

I think it was at the Warrens' tea that we met the Hon. George Brodrick, Head of Merton, whom they seemed to think was an important person.

Monday, June 22. Perfectly heavenly day at last. After a late breakfast we wandered out to see Oxford at its perfection. It probably doesn't look as it did today but once a year, and that is one day in June when everything is right. Everything was looking brilliant after the rainy week. We went to Wadham and Magdalen Gardens which are the most beautiful in different ways. Wadham is small but perfect as far as it goes. The long, low façade of the college, by Christopher Wren, I think, and the ivy-covered wall all around the square plot of lawn made a fine background, and the tall larkspur, golden glow, poppies and

---

* William Archibald Spooner (1844–1930) was a beloved Oxford figure whose tendency to confuse the syllables of words led to the coining of the term "Spoonerisms." "You have, sir, tasted a whole worm"— (wasted a whole term). [Ed.]

other flowers which bordered it stood out brilliant by contrast to the crumbly old stone. Four wonderful trees in a
mass threw their long shadows across the velvet lawn.
There were a cedar of Lebanon, a purple beech, a curious
silvery-grey American product, and a perfectly shaped,
huge English oak. One rich shade stood out against the
other and the whole clump would have made wonderful
study in color for some lucky artist. Magdalen, of course,
has everything; a fairyland forest of great giant trees, with
deer browsing about under their deep shade; green lawns
and cloistered courts; Addison's shady, peaceful walk with
views between the trees on either side of wide meadows—
now almost entirely under water; and finally a shady river
running under a line of willows on one side and on the
other a high stone wall, and over the wall bright flowers of
another herbaceous border turn their faces to the sun. Ivy
was everywhere, and endless variety of picturesque bits and
brilliant color showing against crumbling old stone. It
was agonizing not to have time to sketch everything.

Tuesday, June 23. We all went to a deadly lunch at the
Cairds'*. These lunches are getting to be too much! Nobody talked, there was nothing to eat, most of the people
were dusty, to say the least, and I thought Mrs. Caird
would never rise from the table. I really thought she had
forgotten all about it, and by the time she did get up I had
forgotten all about my lunch. There wasn't much of it to
remember—except the cheese. From this lunch we adjourned to a still worse tea at the Dyers'. There was one
clean man there, but we met him going in as we came out.
One woman there was so strange-looking that I watched
her closely. She did not make one remark the whole afternoon, except that she leaned forward to another lady once

* Edward Caird was Master of Balliol. [Ed.]

and said in a hoarse undertone, "Have you cut your hay yet?"—if that might be called a remark.

After lunch we set out with Mr. Dyer and Mr. Spooner to *do* New College. I have written enough guidebook stuff for one day, so I will not attempt to describe New College . . . The old warden of New College died this last winter, at the age of ninety-eight or so, and Mr. Spooner has got to make over the warden's house entirely, as the old man lived only in two rooms, and these were quite unspeakable. He showed us over the quaint old building and, though he has a colossal job before him in making it livable, I envy him the doing of it. One feature of the house is a bridge that runs right over the narrow street and joins the two parts of the house; another is a long flight of stone stairs, that dives through a narrow stone doorway, right straight down to the garden. Then, last but not least, it has a stable yard that has not been touched since before America was discovered! This may not seem to be an enviable possession but it certainly was the most picturesque thing I ever saw.

Papa and I took a cab over to Dr. Broderick's. He is a very tall, ugly old man, but he had the most courteous manners and made us feel immediately at home, he was so cordial. With him in his library were a chatty Lady Somebody and a pleasant gentleman and a most beautiful and charming girl. Altogether this tea was a great improvement on the other, and was quite a different atmosphere from any we had yet struck at Oxford, except possibly at the Warrens' on Sunday.

Prayers at New College. Directly opposite us in the stalls I noticed a distinguished-looking young girl and immediately decided that she was Princess Alice. Next her was a middle-aged women with a placid German face, hand-

some clothes but not style, and she of course must be the
Duchess of Albany.* The girl stood very straight and just
escaped looking prim by being so young and pretty, but in
spite of her youth and small stature the impression she gave
was of great dignity. She had a sweet face with fair skin
and eyes and hair. She wore a light foulard dress, big white
hat and little pearls in her ears, but she wore light tan
gloves instead of white, and this little German touch made
her seem all the more attractive, because it was so sensible.

After church, the Spooners, the Royalties, and we stood
around awkwardly together in the antechapel. Papa was
presented to the Duchess, and talked to her; the Princess
and the Warden wandered around looking at the stained
glass, and I was left to talk to Mrs. and Miss Spooner and
old Mrs. Temple. To my great amusement they wouldn't
listen, or even look my way—all their eyes and ears were
for the Royalties, before whom they actually cringed. It
went against my grain to see old Mrs. Temple bobbing
like any old apple-woman when the Princess condescend-
ingly extended her hand.

Wednesday, June 24. Papa took me to the Encaeria. This
takes place in the Sheldonian Theatre and corresponds to
our Commencement exercises in Sanders Theatre. We had
fine seats, though not together. Papa was "inside the ropes"
with dons and distinguished guests, and I was in one of the
temporary side galleries built for ladies. Just below me
was "the floor" of the theatre, which was all left open,
but which rapidly filled with men, mostly in caps and
gowns, who stood, or wandered and jostled about, during
the whole two-and-a-half hours of the proceedings. They
seemed exactly the same crowd that goes to Sanders Theatre
—only English. The organ was playing and there was a

---

* Helena, Princess of Waldeck-Pyrmont, married Leopold, Duke of Albany,
youngest son of Queen Victoria. Princess Alice is their daughter. [Ed.]

pleasant flutter of expectancy, mixed with a dignified hush
—when a loud voice from the upper gallery addressed the
organist in a clear, drawling tone, saying, "That's not much
good, please give us something from the 'Toreador'." This
was not funny but it caused a rustle and titter, and from
that moment there was more or less of a running comment
on all the proceedings. Each pause teemed with excitement
to know what the next calm impertinence would be. Occasionally they were really funny and showed quick wit and a
ready tongue. More often the wit was in the saying of them
—patronizing, sarcastic and just impertinent enough. Dignified dons reddened and writhed under their taunts, the
Vice-Chancellor "shshed" and waved his hands in vain—
if the students wanted to make an uproar and break up the
meeting they apparently had it in their power to do so—
and yet there were only a few of them there, and they were
scattered in amongst girls and relatives in the upper gallery.
Imagine President Eliot in such circumstances. Impossible!

After we had been in our seats nearly an hour there was
a stir in the crowd, and the big doors at the end opposite
the Chancellor's throne opened. The crowd of men separated, and through them walked the little Princess Alice,*
all in white with head erect, but in a great hurry and
blushing furiously. Behind came her mother and Lady
Collins, etc. Everybody stood until they were seated in
their big gilt armchairs on the right of the Chancellor's
throne. After this everyone who came in bobbed a curtsy
or bowed to the Princess as they passed her, whether she
noticed them or not. Soon after the Royalties had appeared
on the scene, the doors again opened to admit the Vice
Chancellor, with maces before and maces behind. Lord
Salisbury is the Chancellor of Oxford, but, as he was too
ill to attend, the Vice Chancellor had to preside. After him
came a long procession of dons, waddling in in their red

* She was 20 years old in 1903. [Ed.]

gowns; then there was another breathless pause, during
which everyone remained standing—and then finally came
Sir George White*, the hero of the day, amid deafening
roars and cheers. He looked every inch a soldier, and yet
the bright red gown over the scarlet uniform was not un-
suitable either, as he looked a scholar too, and had a fine
face and head. He kept "eyes front" and walked very
straight, though he seemed quite moved by his warm reception. He held his plumed hat on one arm and his other
hand was on his sword which kicked his gown out in rather
an absurd manner. His sandy hair and moustache, his sun-
burnt face, his uniform, his gown and a crimson order
which he wore across his chest, were each and all a different
shade of red, but though all swore audibly together, all
combined to make him almost a dazzling sight.

After him came the other men who were to receive
degrees but their entrance was flat after the enthusiasm
over Sir George. The Royalties meanwhile were the only
people in the theatre to remain seated. It seemed to me
that they should have been able to join in this small way
of showing honor to one of their country's leading de-
fenders, and the other learned and distinguished men.

Sir George had stopped before the Vice Chancellor's
throne, and the thrills we had been feeling over his splendid entrance died down, as the Vice Chancellor began to
gabble some Latin at him. When he had done, he leaned
over—almost losing his balance in doing so—and they
shook hands. Then Sir George climbed over some people,
and finally found his seat in the front row of the lower
balcony. This process was repeated with each of the honorary degrees, with more or less enthusiasm on the part of
the audience. Comparisons are odious, but for dignity,
impressiveness and general efficiency give me President
Eliot's way of doing things at Commencement!

* A famous general of the Boer War. [Ed.]

After this all is confusion in my mind about the proceedings of the next hour-and-a-half—one old man after another got up and talked in some dead language; and then the students began, and they popped up in turn in either one of the two funny little pulpits in the upper side galleries, and recited Latin poems, Greek odes, English theses and Latin essays to our long-suffering ears. One old man paused for applause, and got so much that he couldn't begin again, and none of the rest of his essay was heard in the continued stamping and clapping. Another old man talked too low, and repeated calls of "Louder! louder!" had no effect, until a clear voice in an injured tone said, "My *deah* fellow! can't you speak louder? I haven't heard a word." The Vice Chancellor rattled off a dreary waste of Latin, during which he and his two satellites, or whatever they were, took off their hats and bowed their heads about every twenty words. This fascinated the upper balcony and they began to count the times the hats came off. They counted in chorus and were way up in the "teens" when suddenly a triumphant voice sang out, "Ah! you forgot it that time!" and the satellites were visibly disconcerted. Every time a student got up to recite his life was made miserable unitl it was discovered what stuff he was made of. Most of them fought their way through the first difficult three minutes of jibes and jeers, coming out triumphant, neither laughing nor crying, and still talking! But it must have been torture to them! One poor boy, who had a nervous habit of winking, almost broke down and gave it up. The Greek odist brought down the house. He was a good-natured fellow who *couldn't* be rattled, but some of the Greek sounds he made *were* ridiculous, and the way he said them would have amused any assembly.

Friday, June 26. Mr. Parry asked us weeks ago to come and see the Trooping of the Color from his office in the

Treasury Building, so we started out for there immediately after breakfast. It was a brilliant day, such a birthday as the poor King has only once in ten years probably
—and all London was out to see the soldiers. Arrived at
the Foreign Office at last, we met the Parrys, and after
clambering up many flights of stairs and along passageways, we found ourselves in a room with big windows and
convenient, wide ledges to sit on overlooking the whole
Parade, and giving us a perfect bird's-eye view from about
three flights up—quite near enough to recognize all the
interesting people.

The King*, looking very fat on his huge horse, was
escorted by the Prince of Wales and the Duke of Connaught, who rode a step behind him, the former an insignificant and much shrunken copy of his father, and the
latter well-set-up and soldierly. "Bobs"† was also there on
his gray charger, looking dignified and alert as ever. The
people around me thought the King made a splendid martial figure, but he looked to me like a round, red, roly-poly
barrel, balancing an enormous black muff on end.

It was the most brilliant military spectacle I ever saw.
The English know how to do this sort of thing to perfection
and it's something in which we shall never be able to rival
them. After it was over we waited for the crowd to scatter
below and meanwhile we ate delicious strawberries and
cherries. Then Mr. Parry suggested taking Papa and me
over the Prime Minister's house, 10 Downing Street, which
adjoins the Foreign Office building. So we went down the
many flights of stairs and passageways again, and suddenly
found ourselves in a large homelike room, flooded with
sunshine, and on the walls crayons and portraits of the
Balfour family—a good one of the Prime Minister and a

* Edward VII. [Ed.]
† Field Marshal Lord Roberts. [Ed.]

very handsome bust of his brother who died. We went through this room to the study where we were welcomed by Mr. Balfour's private secretary, who showed us many interesting books and documents, and bills signed, or to be signed, by the King. He was a very polite and good-looking young man named Ramsey, and on inquiry, proved to be Fairie Ramsey's first cousin. He took us over the rest of the house, showed us the big banqueting hall, with the curious Burne-Jones frescoes, where the Prince of Wales dines tonight, another room in which were portraits of past Prime Ministers, and also the little garden under the wall of the Horse Guards with the hole in the wall where Mr. Balfour slips through when he wants to play golf, and unwelcome visitors, like suffragettes, are at the front door. Really, 10 Downing Street is the most interesting house in London and especially to us Americans. Here it was that the cabinet sat during George IV's reign, and it has far more history attached to it than any of the London palaces or in fact any of the palaces in England.

Saturday, June 27. To Lambeth for the Royal dinner party at a quarter-to-eight. Mrs. Davidson was in a becoming dress with a few handsome jewels and an order and looked very pretty, and the Archbishop was gorgeous in his short purple silk apron, jewelled cross and light blue ribbon of the Order of the Garter across his chest. The Archbishop did not forget us among his more important guests, but came and told me who I was going to sit by, and what to talk to him about. He then went and got "him" and introduced "him" and he was a Captain Swinton, very pleasant, good-looking and exceedingly tall. The Archbishop said he picked him out for his height as he knew I didn't like to walk in with little men! When everyone but the Royalties had come the Davidsons left the room, soon appearing again with a large bland lady who was, of course, the Princess Christian.* We all stood back from the centre of the room, leaving a broad open space, and, as she walked down it, Mrs. Davidson mentioned each person's name, the Princess bent a little and the victim curtsied. After her came the Prince, a very tall, straight, white-haired old man with an eye glass, or a glass eye, I forget which. They were both fine-looking and had great presence, and Princess Victoria† was pleasant-looking too, but they were all very stiff. I suppose it was *"le grand air."* They had with them a handsome young equerry in court dress and a charming-looking lady-in-waiting, Lady Dick Cunningham, who has had a pathetic history, but it is too long to write here. As soon as possible after their arrival we all went in to dinner, Mr. Conybeare arranging us in correct precedence. I liked my seat immensely. The dashing Captain was fond of music and art, and proved to be a friend of Sargent, so there was plenty to say to him, and on the other side I found a most genial neighbor who was easily amused, and a great admirer of Mrs. Julia Ward Howe and things American. Mr. Banks, the Captain, and I got so excited over an automobile discussion toward the end of dinner that poor Mr. Banks forgot to say grace, until the butler jogged his elbow, when he jumped as if he had been shot, and we saw the Archbishop looking sternly down the table toward our end.

We all filed out after the Princesses, Mrs. Boyd-Carpenter kindly asking me to join her. The Princesses stood for nearly an hour after dinner and I almost dropped. I leaned on the tables and the chairs and tried one foot after the other, and got crosser every moment. It seems to me that if I had

* Queen Victoria's daughter, Helena, who married Prince Christian of Schleswig-Holstein. [Ed.]

† The daughter of Prince and Princess Christian. [Ed].

been a Royalty for nearly sixty years I would have learned
to be a little more considerate. Poor old Lady Kelvin
looked exhausted when Her Royal Highness finally con-
descended to try a chair. We all flopped immediately.
English people *are* so gawky! When the men came in they
all stuck right in the doorway except the two Americans,
Mr. Choate and Papa, who came into the middle of the
room and talked to the ladies all alone for some time. The
rest had to be inveigled in by Mrs. Davidson, and shoved
from behind by the Archbishop. It was my lot to entertain the good-looking equerry which proved a difficult task.
He obviously took not the least interest in me, nor could
I please him with any remark. Still I struggled on, little
thinking that worse was in store for me. I saw the Archbishop coming towards me across the room from the young
Princess's direction. I divined his intention but was power-
less to stop him. He bent down and said solemnly, "The
Princess Victoria would like to meet you," and I had to get
up and be led back by him. He introduced me, the Princess
of course remaining seated, and I had to accomplish the
difficult task of curtsying and shaking hands at the same
time, which I did awkwardly enough. She asked me to sit
down next her, which I was just going to do anyway—only
I hope she did not notice my intention. Some stupid person had told me at Oxford that one should only reply to
their questions in talking to Royalty. This rule I followed
rigidly, so that after she had asked me when I came, when
I was going and if I had ever been there before, conversation flagged, and we sat and looked at each other in total
silence during the longest moments of my life. I wish I had
never heard the silly rule because then we might have had
a very nice time, instead of which it was hideous, and after
five minutes, which seemed an hour, I could have screamed
aloud for somebody to come and take me away. I tried in

vain to catch the Archbishop's eye and looked frantically around the room for help. No one would come near us, any more than if we had had the plague, though I saw that Papa had noticed my strained attitude. Finally Lord Stanhope came up and the Princess turned gratefully and talked to him. Then I didn't know whether to go or stay. I believe Lord Stanhope is not considered clever or interesting, but I shall always love him because he turned and included me in the conversation. He must have had a good time, too, as all his polite and rather vapid remarks were welcomed and seconded with much cordiality and appreciation. Then old Mr. Goldschmidt, Jennie Lind's husband, came up to speak to me, and soon after this the Royalties left.

Princess Victoria shook hands with me again when they left, and I wished I could tell her that I was not always so stupid and that I liked her looks. I suppose she had thought that, being an American, I might meet her in a more equal and democratic way, and give her a little change and amusement, and I had proved quite as dull, if not more so, than the dullest English girl could be.

One funny thing about this dinner, I must add, and that is what Lady Dick Cunningham told Papa. The list of the guests was sent to her to show to Princess Christian, according to custom, to see if she "approved." Lady Dick Cunningham said she was looking over it with a friend (who may or may not have been the Princess) and the friend said, "That should be a rather jolly dinner, because of course the Bishop of Massachusetts and his daughters will be black." We must have been a sad disappointment all around!

Sunday, June 28. Papa and I lunched with the Archbishop of Armagh and Miss Alexander. The Irish are so

different from the English! They are much easier and jol-
lier, and meet you cordially halfway. Miss Alexander is
attractive and really *smart* looking. She is the first handsomely and tastefully dressed person that I have seen. The
old bishop is a lovely genial soul, perfectly helpless even
with two canes, but with real Irish blue eyes that twinkle
all the time.

Monday, June 29. To Fulham Palace, where the Bishop
of London had asked us to visit him for a day or two.

Fulham is much prettier than Lambeth and the grounds
are even larger and more beautifully laid out. The palace
of course is small comparatively, but much more picturesque. We drove through the gates into an old square court
with a charming fountain in the middle. The usual number of footmen opened the doors and showed us through
interminable halls, finally out into the garden behind which
we came upon a charming view. Four or five acres of green
lawn stretched away on all sides, broken here and there by
fine old trees, some overgrown with ivy. Beyond, to the
left, was a real country scene. Fields and meadows stretched
as far as you could see and in them people were making
hay, and piling it on the carts, while cows browsed in the
shade of trees, all this right in the middle of the biggest
city in the world. Off to the right we could see greenhouses
and a garden, and then a wall and an old church tower
beyond; and right in the foreground was a well-laden tea-
table with an elderly lady making tea and four young men
partaking of good things. The Bishop was in town and
would not return till eleven o'clock at night. Apparently
he always keeps open house, though Lady Wilson said he
was almost never at home himself. He is in town all of
every day, and dined at home *once,* during a visit of two
weeks which his mother had just made him. He must be

as busy as the Archbishop! I am coming to the conclusion
that Englishmen who do work—such as Bishops or cabinet
ministers—work harder and longer than anyone does in
America.

Tuesday, June 30. Was waked by the sun pouring in my
open windows, and looked from my bed right out towards
the hayfields. We had three large rooms on the long
façade of the palace overlooking the gardens. It was so
peaceful with only the country noises, that I had to think
twice before realizing where I was. We met the Bishop
in the hall when we came down, and he came up with
the most cordial welcome, apologizing for being such a
"shabby" host, and looking as happy and serene as if he
had nothing in the world to do. After prayers in the chapel
he asked if we wouldn't take a walk around the garden with
him. We stepped out of his study window and walked all
around the place very leisurely, and he talked all the time,
and seemed to be keen on nothing more than gardening.
At breakfast he entertained the whole table. I never saw a
man before in such spirits at breakfast time and he quite
fascinated everyone. We asked him about the squash
match, which he and the Archbishop played against their
two chaplains; about the result of which there seems to be a
difference of opinion, according as you ask the bishops or
the chaplains. He didn't seem to eat any breakfast, and left
the table before I was halfway through. He was to drive
us in to town, in time for the consecration service of a
church in Kensington, which Papa rather wanted to see.
Five of us piled into the most enormous barouche I ever
saw—the Bishop, the Chaplain and I on the back seat and
Papa and Sally opposite. The Bishop read his mail and
dictated to the Chaplain in fits and starts, and filled up the
gaps with pleasant and amusing conversation. The secre-

tary was also interesting to talk to, and I think the Bishop's
correspondence that day must have been a little vague, as I
often found myself chatting away on one side of him without knowing that the Bishop was dictating on the other.
We drew up before a brand-new church, where a lot of
bustling dignitaries immediately fell upon the Bishop and
hustled him away before we could half say good-bye. We
were shown to very "high seats in the synagogue," which
were fine places from which to watch all the elaborate happenings which presently began. There were anthems and
organ recitals, and processions of mayors and other gold-
lace people. After a great deal of distant intoning a clear
voice from some unseen source suddenly said, "In Heaven's
name let us begin!" Actually, that was in the service, and
of course it was not meant to be amusing at all. Then the
choir and the clergy began to march up the aisle to a slow
chant, and sentences read by the Bishop. Slowly the gold
cross came nearer and then we could see the tall Chaplain
towering above the rest, clad in wonderful clothes and
carrying the Bishop's heavy gold mace. Just behind him
came the Bishop dressed entirely in red and purple and
gold, and weighed down by his heavy mitre. He had a stiff
gold thing on, something between a cape and a pair of
sandwich boards, and on his hands were red gloves. We
did not stay all through the service which threatened to
last the rest of the day—but stole out and found the big
barouche waiting to take us to the Berkeley. We have all
caught the Bishop of London craze, and his ears must have
burned under his mitre, all the nice things we said about
him. Papa thought he had more humor and fascination
than any man he had ever seen, and he could not help com-
paring this little visit at Fulham with the last one he made
in '97. Our present host was the exact opposite of his then
host and hostess, who said, "You might as well say good-bye

to your guests when they're leaving. It is worthwhile to be
polite as one never knows but one might want something
of them some day!"

We had just time to change our clothes at the Berkeley
and get to the Chamberlains' where we were to lunch. It
was not a lunch party, as a handsome Lady Alice Stuart
was the only guest outside of the Chamberlain family. A
place was set for her husband too, but neither he nor Mr.
Chamberlain, nor Mr. Austen Chamberlain turned up at
all, which was quite a disappointment to us. They were all
kept at the "House." I suppose it is quite the usual thing
among Parliamentary people never to know whether the
men are coming or not. Lady Alice and Mrs. Chamberlain
both spoke as if they didn't see much of their husbands and
I expect that this crowd of people are probably as busy as
the ecclesiastics. The interesting people in England—or
anywhere—do not loaf.

In the evening Lord and Lady Ashcombe gave us a dinner party. They have a typical big house in Prince's Gate
of the last generation style, like the Baroness Burdett-
Coutts' which I think I described last year. They had a
dinner of twenty-two and they had taken pains to get
together people who would be interesting for us to meet.
Many of the guests had affiliations with America. The
Duckworths had stayed with the Weir Mitchells; Mrs.
Cutler's brother, Col. Foster, is at Bar Harbor now with
the English Embassy. My two neighbors were Mr. Cole of
the Bank of England, who is much in America, and knew a
lot of people I did, and Sir Lewis Dibden, who is the
Archbishop's lawyer and who breakfasted with us when we
were at Lambeth. The Rt. Hon. John Talbot is the Bishop
of Rochester's brother, and his wife was a Lyttleton and
Mrs. Talbot's sister. Altogether we felt very much at home
and found everybody pleasant and cordial—Lord and Lady

Ashcombe particularly. It was the "best appointed" dinner I ever went to, and never have I tasted such good food! The fruit was magnificent, and looked like fairy story fruit —nectarines, wonderful peaches and Black Hamburg grapes as big as our apples. There were about sixteen men to wait on us, all in maroon livery with silver buttons and pink stockings. As a feast it was certainly magnificent—an example of old-fashioned, high-toned English hospitality.

Wednesday, July 1. Mr. Macmillan,* the publisher, gave a dinner for us. In spite of his attractions the dinner was a dull proceeding. His wife and daughter were picturesque but lackadaisical, and the other lady there was the widow of the author of Green's History of England who looked like Mrs. Gordon Dexter, and talked like a teapot. Poor Green! I suppose he wrote so much because he never got a chance to speak. She is a wild Irish enthusiast and as a "type" was interesting to listen to at first. I sat between Mr. Macmillan, to whom I tried to be agreeable, and an unknown man who took no interest whatever in me and I am sure I reciprocated his feelings. He talked Irish across the table to Mrs. Green, and they almost came to blows. After dinner Mrs. Green *wouldn't* go home. She got Papa pinned into the corner of a sofa and talked Irish to him till eleven o'clock, while the rest of us tried to conceal our yawns from each other. Finally I could bear it no longer and catching a desperate glance from Papa, got up and said goodnight with many excuses about having to pack, etc. It was such a pity, when Mr. Macmillan had been so hospitable to us perfect strangers that we should have had to outstay our welcome in this way.

Thursday, July 2. Still perfectly lovely weather. It suddenly occurred to me that I hadn't clapped eyes on St.

* The father of Harold Macmillan, the recent Prime Minister. [Ed.]

Paul's or the Strand this whole trip, which mustn't be, of course, or I shall not feel as if I had been to London. So I took a hansom and drove up the Strand till I saw the Cathedral looming up ahead. When I got to exactly the right spot I made the man stop, so that I could look at it, and then I told him to turn around and drive back. He must have thought me an exceptionally crazy American to drive up the Strand through the dense traffic, stop a moment, and then drive back. In the afternoon we took Rosamond Peabody out to Lord's to see the Oxford-Cambridge cricket match, and of all the stupid things it was the slowest! One of them had got several thousand runs, so they had kindly "resigned" to give the other side a chance to run before it got too late in the year. We had members' tickets which put us in a very select stand, I suppose, but the only person in it we knew was the dirty old M.P., who said he was a friend of Lord Tankerville. Between the halves everyone wandered around on the cricket field. I never saw such a crowd in my life—and they were all nice-looking and quiet, the men immaculately set up, and the women all in light frilly things with parasols and one and all with charming refined voices. Think of our professional baseball crowds, or even our big football game crowd in comparison! There were tents for tea around the field of course, and the players were all immaculate, too, in their pale blue and pink striped flannels, all so clean and white against the green lawn. The umpires, in their glittering white caps and aprons, looked like the butcher of Spotless Town, and even the bats and balls were clean and white. We got so bored looking at the game and everything was so quiet and silent all about us, that we went out and wandered in the promenade behind the stand, and here we met quite number of people we knew, or knew by sight. Mr. Alington of Eton spoke to us, and even one or two men we had met at the Cambridge balls.

CHAPTER 18

INTO THE TWENTIETH CENTURY

⊷҈

A RESUME of the Glorious Year of 1901: No year that I
have lived has come up to 1901. First a wonderful winter
season ending February 14 when we sailed on our wonderful Italian trip. After that two months of the most beautiful spring in Cambridge, the pleasantest spring I ever had,
and why? Because somebody—and a very attractive somebody—was always *there,* except on the very few evenings
when he said he thought the doorbell and I might like a
rest. Well, it all ended on a perfect Class Day evening.
We *did* Class Day under perfect auspices—full moon,
"Valse Bleu" and all, and it is good to look back on.

How nice it is to write a diary again!

Then in September came our wonderful western trip
and the trip South. Whatever happens I should always be
grateful for such a Happy Year.

1902 has not been so bad either. Ruth and I have been
taking singing lessons at the Conservatory and our teacher,
who is young and charming, is most encouraging. Carrie
and I took private painting lessons of a Miss Taylor at
Mr. Tarbell's suggestion, and got on faster than at Art
School. Skating was more fun than ever as I learned more
and more figures. The Lawrence Club has been a real

success, I am glad to say. They are all dears! Tom Connelly is the star, but our handsome President, Joe Murray, is fine too and so are the two Howards, and faithful Mike O'Donnell and James Mitchell (the wag), Frank Crowley and Frank Conley, our gentlemanly little Secretary.* I thought I should lose interest when they got as old as this, but I don't seem to and I am glad of it. Besides my former charities I have become a Manager of the Church Home. Mostly because Grandmas Lawrence and Cunningham were both on the Board for years and so was Mamma too.

January ended with Marjorie Robbins' wedding at Emmanuel at which I was a bridesmaid.

Decoration Day, 1902. On Brattle Street I saw a little boy about five years old all dressed in his best and clean and sweet and cunning carrying a small bunch of flowers and evidently on his way to Mt. Auburn Cemetery. He was patiently waiting for his father who was sitting on the wall so drunk he couldn't walk or stand. He tried to get up but after a few steps fell on the wall again. Finally he got going and staggered on to Mt. Auburn, which was still more than a mile away. Poor tired hungry little boy before he gets home if he ever does.

What a sad old world it is and what a mess people can make of their lives.

Dec. 1902. Art, Art, Art—also the Bazeleys' Xmas dinner with pig's head, blazing Plum Pudding, sparkling ices, holly, snappers and mistletoe. I never saw a prettier table. Then Xmas with church and in the evening Carrie and I went to the Messiah Oratorio. I have been learning to sing some of it which made it more interesting for me than

---

* Tom Connelly ended up a judge on the Massachusetts bench, and Frank Crowley was postmaster of Boston later in life.

usual. Harold came in after church. He had sent lovely roses to Mamma.

Feb. 4, 1903. The great day at last! Dined at the Endicotts' to meet *Sargent!** It was awfully nice of them to ask me, but they knew (in London last summer) how much I wanted to meet him. He was disappointing looking. In fact I may as well say at once that though he is tall, he is not well made and is in fact a little fat, his face is red, and his eyes rather goggly!!! He has a small brown beard and moustache and dark hair beginning to thin and turn grey. It was a dinner of fourteen, all much older than I.

I was talking to Mr. Preble Motley after dinner (with whom I always get along swimmingly) when Mrs. Endicott brought Mr. Sargent up and introduced him and as soon as he spoke to me I forgot all these discrepancies and, though I was saying nothing but disagreeable and tactless things about our disappointment in not getting to his studio last spring, and he was only regretting and apologizing and asking after Aunt Sally, I liked him better and better. He seemed so anxious to please and so unspoiled and simple. He talks fast and much and his eyes do look on closer acquaintance as if they could see right through people, as they do.

In March Sargent began a portrait of Uncle Caleb. The sittings took place at their house on Gloucester Street, and he didn't mind a bit if people watched.

March 24, 1903. Went to Aunt Sue's to *watch Sargent paint Uncle Caleb!* He was doing his judge's gown today and he dashed right ahead as though he was painting a fence until he finished it and he never made a mistake

---

* John Singer Sargent, the painter. [Ed.]

once! I suppose he was thinking all the time, but I know he was talking all the time and very pleasantly and amusingly. It was wonderful and he is a wonderful man.

March 28, 1903. Up to Aunt Sue's to see Sargent paint. This is his seventh and last sitting and the picture seems perfect to all of us. He was working on a background and put in rows of law books and a big bronze of a jockey on a horse. Then he offered to take it out if we (Aunt Sue, Miss Louisa Loring, Uncle Peter and I) did not like it. He had put in Uncle C's watch chain and when we decided against it he whisked it out again in a jiffy—mixing the gown color perfectly accurately in no time at all. I watched it all very carefully in order to tell the Portrait class about it later. They are thrilled that I am actually seeing him at work.

He was much interested to hear that I had just seen the *Commonwealth* sail and disappointed not to have been there himself as he had a book he wanted to give General Wood. He had been to the Tavern Club dinner for the General last night and was full of excitement about it. He is as crazy as a schoolgirl about General Wood and raves about his looks and his achievement. He gave him the portrait he did of him—thereby losing some four or five thousand dollars.

While we were all talking Mr. St. Gaudens* suddenly walked in upon us and made a call. Mr. S. had asked him to come and criticize the picture. The two great men reviewed the dinner last night, talking it over like two Harvard boys. They thought all the speeches fine but were amused by Mr. Curtis Guild's rather exaggerated and excitable oratory. Both seemed so simple and unspoiled it made me squirm to hear Miss Loring flatter them. She lays it on so thick to Mr. Sargent and he pays no more attention

---

* The famous sculptor. [Ed.]

to it than so much air. This morning he got belated and, as my cab was at the door, I told him to take it to go to his lunch party (to which he was already almost an hour late), and I told him I would clean up his palettes and brushes. I wouldn't have done this if he had been a different sort of man, but he was so flustered at being late and so unaffectedly worried about taking my cab, and so insistent about my *not* cleaning his things that I almost told him that I considered it an honor!

This was a great morning. Told the family about it at lunch.

In April I went to New York to stay with the Morrises. They always had the most remarkable automobiles. The year before Angela met me at the station with a "new automobile which came banging and puffing towards us. It is dark maroon color —lots of room for four to lounge in it—foot-warmers, beautiful fur rugs, bells, tubes, electric lights, and the chauffeur sits up behind in maroon livery and silver buttons as in a hansom."

April 9, 1903. Lovely day. Went out in the motor to do some errands for Angela. Van Valen is a wonderful driver and we went lickety-split down Fifth Avenue weaving in and out amazingly. It was great fun! The Morrises think he shows off with me and that I egg him on—but I don't —only he probably knows I enjoy going fast and taking risks and I expect he enjoys it too. I bought seven wedding presents for Angela—among them one for her first cousin Reggie Vanderbilt who is marrying Miss Neilson. It was amusing ordering all these gorgeous things.

P.M. We went out in the big Rochet-Schneider car stopping for Edith Fabbri and then driving all the way to Westchester Country Club where we had tea. It was so luxurious lying back on our cushioned seats with the wind

on our faces and rushing past! It was more like flying than
anything I ever imagined.

April 10, 1903. Went out in the Franklin and made
some calls. Went to Dr. Rainsford's three-hour service. He
spoke six times and each time finer than the last and it
seemed no longer than an hour.

We dined at the Fabbris' in their *beautiful* house. It is
just like a palace and I don't know any people who *become*
luxury as the Fabbris do and luxury becomes them. We
drove down and back in the Rochet and coming home there
was a full moon and a perfect evening—just warm enough
and no wind, no dust, and the trees just coming out, looking so delicate and feathery in the moonlight that we took
an extra turn all around the park it was so lovely.

April 11, 1903. I am having great luck with the weather
and took another drive this morning, through the Park
where all the buds were bursting and the grass like green
velvet and down the Avenue where I met Eleo Sears who
looked astounded at my sporty appearance. I spent an hour
at the American Artists Exhibition, and was much interested to see Bay Emmet's things. Charlie Hopkinson also
had several in it and there was a good one by Leslie
Thompson—a boy at Art School who got the prize for
water colors at my Students Club Exhibition last year.
Went home on 3 o'clock train after a lovely visit. I did not
see many people but I did not let anyone know I was coming. The Morrises did not think I saw much of *them*
either, or the children, but they were glad I enjoyed the
autos! I did have some lovely times with them and the
children too.

When I got home I complained about a friend's new motor
that it was pretty but not nearly so big and comfortable as the

Morrises' big Rochet-Schneider. Furthermore, I didn't have the same confidence in my friend's driving as I did in Van Valen's —"far from it!" said I, "and in the second place, we did not go fast enough to be amusing." On Boston streets in those days the traffic was almost all horse-drawn carriages or hansom cabs, with an occasional motor car. And taking a trip in one of the new contraptions was a real adventure. A year or two later I set out with Frank and Louise Crowninshield in their new Hotchkiss for an expedition across the state.

Sept. 29. Another lovely day and tremendous preparations completed, we finally got started for Lenox. The automobile looked, as Frank said, like a bird's nest. There was a trunk on behind and in the tonneau were Louise, her guest and I, 3 valises, 3 fur coats, a big flowered bandbox full of hats to wear Sunday in Lenox, a lunch basket and many goggles, veils, maps, etc. Frank also carried on his person a bottle of whiskey and a pair of pistols! Benny jeered us off saying he would expect us back to lunch. Alas, we did even better than he expected. After a beautiful run of three miles the tire (under me) exploded with the most awful report and the inner tube appeared like a large watermelon beneath it. We sat an hour by the roadside and then crawled slowly home again—buying a beefsteak on the way for dinner. Frank and the chauffeur dumped the contents of the automobile onto the lawn and then retired in it to the stable. We were all seated at luncheon when we heard Benny's laugh in the distance. It came nearer and nearer and was most infectious. "Ho-ho-ho, haw-haw-haw," he came on through the hall and nearly deafened us in the dining room. I couldn't help joining in though Frank and Louise did not smile. Benny said, he thought when he came home that gypsies had encamped on the lawn.

Sept. 30. We started again at 9 A.M. We got as far as
Lynn and there in the middle of the city right on the car
tracks the same thing occurred again. While Frank and
the chauffeur worked on the machine Louise and I sat on
the step and read, much to the amusement of the inhabi-
tants of Lynn. We all voted *not* to return to Benny so we
crawled into town to the Automobile Club and Frank went
off to see the Michelin agent.

After lunching at the Club we started again. The
Michelin agent had come and put a new tire on himself
and said it would be all right now. George Tyson was at
the Club with his car and offered to accompany us, so he
took Louise in his machine and off we went again. In
about three miles, fortunately after we had come down a
long steep hill, it happened again. Frank and the chauffeur
looked at each other with rather sick expressions and Frank
said that was as far as he was going to drive that machine.
He had burst four inner tubes in three days, at $21 apiece.
George Tyson and Louise, missing us, returned and greeted
us as if they had never heard of such a thing happening
before. The chauffeur put the old worn-out French tire on
the car and we returned to the Michelin agent with whom
Frank had quite an interview. Frank said the agent gave
him a new shoe and two tubes and was "fairly decent."
Done out of her trip, Louise suggested dinner at the Touraine and then the theatre but this was too much for me
who was tired out from waiting around and as long as I had
my luggage right there I decided to go home. Frank was
very nice about it and most apologetic and sent me home
in the machine.

Oct. 1. Geo. Tyson's machine came out for me with his
little Negro chauffeur to take me to Marblehead. I was
rather worried about the ride as I had been terrified by the

way Frank's chauffeur drove me home last evening. We
came within a hair's breadth of killing several people and
I only hope they did not die of shock afterwards. But the
little Negro was a wonderful driver and I much enjoyed my
luxurious ride alone in a huge Pierce-Arrow.

In November 1905 I had the adventure of driving all the
way from New York to Boston in the Morrises' car with Angela.
The first day we traveled from New York to Middletown, Conn.
It was a lovely day and a fine run. Almost too exciting after
dark in unknown country. Twice we came upon and crossed
a railroad track before we knew it, and both times a train went
by immediately afterwards.

The next day I ached in every limb but we got off to an
early start at 8:45.

Enjoyed every second of the run. We ate lunch at a
dreadful little town and filled up on some delicious sandwiches which Katharine Wadsworth had pressed upon us.
The roads were excellent nearly all the way, and when they
were not good they were very pretty. We passed every
machine on the road, and there were a great many coming
along for the game.

It is strange to come into Boston from New York by the
road, and I was interested to see just where and how we
should come. Arrived at 122 Commonwealth Avenue at
6 o'clock. We astonished the family by our awful looks—I,
in a grey silk Paris novelty of Angela's, looked more like a
dusty knight in chain armor and helmet, and I don't know
what Angela looked like, though of course she managed to
look pretty in spite of every attempt not to.

I escorted Preston around to the Automobile Club and
introduced him as the chauffeur of Mr. D. H. Morris, President of the Automobile Club of America.

I shall always remember the delight of this first long-distance auto trip, which seemed to do me a lot of good for a long time afterward. We averaged 22 miles an hour from New York, which was considered great going.

1903. Every pleasant afternoon in winter found me either taking a skating lesson or skating with friends. My usual place was a skating club called the Chutes, with a rink on Huntington Avenue where Northeastern University now stands. George Atkinson was often my partner and kindly helped me to learn to waltz, and Lawrence Haughton, Harley, and Cousin George Meyer frequently went. Cousin George asked me to waltz one day and though I was a little timorous, not being sure I could waltz with anybody but George Atkinson, I tried it. The result was disastrous. Down came the Italian Ambassador on the back of his head with me on top of him.

Dec. 17, 1903. After lunch met Harold at the station to go river skating on the Charles. First we took the wrong train—then we went three stations too far and had to wait for another train back to Riverside, so by the time we got to Newton Upper Falls it was almost sunset. Then we had a long walk, and got lost before we finally found the river which alas! had no ice on it—but we persevered and finally came to a part that was frozen but was covered with snow and it didn't bear us anyway when we tried the edge. So on again we went and at last found a pretty place where the ice was smooth and black. H. put on my skates and I ventured on—it was delightful! Then H. came on and skated around to see if it was safe and it seemed to be, but for a precaution I made him cut down a small tree with his knife, and this I pulled after me in order to rescue either one of us who fell in. We skated happily along, H. insisting upon leading me by about 30 yards, which was very unsociable. Once I saw a lovely patch of ice and struck off

toward it but no sooner had I got to it than frightful
cracking began all around and I did not know in which
direction safety lay. I yelled lustily for Harold who in a
second had turned, rushed over to where I was and shot
by me in the direction I was headed. I was delighted to
find that he was so "sandy." We skated on but it was not
all joy as it was very dangerous. We often came to patches
of open water and when the ice was snowy we could not
tell whether it would bear us and there were *no* skate
marks, showing that no one had tried it before us. In
places where there was black ice it was hard to tell it in
the dusk from water and it was disconcerting to see leaves
and bits of newspaper floating briskly not more than half
an inch below one's feet! The current was very strong and
the ice appallingly clear. And I had all I could do to
struggle after Harold, who was going very fast, and the
wind was dead against us. I called to him to tow me but he
only redoubled his efforts saying, "Don't come any nearer
me, the ice will break." At last we came to a bridge and
underneath it a sea of rippling water from shore to shore
and I was very glad to see it as it most effectively barred our
way to Dedham. So we turned and skated back slowly, and
more sociably, with the wind—stopping occasionally to
waltz or try some fancy figures or admire the pretty river-
sides and the sunset. At Newton we took an electric car for
home after a pleasant afternoon. The exercise was fine and
it was beautiful being in the country again. I was pleased
with Harold too. He had been nice, very polite, plucky,
skated well and looked very handsome. He stayed to supper and we related our adventure, which the family rightly
thought was crazy.

Dec. 18, 1903. Church Home meeting and Papa presided
and it was a very amusing occasion. Dr. Van Allen and
Dr. Parks had a set-to—Dr. Van A. in his mild old-woman-

ish manner was so calmly cheeky it was exciting to see how long Dr. Parks would last without exploding. As it was, he hung on to the ragged edges of his temper and insulted Dr. Van A. in a most punctiliously polite manner. This excitement was interspersed with long-winded and pompous remarks from Mr. Paine which he intended should pour oil on the troubled waters but wandered far from the question and served only to irritate the contestants rather more. Mrs. Oliver with her perpetual grievances added to the fun and I had difficulty suppressing my giggles and finally guffawed several times. Papa thinks they are the stupidest, longest and most useless meetings he goes to.

Jan. 22, 1904. Doctor came. Said I had anemia again and must give in. Evening, went to a very nice dinner at the Crowninshields'.

Jan. 23, 1904. Snow, rain and sleet but I *will* go out. Dyer is staying with his sister Anna Stillman and asked me to go to the Horse Show at the Riding Club. Everybody was there and it was very amusing and gay.

Jan. 28, 1904. Sleighing and then singing. My attractive teacher, Miss Woltman, is engaged and will stop teaching, alas. I told her I thought I would stop taking lessons but she said I must not, that I might be a second Schumann-Heink one day!

March 16, 1904. The streets are in the most awful condition. The ice is two or three feet deep with deep ruts in it in which some unfortunate cart is always stuck. People have arranged little bridges of planks on boxes from the sidewalk to their carriages. You can tell the character of the inmates by their boxes. Soap and champagne boxes are the most common.

May 23, 1904. Baby is five years old and we *must* not call him "Baby" anymore. When he was asked the usual silly question that grown-ups ask children the other day, "What are you going to be when you grow up?" he sighed and replied, "Oh, I suppose I'll have to be a bishop!"*

I took the night off and went to the ball. I stayed till 3:00 A.M. and got ten favors. It was fun to show the buds there's life in the old dog yet.

That spring, the beautiful old estate of Governor Gore in Waltham was left to the Diocese of Massachusetts. For months we wondered whether we could possibly be going to move into the famous old residence.

June 3, 1904. Harold and I drove to Waltham to see the "Bishop's Palace." It was quite like a fairy tale and the day being of the misty Corot sort heightened the unreal feeling. We drove up a straight, narrow country road, between farms and pretty rolling country and after a half-hour or more came straight into a grand old English Estate of over a hundred acres with a handsome Georgian Mansion. It is the "Governor Gore" place and has just been left by an old Miss Walker to the Diocese for a Bishop's residence. The trees were superb, being so old and always having had good care. There are straight English-looking lanes, shaded by tall elms very close together and we drove down one of these and entered the avenue. A youth—who could speak no English—ran out of the lodge to open the gate for us and we entered our domain, which has always been so near us and yet I had never seen or heard of it before! It seemed incredible when it is one of the finest historical places in the country and certainly the finest in New England. The house is of brick with two long wings and a fine façade, both facing the avenue and in the back

* This is Bishop Frederic C. Lawrence.

which looked over acres and acres of lawn to the oblong
artificial lake. There is a beautiful old-fashioned formal
garden—a large prosperous farm, orchards, graperies, greenhouses, a deer park with lots of deer—and rarest of all, I
believe, some fine fig trees. In the house are many wonderful things too—ballrooms, picture galleries, and a billiard
table which had been played on by George Washington. In
the billiard room was a fascinating old wallpaper with little
black devils on it.

More than a year later we were still trying to make up our
minds.

It was such a lovely afternoon the whole family went
up to the Waltham place in two carriages to try to make
a final decision as to whether to live there or not. It is
so beautiful it is to me like an enchanted place, hidden off the road behind its tall old trees. One wonders to
find the caretaker and gardeners really awake. It is a bit
of old England or our own Colonial times set down in this
hurrying 20th-century and apparently unknown and unseen. I longed to make sketches everywhere and we were
all much tempted to live there, but alas! it needs many
bathrooms and many servants and is much too far away
from Papa's office.

The final decision was No, but the house was preserved after
many vicissitudes and is now open to the public, and main-
tained by the Gore Place Society.

Nov. 3, 1904. The ball at the Somerset to celebrate the
Mikado's birthday and Baron Kaneko's visit. They hoped
so much that Port Arthur would fall today* and the Japs
did their best to present it to the Emperor with the result

* This was during the Russo-Japanese War in which American sympathies
were chiefly with the Japanese. Port Arthur surrendered to the Japanese on
January 2, 1905, after a siege of seven months. [Ed.]

that thousands of them were killed and no news has yet arrived that it surrendered. The reception was beautiful and a lot of distinguished people were there with quite a sprinkling of uniforms. The little baron received with a row of eight patronesses, one of whom was Mamma, and they all bowed simultaneously and you tried to include all in your curtsey. Kaneko looked very dignified in spite of his tiny stature. The hall was decorated with U.S. and Japanese flags and the entrance hall and porch were simply a bower of wisteria hanging down through lattice and there was a cherry tree fifteen feet high all covered with pink blossoms at the ballroom door. The chrysanthemums everywhere were gorgeous and in the supper room was a miniature Fujiyama six feet high made of white chrysanthemums and greens; life-size storks and some wonderful pagodas were on the supper tables—the pagodas made of frosting and lighted inside so that the red light shone through their little windows. Altogether it was a very handsome ball and I should have enjoyed staying longer but had to go home with Pa and Ma.

So many of my friends were getting married in these years. At least three of them had settled in Milton, where we later had a house, among them Tradja, my sister-in-law Marion Peabody, and Nellie. . . . Once talking with Nellie about all the marriages, "we agreed that all the girls had married the very opposite kind of husbands than we would have supposed they would, and the ones we didn't think would get married had, and vice versa. She said if anyone had told her ten years ago she was going to marry El. Whitney she would have thought them crazy but I can see that nobody is happier or more contented with her lot than this *changed* Nellie who is so much nicer and sweeter and simpler than she used to be. It's a queer, unexpected, humorous, terrible, beautiful sad old world."

I made one of my exciting trips to New York that winter of
1904. For a wonder, Dave Morris was feeling poor and had sold
all his automobiles (though not for long). We got about quite
a bit in an electric hansom that you could hire by the hour.
"There is nothing so delicious to ride in as an open electric hansom which glides along so quietly and swiftly with nothing in
front of you to impede the view and fresh air, and is so comfortable and cosy."

Nov. 17, 1904. I met Dyer at Sherry's for lunch and he
was as handsome as ever and made all the other men there
look like thirty cents. He and I had quite a wait for Mrs.
Wadsworth but she finally came and we had fun picking
out and rubbering at the celebrities. Anna Held looked
like a bad dream and Mrs. Pat Campbell like Lady Mac-
beth. John Drew was flitting about like a fishy-eyed butter-
fly ogling at everyone. Mrs. Willie Vanderbilt was there
and many others with wonderful coiffures, jewels and
clothes. After lunch we took an electric hansom by the
hour and Dyer and I waited in it while Mrs. W. shopped.
We ended up at the Horse Show where all the notables
appeared again—only many more of them. Never have I
seen such extraordinary looking people in such quantities.
A person resembling a lady or a gentleman was a rare sight
but I did see a few old friends.

In May 1905 my long-awaited visit to the Duponts took place.
My friend Louise Crowninshield was Harry Dupont's sister
and they were going to be down there too.

May 8, 1905. Arrived at Wilmington at 7:00 P.M. and
found nobody to meet me—in fact an empty station except
for a disagreeable man who followed me around even to
the telephone booth. It was lonely and getting dark and I

knew the Duponts lived seven or eight miles away. Fortunately I got Louise on the line and she was aghast to hear my voice as she thought I was coming tomorrow. She told me to take a cab and their carriage would meet me half-way out on the pike. I did this but left my trunk in my agitation and had to go back for it. I was just paying toll on the pike when a station wagon and liveried man drove up and the rest of the way we *flew*. I never saw a horse go so fast unless he was running away. It was delicious driving through the dusk in the soft gentle summery air and scents. We came to an iron gate which sprang open for us mysteriously and after what seemed an endless avenue through very tall trees drew up at a huge porte cochere and in it was Louise waiting for me. The house seemed enormous! The halls solid marble with marble pillars and staircases with bronze railings all the way up to the third story. Large azalea trees in full bloom were set about in the hall in pots.

May 9, 1905. Waked to a gorgeous day. I have two large windows in my room opening out onto a balcony and the sounds of birds and scent of flowers that came floating in were quite intoxicating after a long northern winter. Harry Dupont, Louise's nice younger brother, asked me to go to drive and we drove for an hour or more without going off their grounds. His father* was in New York so he is now the boss and he stopped to speak to the workmen. There are two or three hundred working on the place all the time doing and undoing the orders of the Colonel. Frank says they build a terrace of solid masonry and then

* Henry Algernon Dupont graduated from West Point in 1861 and had a distinguished career in the Civil War, being promoted to Lieutenant Colonel and winning the Congressional Medal of Honor. He retired from the Army in 1875 to enter the family firm. He was United States Senator from Delaware 1906–1917, and died in 1926. [Ed.]

the Colonel decides it would look better a few inches to the right or left so they do it all over again. It made me sad to see so much money wasted with such poor results; but the woods and fields full of flowers were a delight. Shimmering white dogwood grew thick amongst the tall trees, and azaleas and Judas trees made a colorful underbrush. Harry Dupont told me to pick all the lilies of the valley I liked, write the addresses of people to whom I wanted them sent and the butler would box and send them. This is luxury! I picked until I was tired and sent them to the family and aunts at home.

May 10, 1905. Colonel Dupont arrived and one of Louise's aunts gave a tea for us. Her place was lovely—like an English place—the Carr-Gomms' for instance.

Evening. People came to dinner and the man who took me in said he knew me when we lived in Lawrence—the world is small. He was one of Papa's few tennis companions there. After dinner the Colonel talked to me and said I reminded him of one of his early flames—Miss Ellen Mason!—which pleased me very much.

May 11, 1905. We drove to Philadelphia where I had never been and while Louise and Ethel had their hair waved I took a hansom and drove about the city. I thought Rittenhouse Square and the residential quarters were beautiful and much like London with the comfortable looking houses—so handsome, homelike and dignified. We did not get home to Montchanin till 4 and had to go back to Wilmington for dinner at Judge Gray's.* He is the man who was talked of for President this last campaign

---

* George Gray (1840–1925), Attorney-General of Delaware, United States Senator (1885–1899), Judge of the U.S. Circuit Court for the Third Circuit, Member of the Permanent Court of Arbitration at the Hague. [Ed.]

and is a very agreeable and handsome gentleman and father
of Nanny Gray. Besides Judge and Mrs. Gray and Nanny
and the Colonel and Louise, Frank and myself, there was
a Dr. Riddle and the Baroness von Hutten* and Alexis
Dupont. I never liked the Baroness and she has not improved. After dinner she sat herself down by me and began
on all her Boston friends and how she got the better of
Mrs. Jack, etc., but I put on a cool, uninterested manner
and used all my wits to give her no satisfaction. As soon
as she heard the men coming in she sprang at the piano—
nobody had asked her to—and there she remained playing
and singing and enjoying the center of the stage.

Later I saw Frank having an intense time with her and
she looked a little baffled. He told me about it afterwards.
She began telling him about all her Boston friends thinking to impress *him* and about how stupid it was of Mr.
Mifflin (Frank's cousin) not to publish her book and called
everybody by their first names and he led her along in the
most innocent-seeming way—but she was fair game. She
has just written a new book which I am glad I had not yet
read.

May 12, 1905. Mr. and Mrs. Dick Elliot arrived. She
was Bessie Wheeler of the big family who lived next to us
at Newport nineteen years ago. She was engaged then
though only eighteen, and she is now a most charming and
popular person. Louise has always said she would rather
look like, *be* like and *talk* like Bessie Elliot than anybody
in the world. I don't by any means always agree with
Louise and my reaction to this remark was, "Oh well! that's
only Louise's opinion" but now I wondered why she hadn't
said it stronger. My first glimpse of Mrs. Elliot won me

* Betsy Riddle, Freifrau von Hutten zum Stolzenberg, a popular novelist of
the time. [Ed.]

completely. She had such a sweet smile and direct cordial look. She is tall and very straight with a perfect figure and curly reddish-gold hair. She is always pleasant and always says the right thing—exactly. She doesn't talk much but when she does everybody listens, her manner is so charming and her voice low and soft, as different from everyone else's as her looks are and her way of looking at you. She doesn't look a day older than I but her oldest son has just entered Annapolis!

After dinner most of them played bridge and the Colonel showed me every book in his library and I thought I should go crazy admiring them one by one.

May 13, 1905. We all went over to the Brandywine to canoe. Mrs. Elliot and I were walking across a field to the river where cows were pastured and suddenly a bull stood right in front of us and stared. After an awful moment I turned and fled but Mrs. Elliot bravely went by him. Of course I had to do it later but I skulked along near the fence. The canoes were bright red and the men had to carry them across the field, but finally we were off. The Brandywine was lovely like the Thames and made me quite homesick for England. I drove back with Harry Dupont and I like him better all the time—he is such an easy, friendly person and has a great sense of humor and is a most thoughtful host.

May 15, 1905. Frank Crowninshield kindly changed his plans so as to escort me home. He said we should travel as father and daughter. I don't know whether the people on the train thought we were father and daughter or not but certainly they thought a good deal about us and had a right to. Frank was *so* funny. In his hesitating, almost childish but most expressive manner of speech to the waiter at lunch, the conductor, etc., he was so absurd that I giggled all day long. Crossing the ferry in New York, we had an interesting sail as some of the yachts were there waiting to be towed down stream for the ocean yacht race that begins tomorrow. Frank knew them all intimately and he told me which would win and what chances the others had.

I reached home just before my sister Julie's wedding. She was marrying Morton L. Fearey, a law student who had lived "in our back yard"—that is to say, in Winthrop Hall which was just behind our house. My father built Winthrop Hall when he was dean of the theological school to take the overflow from Lawrence Hall. He rented most of it to Yale men who came to the Harvard Law School but didn't want to live in Harvard College. Two of my sisters married law students who lived there.

May 20, 1905. A good day for the wedding, thank goodness! Morton and the ushers arrived in the morning. The place was decorated with bay trees around the front terrace and on the porch, and we had the steps carpeted again down from the oval room to the lawn. The church was dressed with white lilacs and green; when we drove over at 3:30 there was quite a crowd all along our wall and around the church door. We had not expected this in Cambridge. The chapel was full already and I was rather annoyed to see no one practically in the seats I had so carefully allotted to them. All the servants and John Herlihy and Mary Ann were up in the balcony and what was my amusement to discover Mrs. Jack Gardner up there with them—Reese, the coachman, looking over her shoulder. She was not invited to the church but that makes little difference with her. The servants were quite excited afterwards when they heard who their companion had been.

Julie came in on Uncle Amory's arm after the ushers and
Sally—the only bridesmaid. She looked very pretty in the
regulation white satin, tulle veil and orange blossoms.
Dean Hodges had the betrothal service and Papa married
them. Morton, after being absolutely calm up to now,
couldn't get out the words "with this ring" for a moment.
He looked handsome and fine coming down the aisle and
Julie looked beaming. Everybody walked over to the house
and Mrs. Jack stood on the terrace and received them!
Mamma and Mr. and Mrs. Fearey were with the bride and
groom receiving in the parlor.

Five-hundred-and-thirty came according to Geo. Becker
at the door. I was pouring tea in the dining room. Just at
first no one came in there—the drift being through the
parlor and then out on the lawn so Papa told Barkie
Donald (who was an usher) to go about and tell people
there was tea in the dining room. Just as B.D. was starting
to do this Evans, the caterer, caught him and said, "Don't
say tea, say champagne, that'll bring 'em," which amused
Barkie very much. Everybody said Julie "looked lovely"
and Morton was "very fine looking" and they had "enjoyed
the lovely sight and had a good time"—but the main thing
is that Julie is happy and we have an A.1. brother-in-law.

CHAPTER 19

SOME IMPORTANT VISITS
AND VISITORS

✒

In February of 1902 I went to New York again to see the christening of a yacht designed by our friend Harry Barbey for the Emperor of Germany.

Feb. 25, 1902. (At the Morrises') We all got up at 6:30, ate a hasty breakfast, and were off to the 23rd Street dock. We were going to see the launching by Alice Roosevelt of Emperor William's Yacht *Meteor.* The Fabbris and Harry Barbey, who was architect of the *Meteor,* were taking us to see it from the deck of the Fabbris' yacht, *Teckla,* which Harry B. had also just built. We got onto the wrong dock first by mistake so by the time we got to the right one Sandro was fuming up and down and said they had almost gone without us. He had chartered a tug, and we were going to land at Shooter's Island where their new yacht was to be from which we were to view the launching. About halfway down the river we got abreast of the ferry boat which was bringing the Presidential party. On board of that were President and Mrs. Roosevelt and Alice, Prince Henry, the Emperor's brother, the German Ambassador, Chauncey Depew and his bride, and a lot of gold-lace individuals. All the boats whistled and tooted as they passed and it was almost as much of a hullabaloo as Dewey Day.

Nearing Shooter's Island we noticed several officials on the dock and police on boats, gesticulating to us to go back, but we thought little of it and went on. We were just ahead of the President's boat and we now discovered that the only empty place left for landing was that where all the officials were waiting for the President! This space had a double line of Marines standing at attention all along it. Apparently our being late had lost us our chance of landing and naturally Sandro was disgusted. Now things began to be *exciting*, for land we must, and immediately. Of course, Harry Barbey had a place reserved for him and would have been on the President's boat if he hadn't chosen to come with us, so he told the pilot to go right ahead through a lot of imposing-looking boats, which caused a great sensation.

Huge megaphones were turned upon us roaring out, "Go back, go back, you can't land there." "Back out at once or I will send a police boat to make you." "You are delaying the Presidential party." "We will arrest you."

Our pilot was scared to death and reversed the engines but H. Barbey was yelling madly that he had a special permit, but they only replied, "That makes no difference— you are too late—we will arrest you if you don't back out at once."

Harry Barbey then took the wheel away from the pilot and steered right in up to the dock next to another tug. The very irate officials came down and pulled us one by one over the other tug and shoved us in behind the line of Marines. It was all done in a moment and we found ourselves scuttling along behind the motionless Marines, the observed of all observers. Louise Schieffelin was pale and shaking from the excitement and we were all pretty nervous running the gauntlet of those awful megaphones.

We found the beautiful new *Teckla* all arranged for our comfort, with staircases to board her, and we couldn't have had a more perfect place to view everything as the *Meteor* was lying right alongside us and the platform with the decorated table, the silver hatchet and the two bottles of champagne done up in red, white and blue was directly opposite us. It had now begun to rain and below us in the rain huddled the President's New York guests, awaiting his arrival before going up on to the covered platform. Ernesto was much amused at their sad plight and wanted to throw pennies down to them. There were rows of sailors and soldiers on guard duty and the German ones in their big round straw hats looked like pink-cheeked children. There was an enormous crowd all around and military bands both German and American.

Finally, through the lines of sailors, came the President and the Prince, the Emperor's brother, bowing to right and left in answer to the cheers of the crowd. Prince Henry, a very tall distinguished-looking man, made the President look a little small and ordinary. After them came Admiral Bob Evans and the Prince's suite and finally Mrs. and Miss Roosevelt looking pretty and ladylike in velvet suits and furs. They all mounted the platform followed by the New York guests and Harry Barbey left us then to join them and see how his boat behaved. It must have been an exciting moment for him.

At a given word scores of workmen began hammering at the wooden supports and the noise was quite deafening and drowned out the bands. Then Alice Roosevelt broke the bottle on the bow and christened the yacht "Meteor" and she glided down and out into the water with all her flags fluttering while guns roared, people cheered, and the bands played the National Anthems. Such a din as there was! Then came speeches by the President, the Prince, and

others and the sending of a telegram to the Emperor. Finally they all filed down again and Harry Barbey came back
and led us all down to follow them which, with difficulty,
we succeeded in doing through the dense crowd. The notables all boarded the *Hohenzollern* for a lunch party and we
boarded our tug, the *Annie Ellis,* and Harry Barbey went
back and joined the swells on the *Hohenzollern.*

The poor *Annie Ellis* seemed to be still in everyone's
way. There were shouts of "Hurry up, *Annie Ellis,* get out
of there" and we were almost run down by the Presidential
party as we hurried to get aboard. We were pulled and
hauled over the *Annie Ellis's* bow which was very high and
covered by a thick wad of dirty rope and tarry straw. It was
not at all easy to climb over it but finally we were all on,
though Will Sloane barely made it with a flying leap, the
other men pulling him in as we started.

It was fun going home. All the East River tug men and
"Hefty Burkes" called out to us, saying, "Did ye see
Henery?" "How was Alice looking?" "Was she sweet to
Henery?" and one pointed to a stolid-looking German
sailor standing high up alone on the *Hohenzollern* and
said, "That's him, that's Henery with the round hat on."

Carriages were waiting for us at the wharf and we all
went to lunch at the Fabbris' gorgeous new house. I sat
between Ernesto and Sandro who were in their best moods.
In the evening the Morrises had a dinner for fourteen and
I sat between Marquis Guardini and North Duane and
after dinner had Ed Harding so it was a really great day.

Feb. 27, 1902. Lunched at the Mahans, and then Angela
came for me and we went to the Opera with the Sloanes.
Their box is next to the J. P. Morgans' (his is the centre
one) and we found Mrs. George Vanderbilt and Leila
Sloane already there. The Opera was *Walküre* which, of

course, was wonderful but we could not stay all through it
as the Morrises were having another big dinner in the
evening and Angela had to rest.

Feb. 28, 1902. I went way down to the Criminal Courts
with Van Valen in the steam runabout. It was almost too
exciting going through those crowded streets but Van Valen
is a wonderful driver and has a steady head and sure hand.
Arrived at the Courts I entered in fear and trembling and
found crowds of men all with their hats on the back of
their heads and smoking and spitting. I went upstairs to a
door marked "Special Sessions" guarded by a uniformed
majordomo, to whom I said meekly, "May I go in here?"
He said, "Certainly, walk in."

Inside were a lot more busy tough-looking men. Through
this noisy crowd I saw on the other side of the room a
group of women and fled to them, sitting down amongst
them. Then I saw a figure with flying coattails jumping
over the rail in front of me which separated us from the
judge and the lawyers and to my amazement it was Sam
Thorne who came right up to me and said, "You must not
sit here—you are among the prisoners' families—come inside with me." But nothing would have induced me to
leave my lady friends and go inside the rail with all the
men. *Finally* Angela arrived and seats were arranged inside
for both of us. Next to me sat Evert Wendall and beyond
him Anthony Comstock!

We had come there to hear the Probation System and see
how it was working. It started in Massachusetts and seems
to be a success there. It was most interesting to me to see
all the boys and watch their faces, trying to judge their
characters through their face and manner. We were lucky
to come today as Judge Jerome was in the chair and after
the Probation part was over he cross-examined some police-

men as he is trying to do what Roosevelt did—enforce the
law on shutting the saloons on Sundays. My, how sharp he
was and how quick! It was not hard to judge which policemen were honest and which not. One especially got rattled
and blustery and kept contradicting himself. Another one
caused much merriment when Jerome was trying to show
that the saloons which were open on Sundays were usually
those patronized by the Irish while those belonging to Jews
and Germans were raided and closed. The policeman
couldn't understand this at all and thought it must be just a
coincidence as how could anyone tell before raiding a place
who it belonged to? Jerome suggested that the name on the
sign might be a clue but the policeman couldn't see that.
Jerome wanted to know if the name Cohen would suggest
that it belonged to an Irishman or German. The policeman "couldn't say." "Well," said Mr. Jerome, "supposing
you saw the name O'Brien over the door, would you think
it was kept by a German?" "Yes," said the poor policeman
and immediately blushed crimson at the laughter of the
crowd which was peremptorily hushed.

Prince Henry came to Boston immediately after his New York
visit.

March 6, 1902. Perfect, clear winter's day. Flags are out
everywhere and we are proud to have the Prince see Boston
looking so beautiful and gay. I followed him around taking
photos of him and his escort and the crowds. His escort was
absurd. In order to keep all his engagements for today he
had to be driven about very fast and the poor escort—
mounted on fearful horses of every description—came
floundering along in the deep snow having the greatest difficulty in keeping up with the barouches. From Carrie's
steps we saw three men fall off, one horse bolt and one go

down, and after the procession passed the street was strewn with trophies in the way of capes, hats and swords which were picked up by the stragglers who continued to come along for ten minutes or so. What *must* the Prince have thought of our cavalry—used as he was to the German?

Papa, Julie, Sally and I sleighed out to Cambridge later in the morning and saw the Prince get his degree. The Prince is a fine-looking man—tall, slim and straight with a light beard and pleasant expression. He looks more like a Naval officer than a soldier—which he probably is. The ceremony was very short. President Eliot presented the degree with one of his inimitable, precise and elegant little testimonial speeches.

Papa went to the Thursday Evening Club in the evening to meet him again. He talked to him and thought he was fine. He is keenly interested in everything, and Admiral Bob Evans has to *drag* him away from each place in order to keep his next engagement—he seems to enjoy it all so much.

When we stayed with the Archbishop and Mrs. Davidson in England in 1903 we became very fond of them both, so we were delighted to learn that they were going to make us a visit in Bar Harbor on the occasion of the General Convention of the Protestant Episcopal Church, which was to meet in Boston in the Fall, and my father and Mr. Morgan* had persuaded the Archbishop of Canterbury to come to it. No Archbishop of Canterbury had ever "left" England for foreign parts officially before and the English usually think if anything has never been done, that is sufficient reason for not doing it, so it took some persuading. In fact, I believe it was necessary even to get permission from the King.

So the Archbishop and his party were to come first to

* Mr. J. P. Morgan, the great banker. [Ed.]

Canada of course, then to Mount Desert to visit Bishop
Doane at North East Harbor and then us at Bar Harbor.
Later to visit us again at Boston during the Convention.

Bar Harbor, Sept. 11, 1904. At 8:30 after a hurried
breakfast we drove to the Anchorage Moorings (Secretary
Whitney's place) and there met Mr. Morgan and the launch
from the *Corsair.* We were going over to North East Harbor to hear the Archbishop preach.

Besides our family of four there were Mrs. Douglas, Miss
Townsend, Mrs. Wright, Molly Coles and Annie Morgan.
We, having had our breakfast, would like to have sat on
deck and enjoyed the lovely sail but fate and Mr. Morgan
decreed that we were to go down in the close dining room
where a sumptuous repast of six courses was set before us.
Mr. Morgan ate it all heartily and slowly from melons, oat-
meal, eggs and bacon to griddle cakes and fruit again.
Papa and Miss Townsend sought the deck and fresh air
halfway through and pride alone kept me in my seat. By
the time Mr. Morgan had finished it was almost time to
land. Of course the church was overflowing but the front
seats had been kept for our party. There were many
bishops in the chancel. The Archbishop wore his scarlet
Convocation robes. It was fine to see him again and Mrs.
Davidson too, who sat right next to me. Directly behind
us was Mr. Morgan singing lustily. They were the observed
of all observers and there was an atmosphere more of the
theatre than of church. But when the Archbishop stepped
into the pulpit right near us and spoke clearly and simply
and strongly as he can, everyone's thoughts were pulled
forcibly out of the little vain and mundane channels that
they were probably in (all except Mrs. Davidson's) and
lifted up to each individual's top plane.

Sept. 16, 1904. Owing to the washouts on the road the Archbishop and his party could not come yesterday to stay with us but they came today with 27 pieces of "luggage" just in time to say "how-de-do" and then go out to lunch somewhere with Papa and Mamma. Dyer asked me to go to the County Fair. We had the Wadsworths' pair and cart and drove to the town of Salisbury opposite Lamoine where the fair was held on a field between the mountains and the bay. There were trotting horses and a ball game and a rope-walker and clowns and contortionists and of course a band. Also prize cows and pigs and sheep—but these, according to Dyer—were all "bum"—but the prize baby was a beauty and so were the vegetables, apples and patchwork quilts. I did so wish the Archbishop could have come (and so did he when he heard about it in the evening) because it was so typically American and so lively and picturesque, and things typically American and still unspoilt and uncommercialized are getting rarer and rarer, alas! The Archbishop said trotting races and ball games were just what he wanted most to see and he was almost peevish about it.

Sept. 17, 1904. Pleasant fortunately for our reception for the Archbishop. I poured tea all the afternoon. We had no idea there were so many people left on the island. Everybody came in their best—from Bar, North East and Seal Harbors, but I didn't have much chance to talk to anyone. The Gardiner Shermans gave them a very formal banquet in the evening and Mr. Ellison (one of the two Chaplains) said afterward, "Next time, Edith, I am going to back in before you, that is the proper attitude for a Chaplain." He turns out to be very amusing and they are all the most easy and delightful guests—always extremely thoughtful and polite. Even the maid is so tactful that everyone downstairs is crazy about her.

Sept. 18, 1904. Grand service—church jammed—Archbishop and Chaplains—gold crozier—four bishops in chancel.

Sept. 20, 1904. The whole crowd was home to lunch which was nice as the week is slipping by and we see so little of them. The Archbishop works mornings on the speeches he has to make later, which seem to worry him horribly.

Sept. 22, 1904. I took Mrs. Davidson for quite a long walk. She was lovely. We got back in time for tea which the English think the nicest meal of the day. We all, from the Archbishop down to Baby, sit cozily around the fire while Mr. Ellison, at the piano, sings the most delightful songs. The children had discovered this hidden talent and seemed to know all his repertoire—which included the Lobster Song from *Alice in Wonderland* and "The Old Black Sow" and what Baby called "the sad song" which was about a bad boy. Papa giggled and giggled and shook himself quite red in the face. Well—today after tea they had to go. The Archbishop shook hands with Katy, Freddy's nurse—because she was Scotch—and was so delightful with her that she was reduced to tears and Mrs. D. bade the whole household good-bye and we all said how we should meet soon again in Boston, which the Archbishop thought an awful imposition to "come down on us again." And the little maid and our exquisite butler kept flying up and down stairs for things forgotten, like Mr. Ellison's umbrella that the Queen had given him—but finally they were off and it would have been sad if we had not had their Boston visit to look forward to. They are going on Mr. Morgan's special train to Washington for a few days and Papa and Mamma got a grand invitation to a dinner at the White House for them which they refused!

Sept. 23, 1904. Perfect day. All the family (except Ap and myself)—and all the luggage went on the morning train to Boston. Ap and I walked down to see them off and outside of Bees were large bulletins which said "Morgan Special wrecked! Archbishop of Canterbury on board! Passengers badly shaken but no serious injury." Imagine our feelings! Everyone stopped us on the way back from the wharf but we could not find out anything more. In afternoon got a paper to read about the accident. Only the poor little maid was injured—about the face. Mr. Morgan must be awfully upset.

Oct. 4, 1904. Cambridge. Spent the morning with Mr. King, Mr. Dewart and Mr. Allen planning a special concert at the Sailor's Haven for the Convention. Went to our town house where the Archbishop and Mrs. Davidson, the two Chaplains and maid arrived this P.M. on the special train with Mr. Morgan. Crowds of reporters were at the station and simply dog Papa's footsteps all the time. The Archbishop had asked me to take him to a professional ball game, and there was a good one today and we had planned to go there right from the station but of course we had not counted on all this bother of reporters and publicity, and Papa said we couldn't do it. Mr. Sullivan asked Charlie Taylor of the Boston Globe if it couldn't be prevented and he said, "You might as well try to stop the tide." Papa said I and one other could come in and have tea with the Davidsons but Sally and Ruth were both set on going, so I had to go back to Cambridge where we young ones are still living.

Oct. 5, 1904. Beautiful day for opening of Convention.
I stupidly lost my ticket and Uncle Robert*—who was running it—wouldn't let me go to my seat so I had to sit in the
transept where I couldn't see a thing and all the time
Mamma and Mrs. Davidson were keeping seats for us,
Julie and me. So we couldn't see the procession except in
glimpses which was said to be very fine. Bishop Doane
preached the sermon which also was said to be fine and I
know for myself that the music was beautiful. Afterward
I escorted Mr. Ellison and Mr. Holden out to Cambridge
to lunch with us as Papa was having a big lunch in town.
We ate a hasty repast and then I drove them in to the
professional ball game—Boston Nationals and Chicago—
which unfortunately was a very poor game and there was
almost nobody there. We sat in the front row next to the
press, and their instruments, etc., interested the Englishmen greatly. We were in imminent danger of getting hit,
and that added a touch of excitement—about the only
touch there was. I thought it was a "put up" game as the
players seemed to take not the slightest interest in it. I was
much disappointed it was so dull but the Englishmen said
it showed them the game. It was just as well the Archbishop couldn't come.

Oct. 6, 1904. Played in Longwood Tennis Tournament.
Then to 122 for instructions. Then lunched at Carrie's and
then to Tremont Temple with Papa and the Davidsons
for the big Missionary Meeting. To my horror we were all
marched onto the stage from the stage entrance while the
whole audience clapped and rose—I in my dirty tennis
clothes and $3.00 Jordan Marsh hat. (The papers next
day had it that I wore "a violet suit and toque to match"
which was nice of them and I hoped there might be a few

* Robert Amory.

people who were not at Tremont Temple who would read and believe it.) Mrs. Davidson and I sank into two chairs behind the chairman (Mrs. Thayer) and looked at the wonderful sight before us. She said she had never seen anything like it. The whole theatre was full of women rising tier upon tier until they seemed to reach the ceiling and the overflow meeting in the hall was just as full, and there were hundreds more who couldn't get in at all. Their offering had been presented at the Service at Trinity this morning at which Papa preached and all were anxious to hear the amount they had raised. First Papa made a welcoming address, then the Archbishop spoke, and then they both repeated their speeches downstairs at the overflow while we heard the Bishop of Tokyo, the bishop of the Philippines and Miss Emery, the General Secretary—all good, but especially Bishop Brent* who has a charming and forceful personality. Then Mrs. Davidson and I went on to the Girl's Friendly tea at the Touraine. This was another jam and poor Mrs. Davidson had to shake hands with a never-ending line of women for an hour and a quarter, when I abruptly took her away leaving the disappointed line apparently just as long as ever. She had told me to insist upon her going at a certain moment, no matter how much she (and they) "kicked and screamed." She wanted to walk back to 122 (for a "rest") so we did and it was a delicious clear brisk evening. She and the Archbishop and I dined at the Jack Peabodys'. It was a very nice dinner, the Judge Grants and Marion and Jim being the only other guests. I sat between Harold and the Archbishop and it was really the first time I had a real talk with the latter since he came to America. I enjoyed it immensely. He really is as easy as an old shoe —goes everyone one better and quicker in conversation and seems interested in anything that comes up. He can come

* Charles Henry Brent, the famous Bishop of the Philippines. [Ed.]

down to your level and really enjoy it apparently and what
is even better he can almost haul you up to his.

Oct. 7, 1904. Once at dinner I noticed such a strange expression on the Archbishop's face as he looked silently and
fixedly at something, that I looked around and found Elsie
behind a sofa and they were having a winking competition.

Oct. 8, 1904. I did nothing all day except that a few
people came to tea—1750 according to the man at the door!
The house was emptied of all furniture downstairs—simply
filled with gorgeous flowers. Mrs. Davidson and Mamma
have been showered with them and Julie is still getting
some. The long glass doors were opened onto the lawn and
fortunately it was a good day. Ma and Pa and the Davidsons received in the study near the front door, an usher
calling out the names. After squeezing the Archbishop's
poor sore hand, another usher (Livingston) said to them
"Pass on quickly, please"—which brought them to the oval
room where Harold was explaining that they could go into
the parlor where there was a long table spread with good
things or they could go onto the lawn—or even into the
Longfellow House which was opened for the occasion—or
they could go across our hall to the dining room where
Ruth, Harriet, Alice Gardiner and Isabel were pouring tea
and chocolate. In spite of all Pa's precautions however
there was a tight jam in the hall and going to investigate I
found a line of people three deep from the front door till it
disappeared around the corner of Lawrence Hall. It really
was funny to see Aunt Sally and Uncle Peter, the Lord
Bishop of Hereford, Stevie Chase, Dr. Huntington all waiting patiently and looking at the gay party from a distance.
I flew around speaking to everybody and trying to look
after the delightful old Bishop of Hereford who seems so

helpless and vague I wonder that he was allowed to come
to this strange country by himself. He has got himself into
a scrape as he has said (not knowing how far New York is
from Boston) that he will speak there Wednesday evening
and he sails Thursday morning from Boston, but he insists
on doing it and will take the one o'clock to New York and
return on the midnight and go straight to the ship.

Oct. 9, 1904. Went to Trinity to hear the Archbishop.
I just trusted to luck and the policeman at the Clarendon
Street door wasn't going to let me in but some official
gentleman nearby said, "That's all right, Miss Lawrence,"
so I went in but every seat on the floor was taken. I tried
the gallery but this was just as full. I was just settling myself on the lowest step of the aisle when a girl in the pew
near me got up and said, "Oh, you must take my seat, Miss
Lawrence." Of course I wouldn't think of it but she made
such a fuss that the people in the pew made room for me
so I got a fine seat but felt very cheeky and mean when
I heard there were 10,000 people waiting patiently outside,
only to find that the doors would not be opened to the
public at all. One old lady who had come all the way from
New Hampshire and waited since 8:00 A.M. was so disappointed that she cried. If I could have found her I certainly
would have given her my seat but my staying out would
not have helped the 10,000, so I stayed in and enjoyed it.

A little grey-haired man read the lessons whom I recognized as the Bishop of Ripon, but I could hardly believe
it, because he had such a funny gentle little voice for the
greatest preacher in England, but his enunciation was
very clear-cut and perfect and his accent decidedly English
—or rather Scotch—and I also recognized him because of
the funny characteristic forelock he wears. The Archbishop's sermon was very fine and delivered splendidly in

his strong clear voice so that every word was heard in every corner of the church. It was a great service and every person there must have been impressed by his grand personality.

I went later to hear the Bishop of Ripon at Appleton Chapel. Mr. Ellison read the service and as I had warned him about the slowness of the responses and the general dreariness of the Unitarian service, he was probably not nervous. The sermon waked everybody up! It was marvelous! The little Bishop led us up to the great broad plane where his mind is at home, and he put his fine thoughts so clearly before us that we couldn't help outdoing ourselves and following him with all our ears. In spite of his very gentle voice, each clear-cut word was heard by every person in the densely crowded building—where every face was rivetted upon the nervous little Englishman with the brilliant mind.

Oct. 10, 1904. Ruth and I went in town to the great mass missionary meeting at Tremont Temple. It was jammed way out into the street and the usher said, "They wouldn't let President Roosevelt in if he came" but Papa was having a word with another usher and the first thing we knew we were being led right up to the front pew where we found Mr. Ellison in solitary grandeur keeping some seats for us and Harold appeared at once with programmes. Papa presided very well and he got off some very good things—though he did look awfully tired. One of the best speeches was made by the old colored bishop from Africa (Ferguson). He was full of enthusiasm and humor —about halfway through the Archbishop came walking onto the stage and everyone rose and clapped tremendously. He had been speaking to the overflow meeting at St. Paul's where the same program was being carried out—only reversed. He sat right down in front of Mr. Ellison and me and grinned a recognition of us. Bishop Brent made a splendid speech, talking very fast about the Philippines and keeping an anxious eye on the quarter-of-an-hour glass where the sand was running much too fast for him. The Archbishop spoke last and made a fine speech, but he spoke longer than usual and Mr. Ellison squirmed about in his chair. He feels more or less responsible, for, besides being an Englishman and a brother-in-law, he helps the Archbishop to write his speeches. Every time the Archbishop began a new sentence Mr. E. would wiggle and the Archbishop would give a worried glance down at him. I was amused by Mr. E.'s distress especially as there seemed no cause for it—the speech being a fine and strong one and everyone talking about it in the most enthusiastic way as we went out.

Oct. 11, 1904. We all were taken to the Art Museum for the big reception for the Archbishop. I felt I was dreaming, it was so funny to be in the Art Museum where I had been a humble student in the squalor of the school studio, and now to be at this brilliant reception which was also a funny mixture of artists and frumps, society ushers like Joe Minot, Hooper-Hooper, Holker Abbott, and quantities of clergymen, then Mrs. Jack in all her diamonds surrounded by Bishops and finally Papa and Mamma receiving with the Archbishop. It was all too queer, but also amusing.

Oct. 12, 1904. Went in town to see if I could be of any assistance as the Davidsons are leaving today. They had to send downtown for an extra trunk they have been so showered with presents from a $500 loving cup to all sorts of flowers, books and silver ornaments. I felt awfully sad about saying good-bye—not knowing when we might meet

again if ever. The Archbishop said we were coming over
next June and for me to talk as if there were no question
about it! Both he and Mrs. Davidson were awfully sweet
and seemed quite sad about saying good-bye too—though
of course they are glad to be going home and they have
worked hard and must be looking forward to a rest. The
Archbishop held my hand in both of his (and I hoped it was
not only done in order to prevent my shaking and crunch-
ing it) and said a lot of nice things and Mrs. Davidson
kissed us all good-bye. Mr. Ellison and Mr. Holden were
unfeignedly glad to be going home to wife and sweetheart,
and dear old England—so for them it was a glad hour but
for me it held many regrets. The next day we saw "the
special" off and got a last wave from Mrs. Davidson. The
poor Archbishop was already being interviewed by some
man who had come from New York to ride back with him.

In 1905 my father happened to be President of the Harvard
Alumni and that was also the year that President Theodore
Roosevelt had the twenty-fifth anniversary of his graduation.
His friend, who was also his Secretary of the Navy, Robert
Bacon, was Chief Marshal. All these happenings were lucky for
us as the President was to stay with us during the celebrations
and commencement. Of course, there were great preparations
and almost at the last moment we received word from Washington that the President would be accompanied by his son Kermit
and seven Secret Service men! This was quite a shock to my
mother, but, fortunately, the students of the Theological School
were leaving that week and so the secret service men could be
housed in their dormitory (Lawrence Hall) right next to our
house. I remember I had to move out of my room as my mother
and father took mine, having given theirs, which was larger and
had a bathroom attached (not so usual in those days as now) to
the President. My brother Appleton also had to give up his to
Kermit, and Mr. Loeb, the secretary, was in the spare room.

My father met the President at the Back Bay Station at 7:00
A.M. with our carriage. They drove to Cambridge, escorted by
at least a dozen mounted police. My mother had been asked to
invite Governor Douglas, Lieutenant Governor Guild, Judge
Lowell, President Eliot and Mr. Cruthers all to breakfast, so
she didn't want us, and I was only too thankful to stay in bed
as I had slept almost not at all in my strange quarters. When
I did get up and looked out there was a patient crowd standing
outside our wall on Brattle Street, and as the morning advanced,
and the time drew near for the President to go out, the throng
increased steadily. The place looked very pretty with the wide
green lawn and the flowering shrubs and a large American flag
waving slowly from the bow window balcony in front. At the
steps were the secret service men and "gentlemen of the press."
There were more police all around the grounds and walking
up and down the street. While eating my breakfast, I saw two
Groton hat bands coming up the street and discovered them to
belong to Mr. Billings and young Kermit. Suddenly a volcano
flew out of the house and met Kermit on the porch, and there
was the President hugging his son like a bear, and gritting his
teeth and laughing, apparently beside himself with joy and excitement. It was very amusing, and, of course, it was a wonderful sight for the crowd in the street.

My father had invited a few youthful relatives to come and
shake hands with the President and now they began to arrive.
Aunt Harriet* and her flock came in their automobile, which,
of course, was stopped by the Chief of Police, who inquired
what their errand was. Aunt Harriet said, "Why-y-y, I'm the
Bishop's sister," to which the gallant Chief replied, "Ah! indeed!
certainly! I see the resemblance! Pass on!" When I went into
the parlor I found a rather stiff assemblage. In the middle of
the room the President and Kermit, still with their arms around
each other, were talking volubly together. In a large circle
around them stood the Lawrence, Hemenway, Brooks and Sal-

---

* Mrs. Augustus Hemenway, Bishop Lawrence's sister. [Ed.]

tonstall families staring in silent—and very gauche—wonder,
and in one corner Mamma and Mr. Loeb, the President's secretary, were discussing arrangements.

Fortunately, this party broke up soon, after the President had
shaken hands with everybody, saying nice appropriate things
to all the children. At 11:30 he and Papa went out in the
Victoria, followed by barouches of secret service men. Just
before this it had begun to pour, but the President would not
have the top of the carriage put up, which was right of him as
the crowd had waited so long to see him. Now it had grown
to huge proportions and Brattle Street was crowded with carts,
automobiles, and bicycles, while the people standing along the
wall were getting drenched. The mounted police were drawn
up in line on either side of the gate and after the carriages had
driven through they all wheeled and cantered after them, making a grand thundering of hoofs, a proceeding which I could see
that Lightning, one of our pair, did not enjoy, but Reese, who
soon quieted him, was the proudest and happiest and most important mortal in the world that day.

The President was going to the Harvard Union, and then to
the Alpha Delta Phi, and then to see his little nephew, Mrs.
Redge Gray's little boy, who had just been badly hurt from an
accident with his pony. After this, he was going to his Class
Luncheon at the Oakley Club in Belmont. Later he went to his
Class Dinner at the Somerset and we went through the same
excitement of the morning—crowds, cheers, police cantering
after, etc. It was very exciting and we did feel so grand and
important!

Mr. Loeb and Kermit dined with us, and Kermit was a most
attractive little boy. He was bright and amusing and talked a
lot, but was not in the least bit forthputting—in fact, he had
no suggestion of self-importance—but seemed quite shy, and
blinked and stuttered a little when embarrassed. His manners
were very good—he was quick to jump and get you something
or shut the door. He almost wept at some allusion Mr. Loeb

made to a check his mother had sent him in reward for winning a prize at Groton which it turned out he hadn't won at all
—through some mistake of the Rector's—so he felt he was getting his mother's check on false pretenses and he got very red,
kept his eyes down and kept saying, "I shall send it back, I want
her to take it back," etc. He was very cunning.

The next day was Commencement and we had just a family
breakfast with the President, Kermit, and Mr. Loeb, and Mr.
Bob Bacon, Chief Marshal for the day—and there never was a
handsomer one. The President kept us laughing all the time
with his tales of last night's dinner. I knew, of course, that he
was a great talker, but I had no idea he was such an amusing
one. He seemed to have a grand time seeing all his old classmates again and the dinner seemed to have been a wildly jolly
occasion. It was fun to hear him and Mr. Bacon talk it over
like two boys, Mr. Bacon not saying much and saying what he
did calmly and slowly and the President grimacing and blink-
ing and gritting his teeth and giggling all the time, accenting
his remarks by pointing at one or the other of us and shaking his
finger. After breakfast he found a picture of himself in the
paper that threw him almost into hysterics. One would have
supposed that he had never seen a picture of himself in the
paper before. He came into the parlor to show it to us, with
the tears rolling down his cheeks and laughing in his high
falsetto way, which was so funny and infectious! His choice of
words was wonderfully good, and his experiences and also his
very rash frankness made him a thrillingly interesting talker.
One of his expressions which pleased Papa was his definition of
the German Emperor—whose admiration and constant messages
bored him a good deal—he called him an "autocratic zigzag."
The Emperor was much struck by Roosevelt's likeness of character to his own, but the President didn't see the similarity.
At about 9:00 P.M. the Lieutenant Governor representing
the Governor arrived, escorted by the picturesque Lancers. The

whole party went off in barouches forming in procession in our
Avenue. Mamma, Ruth, and I were in our victoria by that time
and went with the procession too, though we allowed all the
Lancers to separate us from the President's cortege. It was quite
thrilling to drive through the cheering crowds, preceded by a
large company of cavalry, who were making a great clatter and
looking quite brilliant in their bright red uniforms, long white
plumes, and their lances held aloft.

In Sanders Theatre our seats were next to Mrs. Eliot, directly
opposite the centre of the stage in the front row, so that the
President and President Eliot were right in front of us. Of the
honorary degree recipients Secretary Taft aroused the most enthusiasm. The Commencement orations and dissertations were
excellent and well worth hearing. President Roosevelt seemed
much interested in them and had a word and a handshake with
all the boys who spoke.

Mamma was to lunch with Mrs. Eliot, so we girls came home
and got a bite before returning to the Alumni Meeting where
we all met again in the ladies' gallery at Memorial Hall. It
always thrilled me when the band entered the marble hallway
which made such a loud echoing sound and then the dignitaries
and old graduates marched in. President Eliot and Papa led the
procession—then Mr. Bacon—looking simply beautiful, and
President Roosevelt; but the martial music inspired the latter to
step so lively that he couldn't stay behind, but was striding
brisker and brisker, until he was alone in the lead. Then came
Mr. Bacon's dashing aides, helping the oldest graduates, like
Edward Everett Hale and old Mr. Charles Parker, who tottered
along to the lively, noisy music.

In order to make room for the enormous crowd that was expected this year, the whole dinner had been abolished and the
tables taken out so that the hall accommodated hundreds more
than usual. The head table was kept on the platform and Papa,
as presiding officer, sat in the centre of it with President Eliot
on his right and President Roosevelt on his left. Speeches were

made by Mr. Justice White, Secretary Taft, Mr. Choate and Mr. Agassiz, and all were remarkably good, and not one seemed a moment too long.

President Eliot pleased Papa very much by saying that it was the best Commencement that Harvard had ever had. When it was over, I ran back to the house where Beekman Winthrop, then Governor of Puerto Rico, was waiting to see Mr. Taft. The latter was just arriving in a carriage to see the President. Shortly after, Mamma arrived, and gave them all tea. Mr. Taft was a huge unwieldy man with a face expressive of the keenest good humor. Winthrop and Taft were catching a train in town at 7:30, so we were to have an early dinner, and they all three went off for a talk until then. The President was going to dine at the Somerset Club later, so Mamma had not expected him at dinner, but he came, and sat behind Mr. Winthrop and me on the sofa, and talked like a teapot. Mr. Winthrop and I could not very well turn our backs completely on him so we sat skewed around in our chairs, and in this position it was very difficult to eat. Mr. Winthrop got a few mouthfuls of soup and then Mr. Taft said, "Winthrop, don't you want to do a little telephoning for me just for the sake of old times?" Of course he jumped up, had an undertone colloquy with the Secretary and flew to the telephone, where he spent the next course or two of the dinner.

Meanwhile, the President, in order to talk to better advantage, took his chair at the table, and before he got through at the telephone, Papa had made them all jump by saying they must start right along "if they were going to catch that train." The Secretary made the most deliberate goodbyes all around, while Beekman Winthrop collected all the baggage, umbrellas, etc. The President hardly stopped talking to say goodbye ("Taft's a brick—Taft's a brick," he kept telling us) and then he said, "Why, look here! I'm not going to see you again till October!" to which Taft replied, "No! you sit on the lid good and hard now till I get back!" and then he said, "Well, just a word, there's this other little matter," and the President and his Secretary of War stepped to the window and conversed in undertones, while we all stood in silence and Papa held his watch in his hand, looking frantic. "The other little matter" was either the Russo-Jap peace or the Panama Canal which they settled up in this way—"till next October."

Finally they were off—Secretary Taft still smiling and deliberate and lumbering, and poor Beekman Winthrop looking distraught. With a sigh of relief we turned back to finish our meal and Mamma said to the President, "Well, I don't know what you'd call this, but we should call it a busy day!" To which he replied, "I should call this rather a quiet day, but I haven't got in my two hours' exercise which I generally manage to have every afternoon." At this point the children called our attention to Secretary Taft's carriage galloping back up the street. As it tore up the street, Beekman Winthrop jumped out and burst in upon us with bows and apologies, still smiling, grabbed some papers off the mantelpiece, saying that the Secretary had forgotten them, murmured to Mr. Loeb to telephone to the Back Bay Station to hold the train, made more bows and apologies and was gone. The poor man had come all the way from Puerto Rico to see Taft on business and so far he had not had a chance to talk at all, or get any dinner, so he was now going to accompany him to Worcester or Providence and then return to Boston, provided he had got the advice he came for.

Well, in spite of the President's quiet day, Mr. Loeb said he was tired and rather dreaded this late dinner at the Somerset Club. First the President pressed a coin into Katy's hand, saying, "Thank you for taking such good care of me and God bless you!" Katy, Freddy's nurse, had not taken care of him and gave the coin to Jennie, but would not have parted with the words and handshake for many coins. She had shaken a President's and Archbishop of Canterbury's hands this year which was more than she expected ever to do.

Then the President went downstairs waving a gorgeous neckerchief which he said was a Spanish flag. He put it on, and then his coat, and we all stood around waiting, but a package was handed to him (the police and secret service men having already inspected it), and on opening it he found a wonderfully carved patent-spring match box in the shape of a Swiss chalet from an Armenian admirer. He did not believe in race suicide, but told how many children he had and his whole life history in a very amusing letter.

Just as the President was going to step into the carriage, his private stenographer walked in the door with a thick wad of papers in his hand, saying it had just been received. The President stopped, took it, and standing perfectly still, all ready as he was, read it. He took about two seconds to a page, but his mind was absolutely concentrated on it. When he got through, he told the stenographer in a word or two what to do, then went on with his cordial goodbyes to all of us, got into the carriage with Papa, stood with his hat raised as they drove off, and the still-waiting crowd of people cheered him at the gate, and all the way down the street.

Papa said afterwards that crowds cheered all the way to the bridge, and women threw flowers and things into the carriage, which worried poor Mr. Wylie, the secret service man on the box, as he could not see in the semi-darkness whether the missiles were flowers or bombs. Meanwhile things were very flat at home. The family had all fled, leaving me with Mr. Loeb in the parlor, and he, seeing I fear how sleepy I was, soon went over to Lawrence Hall to talk with the secret service men—and so to bed!*

* In Henry James's biography of President Eliot, he quotes a memorandum "supplied by Mr. G. G. Wolkins" in which Mr. Eliot is reported as saying that Mr. Roosevelt stayed with him over this Commencement, but my diary and memory are confirmed by my father's account in his autobiography, *Memories of A Happy Life*, pp. 225–230.

CHAPTER 20

SAILORS' HAVEN

꿿

THE PROJECT which I worked hardest over in those years was raising money for a new Sailors' Haven in Charlestown. I had been doing a little social work over there for the homesick boys on the training ship *Wabash,* and Stanton King, the head of the Sailors' work, seeing my interest, attacked me persistently on the need for a new building. I spoke to Dr. Parks about it and he said he would appoint a committee if I would be chairman. He did get a splendid committee, all active laymen of his parish and Mrs. Charles H. Taylor of the Boston *Globe* family to keep me company. We met at 122 Commonwealth Avenue and decided to begin by having a parlor meeting to interest people. Dr. William Appleton of the committee said he would ask his sister, Mrs. Arthur Beebe, if she would let us use her big house. My contemporary, Henry S. Grew, was made Treasurer. Our architect member, Mr. Charles Collins, said we should raise fifty thousand dollars. Ten thousands dollars was the price of the corner lot on Water Street we expected to buy and he said we should need forty thousand dollars for the building.

In those days, sailors were real seamen who pulled ropes, climbed the rigging, slept in hammocks, and had a pretty hard rough life. When they went ashore with their hard-earned cash in their pockets, loan sharks and women of the streets were on hand to greet them—and nobody else. They were friendless in the worst part of a strange city, far away from home. After the Episcopal City Mission started the Sailors' Haven, Mr. John Allan and then Mr. King and his staff met every ship that docked and handed the crew cards telling the sailors about the Haven, and often escorting them there and making them feel at home. Nowadays this has changed like everything else. Sailors are well educated and know all about radar, atomic power and jet engines, and are just as well able to look after themselves as any group of young men.

When I first knew the Sailors' Haven it was operating in a small rather tumbledown building near the Navy Yard on Water Street, and Mr. Allan, that fine Scotchman, was the head of it. The man to whom Stanton King gave the credit for changing his life was Mr. Allan. It is hard to describe Stanton King, a character of great force and no little charm. One time when he was in the hospital Elizabeth Andrew and I went to see him:

> He was in bed and very funny-looking, so grim and healthy and sunburned with his tattooed arms. He was smoking a pipe and the room was full of smoke—also with flowers from his many lady friends. On his big brown hand there flashed and sparkled a large solitaire diamond. He explained a friend had lent it to him while he was sick! He said he usually kept the stone turned inside as he thought it looked rather too flashy for him. What comfort can there be in wearing a friend's diamond when you are sick? But he seemed to derive much pleasure from it.

Everything about Mr. King was original. He was born in Barbados, the youngest of twenty-nine children, and he ran away to sea when he was twelve. His father had married three times and perhaps he did not get the loving care that the first dozen or two received. According to his lurid account of his life, John Allan had dragged him up from the depths and eventually made him his chief worker so that it was natural for him to carry on the work when Allan died.

There were weekly concerts Monday nights and some church was responsible for bringing the "shore talent" and the coffee and buns. For a year or two, when I was raising money for the new Haven, I went every Monday bringing different groups of friends, who invariably enjoyed it and I often had difficulty dragging them away. At the end of every concert, Mr. King would shout out a lot of nautical commands and the men would man the topsail. One or two would go aloft (in the new Sailors' Haven we had a real mast with two topsails on it, given by Elizabeth Andrew and made by Lawless who built many of the yachts of the day). A lot of the other sailors in the audience would grab the ropes and then all down the aisle of the concert hall they would sway back and forth, singing "Blow the Man Down," "A Dollar a Day is the Stevedore's Pay," or other chantey songs, while Mr. King, like a cheer leader, would stand on the stage and lead them in a powerful deep bass.

Each Monday evening I would bring friends, trying to interest them in the work, who would sing or cakewalk or do some tricks, and the audience of men would applaud loudly. Sometimes my father or Dr. Worcester, the Rector of Emmanuel, would come with us and give a talk. Dr. Worcester amused the sailors I think, even more than he realized. One old salt said to me, "I have heard some tall yarns in my day, but that man Dr. Worcester, he can certainly top them all."

When the time came for the committee meeting to discuss fund-raising for the Sailors' Haven, I wrote to ten gentlemen, who owned yachts or were interested in shipping, and asked if they would be patrons of our meeting and they all accepted. Then I ordered imposing cards of invitation and addressed several hundred of them. My father was to preside and Mr.

King to speak and it all seemed very promising. Then the great
day came.

March 3, 1903. The long expected meeting at Cousin
Emily Beebe's to raise money for a new Haven for Sailors.
I never came so near to breaking down in a panic before.
Suffice it to say that when Papa and I arrived, there was
Mrs. Beebe standing in her hall all dressed up and ready to
receive. I had sent out 450 handsome large invitations and
I had twelve fine patrons and patronesses. A few of these
were present. Herbert Sears, looking rather unhappy, Dr.
William Appleton, Uncle Augustus, Mrs. Thayer, Mrs. Sargent, etc., then a few of the Committee, Mrs. Taylor and
Mrs. Harry Grew, a few scattered people to whom I had
written personal notes, and all the Lawrence family. The
two parlors and hall were full of little gilt chairs as I had
ordered 100—and there were only thirty people! Oh! it
was too horrible! The man stood at the door—no carriages
drove up. My two ushers, Harold Peabody and Livingston,
had nobody to ush.

Well! we finally had to begin and it seemed as solemn as
a funeral. Papa introduced Mr. King—very nicely indeed,
and Mr. King began to speak, but I could see he was as nervous as I was and he couldn't seem to get going and I became so desperate that it seemed as if nothing mattered any
more—but when he did get going he talked finely for
three-quarters of an hour and Mrs. Cheney and one or two
others were moved to tears. Then Dr. Parks made a short
appeal and was as amusing as usual and then Papa closed
the meeting and said that anyone who felt like giving anything (he suggested the amount for the building or the
amount for the land, perfectly seriously) might come up
and say so to himself or Mr. King—and nobody moved.
Well! finally I moved around and began to chatter to

people—though I felt much more like weeping. I saw
Uncle A. speak to Mr. King and then Mr. K. came and
made a nice little speech to me which I answered gruffly,
but I couldn't help it, and then we thanked Mrs. Beebe and
left. Harold and Livingston walked home with me and
were so kind and polite, asking me to take them over to
the Sailors Haven "any Monday, anytime" that I began to
feel more cheerful.

March 4, 1903. Opened my mail with feverish haste.
There was nothing but $5. from Elsie Beal! That was the
last straw! Went to Art School but accomplished less than
nothing. Telegraphed Tradja that I could not come to
Texas. How could I run away now and leave my poor committee and Mr. King in the lurch? Took a restful drive and
that dear kind Cousin Emily Beebe sent me a check for
$500, and while I was busy writing and working in the
evening, another $500 came from Mrs. Baylies, and my
spirits rose.

March 9, 1903. Made a call on old Cousin Emily Appleton who delighted me by promising $1,000 for the new
Haven.

March 10, 1903. A delightful surprise at breakfast was
a wildly excited note from Stanton King enclosing Uncle
Augustus's visiting card on which was written, "Draw on
me for $10,000." He had gone over to the concert at the
Haven and dropped it in the canvas "draw bucket" when
it was passed as usual for contributions. He certainly is a
corker! Mr. King is almost out of his head with excitement
and I had the pleasure of telling my Committee the good
news at our meeting in the afternoon. Dr. Appleton had
already heard it downtown and on the strength of it had
collected $3,000 more so now we have $15,000.

The way Dr. Appleton said he collected his $3,000 was this: "I went in to see Montgomery Sears and told him we needed a good Sailors Haven in Charlestown and Gus Hemenway had given $10,000 and I was giving $1,000. He said, "All right, I'll give $1,000." Then I went to see Harry Sears and I called upstairs "We're raising money for a new Sailors Haven and Gus Hemenway has given $10,000. How much will you give?" And he said, "How much is Montgomery Sears giving?" I said, "$1,000," and he said, "All right, I'll give one thousand!"

Continuing like this, he brought in his $4,000. Boston, you see, was a smaller and cozier place in those days. Don't think it was all as easy as this, however. The last half of the $50,000 came in very slowly and was hard work.

March 16, 1903. Dinner for the Haven at the Charlie Taylors' with Louis Bacon and an Englishman named Peyton who has something to do with shipping. After dinner we drove over to Charlestown for the Sailors Haven concert. Julie and Ruth and Livingston Davis and Harold Peabody were there too. It was a good concert and great fun and all our guests enjoyed it immensely. Harold P. was so enthusiastic he wouldn't go home when we all did and we left him with an arm around a sailor on either side of him. Mr. Peyton was also enthusiastic and passed coffee and buns and in so doing met several men who said they had seen him in Liverpool. He sent me $25. and said he would like to go over whenever we went.

In April, several of my friends were sailing on the *Commonwealth,* and I thought it would be a good idea to write letters to the people I knew and ask them to get up a concert on board and send the proceeds to us for the new Sailors' Haven. I wrote a long letter to Carrie explaining all this and asked her to make a poster for it and sell it at auction, and I wrote to Lieut. McCoy, Mr. George Gardiner, Mrs. Louis Curtis, and others who were also sailing.

April 28, 1903. I started out right after breakfast to deliver my letters to the ship, but when we got there such swarms of people were coming off the ship they wouldn't let us on! I was in despair as I wanted to leave my note with Carrie but suddenly I saw Mr. King coming down the gangplank and he took us all up the steerage way and we rushed round the decks and finally found Carrie but had only a moment with her, and then had to go down the place that the luggage had been brought up, and I was the very last person off that ship! It was not an easy or a graceful descent and of course Carrie was remarking upon it at the top of her lungs, shrieking, "Sit down and slide," so that everyone on board was much interested in our escape.

Mr. King took us all up on top of the dock again to see the ship off. Here we were right on a line with the bridge and here Mr. King introduced me in stentorian voice to the Captain, and, while everyone aboard and ashore watched and listened, the Captain and I said polite nothings to each other. Then she backed slowly out—everybody waving and yelling—the Captain saluted, handkerchiefs fluttered and we raced to the other end of the wharf to see her turn. It was then I caught a glimpse of General Leonard Wood's erect military figure down on the lower deck with sailors and steerage, leaning against the rail and looking rather sadly at his last view of home.

May 4, 1903. Harold Peabody came to dinner and took me to the last Monday concert in Charlestown. There were a lot of blue-jackets there tonight as the *Massachusetts* and *Nashville* are in, and that often means fights with some of the tougher elements on the docks, and so it was rather a

restless evening with one smart scrap in the outer hall of
the Haven and several outside. One huge nice-looking boy
came in and sat in front of us. He held on to his arm all
the time with his other hand and I saw that his sleeve was
almost entirely torn off. When we left, Water Street was
full of blue-jackets and a policeman stood at the Haven
door.

May 5, 1903. Went to Emmanuel Guild to try to spudge
them up to do something for the Sailors Haven.

P.M. Mr. King spoke at the St. John's Missionary Meeting at Mrs. Cooke's and I went out there to "push on the
good work." He spoke well and I added a few business
words but fear that there wasn't much money there.

Nov. 9, 1903. Stevie Chase invited Lincoln and Katharine and me to dine at the Somerset Club and go to the
Concert at the Haven. He had a grand time and so did I,
but I don't think the Davises did, especially Katharine,
and they left after a short time.

Every Saturday now, from 11 to 1, I spend on the
Wabash with Mr. King talking with the boys. I sit on a
chair—the only one—on a strip of carpet and they gather
around as soon as their duties allow them, their arms around
each other's shoulders in a large circle and we have much to
talk about and some wonderful yarns—some are homesick
but none are fresh. They are all charming and most appreciative.

Dec. 5, 1903. Did not go to Navy Yard but invited some
of the boys to play billiards in the evening. McDonald,
who dances wonderful shuffles for us at the Haven, is
"classed" and in prison on bread and water and for nothing
at all! He saw an old mattress lying on the deck, and when
he washed his own he washed that and hung it up to dry.

A cook came along and said it was his and accused him of stealing it. McDonald explained that he hung it up only for the owner to claim it. The 1st Lieut. who happened to be in an ugly mood—he is drunk much of the time— "classed" McDonald which means he loses his liberty for a month or maybe more. The cook soon discovered his mistake, told the Lieut. and apologized to McD.—in fact, did everything he could but nothing is of any use apparently afterwards.

This incident is not at all unusual and I was always in a state of boiling indignation over the injustices shown to the apprentice boys. Some of them lose their tempers and get into worse trouble, others grow sulky and desert, but most of them, to my great surprise and admiration, take it philosophically and cheerfully and are much amused at my show of indignation. They tell me all sorts of tales of hard luck and then laugh at my rage over them.

Creber, another friend of mine, and a fine manly fellow, didn't come because his pal, Bates, was "classed" and "he didn't think he would enjoy himself with Bates in the brig." There are a good many of these David-and-Jonathan friendships among the boys and another pair of them came to play billiards, "an honest Irish lad" named Caswell and his pal of German extraction named Kohout. Caswell has been in the Navy since he was twelve and must remain till he is twenty-one. Every week since he enlisted, his mother has written him and he to her, and every month he sends her three-quarters of his pay. He and Kohout are hoping for a furlough which they will spend at Caswell's home in Chicago. Kohout apparently has no home and no responsibilities.

Dec. 7, 1903. Aunt Sue invited people to dine and go afterward to the Sailors' Haven. I thought she was only going to have Harold and me, so what was my horror therefore to find Miss Ellen Parker, Mr. Theophilus Parsons, Annie Amory, and Gordon Dexter! I *trembled* at the thought of taking these conventional Boston old bach's and old maids over to that rollicking place, crowded with greasy stokers not to mention the bad air, and tobacco smoke so thick you could cut it. We all went over in the electric cars and fought our way through the crowd at the door and up to the platform. Fortunately they all enjoyed the concert extremely. Mr. Dexter was tremendously entertained, and Miss Amory enjoyed it because *he* did and she was sitting next to him. Mr. Pop Parsons and Uncle Caleb both thought it was great, and the latter sent me a check for $500. the next day and the former sent some more coffee cups!

Dec. 11, 1903. Mr. King telephoned me to say that two of the apprentice boys had run in to tell him that they had all been ordered off the *Wabash* to battleships all over the world. Many had gone without a chance to say good-bye. They left all sorts of messages for me and these two boys— one a romantic little French boy—had obtained special leave to come ashore to give them. This was a terrible piece of news for me and perfectly unexpected and I had a horrid night in consequence. The next morning, which happened to be my day over there, I rushed over, but the *Wabash* was completely deserted except for two or three boys who were packing their kits. I got the addresses of some of my friends from the ship's writer who afterward offered to help me at the Haven or in any way he could. I said goodbye to the old Chaplain and sadly left. I could not imagine the concerts without McDonald to dance for us or to sing "Any Rags" when the other boys would shake the walls by joining in the chorus. What will happen to that quick tempered, loose-jointed rascal and quiet young Ivy Johnson who waited one rainy night at the bottom of the elevated

steps and escorted me gallantly through the toughs and
dangers of Water Street? I hope Bates and Creber got on
the same ship.

Dec. 21, 1903. This was *my* concert and I was responsible for the talent and a terrible time I had getting it! My
friend Harley Parker had been fine and got several people
for me besides himself, and the Jack Sargents had got Reggie Bowles and the Harvard Banjo Club, and the Grews
invited Lena Stevenson to dine and come over. We all sat
on the stage where were also Connie, Amory and the Larz
Andersons—of all people. Well—it was a great success and
they all seemed to enjoy it hugely. Harley made the hit of
the evening by the parody on *Hiawatha* and he had to repeat it several times. Connie sang better than I ever heard
her and the men all joined in the chorus. Lena Stevenson
did an admirable cakewalk which Buck Freeman applauded
to the echo. Larz Anderson and Isabel passed coffee and
rolls with much energy and competence and stayed till the
lights were out and then went home to Brookline in the
elevated! Isabel handed Mr. King $50. for Xmas expenses.
All the guests were enthusiastic about Mr. King of course
and they loved Buck Freeman's dancing and all the sailor
talent. The Banjo Club played whenever they got the
chance and sat on the edge of the stage and played all the
time coffee was served. They all thought it was a wonderful
evening! When it was over we went to Frank and Louise's,
where they had a delicious sit-down supper all ready for us
—just Carrie, Connie, C. Barlow, Harley, Harold and I.
It was awfully nice of them—in fact of Harley, Carrie,
Connie, the Sargents, Andersons, and everybody. I have
fine friends.

April 4, 1904. A delightful concert. Old Professor Ken-
nedy was back after seven years of roaming around the

world and funnier than ever. Gussie loved it—Harold saw
me home. Did I mention the crew of Norsemen who
turned up at the Haven a while ago after a trip of 183 days
from Singapore on a sailing ship? Six or eight huge, fair-
haired, handsome giants. One, a typical Viking, sang in a
most gorgeous voice two songs in Norwegian. Sailors and
guests listened in absolute stillness and then brought down
the house with applause. The young Viking looked so surprised and pleased and his slow smile showed a beautiful
set of teeth. He sang again—a fine Norse sea ballad with
the real true ring to it. He was such a contrast to our shy
or fresh Navy boys—or the ordinary Cockney boy on the
White Star Line. He was a real European gentleman whose
ancestors for a thousand years had sailed the seven seas,
with others like them, on their picturesque ships. When I
passed him on the way out I said, "Thank you very much
for singing," and he smiled and bowed with more dignity
than any of my Boston friends!

Dec. 12, 1904. Charlie Hayden went with us and seemed
to enjoy it. He was very good with the sailors, and was as
amazed as everyone else to see Lem Hitchock there. The
latter robbed him of $10. for the draw bucket and wanted
me to ask him right out for $500. as he said, "Ask him to
give up one race horse and put it into the Sailors Haven."

I sat with my *Missouri* boys as it was their last night and
we were all feeling very sad at parting. Fournier bugled us
out with "Taps" and while his notes were ringing clear and
loud Baker and Jones and the rest were saying goodbye to
me and all thanking me so feelingly for the little I had
done for them.

Dec. 19, 1904. My concert night at the Haven. I had got
Annie Nourse (piano) and Miss Jewell (violin) and they

made really *good* music. Carrie brought a crowd over and
Gus Parker sang and Ros. Gibson played his accompaniments. Hal Movius did some wonderful dances, equal to
any of the sailors and they all were enthusiastic over the
place. I had asked Reggie Bolles of the Harvard Banjo
Club to come again, and he had responded very cordially
and promptly and brought six men with banjos and mandolins and also Billy Dinsmore who good-naturedly played
the piano all the evening. One of the big White Star liners
was in so the sailor talent was excellent, especially the tiny
cabin boy who recites the highly moral parable about
"strong liquor," apropos, the Arab, the camel, and his
"hoomp"—Gus Parker was entranced with him and thought
it was the best part of the evening, so my concert was again
a wild success and I was very happy and thankful.

The best thing about the Sailors' Haven is the spirit of
the place—not only do we have Charlie Hayden hobnob-
bing with the sailors and with Mr. Hitchcock, but we have
officers and navy men mixing with the seamen and stokers
of the merchant marine and coasting steamers—something
that doesn't happen *any* where else and in fact is considered
an impossibility; and most wonderful of all, we have Elizabeth sitting chatting with Annie Nourse. This nearly finished Connie and caused her to remark on the enchanted
atmosphere of the Haven. Really it *is* a remarkable place
and Mr. King is a remarkable man.

Dec. 29, 1904. Xmas Concert at the Haven. Harold had
been there all day and seemed to think I ought to have
been too. The Concert Hall was so jammed there was no
use trying to get in so I went upstairs to the billiard rooms
where there were 60 or 70 playing games or singing to the
Aeolian. Dick was up there playing checkers and Harold
came up and played pool. I played five games of pool with

the writer* of the *Wabash* against two other sailors, one of whom seemed to be considered a shark and we had a most thrilling match. We had a large audience around the table and an umpire who I fear favored the lady a little in his decisions.

Jan. 23, 1905. A dinner at the Taylors which was the greatest fun. The Eben D. Jordans have just rented Inveraray Castle (the Duke of Argyll's place) for the summer and he invited us all over for the shooting season! His talk of the game, deer, birds, etc., as if they were his own, rather annoyed Mr. Paton—who is a Scotchman—and he made some quite tart remarks. He also told Mr. J. that he would have to "live up to the part" which would involve a good deal of hospitality, etc., during the week of the Highland games and he would have to wear Highland dress—kilts, bonnet, etc., and "stand treat for all the Country Side." This delighted Mr. J. who was in great spirits. Afterwards we all adjourned to the Sailors' Haven which was the object of the dinner and a plot laid by Mrs. Taylor to capture Mr. J. and get him over there. Fortunately it was a wonderful concert. Mr. King was in top form and his tactful remarks about the new Haven made a real impression on our guests. The sailor talent was A-1. We had the wonderful good-looking boy who recites so thrillingly about horse races. Then a London music hall sailor who entranced C. Winslow and almost gave Mrs. Taylor hysterics and there were good tap dancers. The shore talent came from Mr. Loring's parish in Newton and they were good too and to crown all Mr. Seabury got Mrs. Cabot Morse to come and sing, and she and her husband were there when we arrived. She has a beautiful voice and both she and Wallace

---

* A training ship had to have a "writer" because a lot of the boys couldn't write, and he wrote their letters home.

Goodrich were *so* kind. She sang in that thick smoke as long as they wanted her to, and he not only played her accompaniments but for all the sailors to sing and dance and even all thru' coffee time he was playing in imitation of a hurdy-gurdy which delighted the sailors.

All the people I take over there are so kind and good-natured and enter so into the spirit of the place that I want to hug them and cry from gratitude. Mr. Seabury sang all the choruses louder than anyone and seemed absolutely beside himself with excitement. He sprang up once and joined an old Negro sailor in a shuffle and at the end when Fournier was bugling "Taps," he borrowed his bugle and played the most elaborate fanfares and coaching tunes upon it. He is coming over again soon to bugle for us on his own cornet and Mr. Jordan is coming to sing! Mr. J. was crazy about it and especially about Mr. King whom he told to come and see him at his office!!! Everybody put all their spare cash in the draw bucket and Mrs. Taylor drove us all home in hacks.

Feb. 21, 1905. Had just got up and was entertaining Evelyn Sears in the parlor when Harold telephoned from the Haven where he said he had been since 6:00 A.M. I had not seen the morning paper so knew nothing of the big fire on the docks. The crew of the *Philadelphia* were waked out of their sleep only three hours after the concert and had to jump overboard and swim for their lives. They came to the Haven for refuge and were given hot coffee immediately and soon fitted out with clothes. It sounded very exciting as Harold told it, so I left Evelyn unceremoniously and went right over to Charlestown. I saw the huge dense wall of smoke from the bridge, and Water Street was all roped off but I ducked under the ropes and picked my way among the fire engines, hose, puddles and general mess. I love the excitement of a fire, the thumping engines, handsome patient horses, the busy brave firemen —it is all so picturesque.

At the Haven Harold and Miss Upham received my "Morning Herald" with delight. Miss Upham had been up all night and so had Mr. King but he had gone home for a rest. There were about 25 men sitting or lying around the billiard room—many asleep. The little cabin boy who had been so clean and happy last night was a pathetic little heap, sound asleep with his head on a hard table. He had been picked up unconscious on one of the docks and carried to the Haven. Mr. Tuttle, the assistant, had gone to see how the man in the hospital was getting on and found that he was not expected to live through the day. The poor fellow had had a temperature of 103 when he jumped into the icy water. The City Mission had sent over some men's clothes. A young man came in with a basket on his arm full of food which he had been sent out to buy. He was a big, fine-looking young Englishman and when Harold introduced him to me as the "Country Parson" he made a grand bow. He was as much amused as anyone and asked me "if they didn't look a band of strolling players." He had on a minister's black suit much too small for him and showing quite a length of white stocking. Below the white stockings were galoshes and he wore a tight frock coat, a red muffler and a brown derby on his head.

Harold and I set to work making sandwiches and feeding the famishing crew. I touched the little cabin boy, and he waked with a jump, apparently always ready to run when called for—though not really awake at all as he flopped right over onto his sandwich as soon as I turned away. Pretty soon he began to stretch and rub his eyes, and I showed him his name in the paper, among the injured, in

large letters. That caused him to smile and forget his
troubles and soon he seemed to be quite himself again.

At last we had our money and the land. When we began
to build, there were the usual unexpected difficulties and
disappointments and red tape with the city, etc. Mr. King
had a new idea every day and $100,000 wouldn't have cov-
ered all of them. Finally, it was done and we had a handsome brick and stone building with a large concert hall
one-and-a-half stories high with a gallery; large billiard and
game rooms on the second floor, reading and writing rooms
and a chapel on the top floor; and of course lockers and
facilities of every kind.

The day we moved out of the old Haven would have
been sad except for Mr. King's ingenuity. The railroad
had lent us an old warehouse until the new building was
ready. The concert started as usual in the old Haven where
the furniture belonging to the City Mission still remained.

Emmanuel was providing the concert so it was an awfully
good one with the same wonderful juggler they had last
year. The sailor talent was excellent too and the audience
large and appreciative. There were many shore people who
had not been there before, and a lot of Emmanuel people.
There were officers from the Navy Yard and from the
ships, and the platform was crowded with distinguished
guests. Papa arrived in time for coffee and after the cups
were cleared away he said a few words. Then everybody
joined in the Doxology which was a splendid chorus of
men's voices. Then John Codman offered to lead off a
song written for the occasion and sung to the tune of
"Marching thru' Georgia," the rest of us joining in the
chorus. Then came the unique—or rather *most* unique
part of the occasion. While the bugler played "Auld Lang
Syne" every person in the building grabbed something to

carry and all marched over to the new quarters. I grabbed
the phonograph and dashed out to see the fun. Water
Street was a strange sight. Hundreds of jolly singing sailors
carrying benches and tables, and ladies and gentlemen following, each carrying a chair or baskets full of crockery.
It was just like Mr. King to think of moving in this way
and everyone seemed to enjoy it hugely. The Boston and
Maine has given us these temporary quarters until the new
Haven is built and everything was prepared for us and
looked bright and cheerful though when I first saw it some
weeks ago it looked pretty hopeless—just an old warehouse
or loft. Mr. King had worked wonders however, and the
sailors swarmed up the rickety stairs and had everything in
place in no time. More bugling brought the noise and confusion to a stop and Mr. King made a short speech of welcome and the concert went on and the Walter Baylieses and
Codmans, etc., sat in the midst of the crowd of sailors and
applauded. They kept it up until Mr. King besought them
to let him go home to bed. Then the attractive young Englishman who escaped from the burning ship the other night
and who afterwards helped us to get food for the crew,
asked to say a few words. Mr. King called him up to the
platform and with dignity and delightful voice he thanked
Mr. King and the Haven staff for all they had done that
night. It was a remarkable and charming little speech. He
seemed such a gentleman that I think the shore people
were much impressed. When Harold left me at home at
about twelve I told him how sad I was that all the good
times in the old Haven were over and he said, with his nice
smile, "We shall have even better ones on the new one."

Sept. 22, 1905. Went to see the new building of the
Sailors' Haven. Mr. King was in Chicago so Mr. Tuttle
showed me over. It is a handsome building beyond my

expectations in every way. The huge hall on the street floor with stage, gallery, and concrete floor had "Lawrence Hall" over the door—named for me at Mr. King's insistence. On either side of the handsome front door were huge ship's lanterns, red and green, and a ship's figurehead was above the door. Mr. T. rather provoked me by pointing out all the little defects; as these mistakes were as much Mr. King's fault as anyone's, it was both annoying and discouraging especially as it is in every other way a fine, beautiful building.

Oct. 4, 1905. Mr. King and I went shopping and completely furnished the new building. Mr. Collins took us to some fascinating places on State and Canal Streets where we found some fine ship's lanterns and fittings. We also did a good job at Jordan's.

Oct. 9, 1905. (First night in the New Haven.) The hall looked fine and was jam full, with crowds standing way out in the entry way who could not get in. The stage was crowded with dignitaries—the speakers, the Admiral and officers of the Navy yard, etc., and the gallery was full of guests and interested friends. My aunts and some cousins turned out in force and Dr. Richardson and Mr. Collins (the architect). I sat next to Mr. King in the middle of the front row, and when Mr. King made many kind remarks about me (against my *express* orders) I felt very conspicuous, especially as, at the same time, one of the helpers handed me a huge bunch of gorgeous roses (from Harold) and everybody applauded.

Financially the evening was a great success. Aunt Sue whispered to me she would give $500. and Dr. Richardson gave me $100. while people clamored to give the big brass bell which —— —— promised but won't pay for! I had

not expected any gifts of money because to my great satisfaction we have quite a tidy little sum in the bank left over
which we can hand over to the City Mission with the new
building. Also I am pleased to death that it is finished
when the architects first promised it! Many a time have I
reminded them and the builders that it was to be done by
the 10th of October and it *is*, and it is satisfactory to everyone and really beyond my expectations.

CHAPTER 21

MARRIAGE

ↄ

Harold Peabody's name kept coming into my diary more and more frequently in these years. He and I worked together at the Sailors' Haven and on other projects, and we came to know and admire each other very much. But even then I was not ready to get married, and used to be cross with my friends sometimes when a rumor would get about that I was engaged to some one. One of my friends congratulated me at Bar Harbor and I turned it off so hastily I didn't even discover to whom she thought I was engaged.

At last on Christmas Harold and I became engaged. It must have been the Christmas spirit.

Dec. 25, 1905. Grandpa Peabody had five children, Jack, Cotty, Frank, Martha and George. Jack, Frank and Martha all married Lawrences, and Cotty married his first cousin, Fanny Peabody. George was the only one who married out of the family, but his marriage did not last long. When the second generation began to marry, Marian married her first cousin, Jim Lawrence, and so we were the fifth such combination without any break, and what then was the use of fighting fate?

We went down to Foss's one morning to get the ring before the engagement was announced. This was an old established jeweler's one flight up on Tremont Street, opposite the Park Street Church. It was a perfectly beautiful ring, just the kind I had always wanted—a large sapphire between two smaller diamonds. On the way downstairs afterward, we met Rosamund Saltonstall and Charlie Auchincloss coming up. They seemed amused and apparently took us all in. We never thought of suspecting them! Their engagement was announced a week later.

As soon as we were engaged, everything became easy and delightful. I was amazed at how nice everybody was. I couldn't see why they were all so interested. Grandma Cunningham, who was always very nice to Harold, said we were "perfectly suited."

Jan. 24, 1906. Hectic day. The engagement came out officially. Flowers and presents arriving every minute all day. Got over ninety boxes of flowers, but it was a pleasant job arranging them. One corner of the room was all violets and another corner was solid gold and another white with roses and jonquils and others. Many people sent their flowers in vases, for which I was more than grateful, and we had to get quantities of vases from the florists and neighbors. Louise sent a pendant moonstone heart surrounded by pearls on a chain. Dr. William Appleton sent the tallest and most gorgeous American Beauties—a regular bush of them. I have a full list in my "Bride Elect," the most useful present from Sally.

Jan. 27. We received our hundredth engagement present today. The parlor is really a wonderful sight and how delicious it smells!

February 16. Went sleighing from two to three-thirty with Aunt Sue. Then made calls with two men on the box. Harold came to dinner and then went off to get me some flowers for the Assembly, my partner, George Atkinson, having neglected to send me any. He sent me a most gorgeous bunch at the last Cotillon I had with him, but I suppose he has lost interest in an engaged girl. It is quite a joke as of course he would not have engaged me if he had known I was engaged! He has paid no attention to me since the engagement came out, not even written a note, and he probably looks upon this evening as an evening worse than wasted.

Harold and I went together to the Assembly and after making our bows to the chaperones he turned to dance with me, but Steve Chase darted in between and bore me off, leaving him standing alone and shaking his fist, which quite amused the receiving ladies. I had imagined I was going to be a terrible pill, so I wore my best dress in order not to make a poor showing before Harold, but to my joy I had the best time I have had in my life. All my old friends came up to congratulate me. In the Cotillon, George Atkinson made a last effort and was fine. He was pleasant, friendly, and pretended to be broken-hearted. We had a terrible seat in a corner at the lower end of the hall, but I got seven or eight favors. At supper time Harold came up seeming furious. I couldn't make it out and it was most unpleasant as he looked and acted like a bear. Mr. Minot had asked us to sit at his table—a great honor, as he was leading the Cotillon and had the big round table in the dining room. I went, delighted, Harold acting grouchy all the time. I had a lovely time in spite of his depressing actions. Then I danced lots more, several perfect ones with Harold, but he didn't unbend even after a wonderful dance to his favorite waltz. Went home with a carriage full of favors and a silent partner after a wonderful evening.

March 9. Worked all P.M. on list, dressmakers, writing and so forth. Then we went to see Gertrude Lawrence who had lovely samples of china and glass for us to choose from.

March 10. Harold and I had our photos taken and then went to Bigelows and Shreves looking at tea-sets. In the evening, Mr. and Mrs. Brooks Adams and our cousin, Mr. Gilchrist, who lives in China, came to dinner, and of course Harold. The latter was so attractive, they seemed to take a great shine to him. Mr. Brooks Adams told Mr. Gilchrist all about China, which was quite amusing for everybody.

All our friends and relations gave dinners for us, and Harold got rather talked out sitting next to Carrie at dinner after dinner—this was not his favorite part of being engaged.

April 6. Went to New York to look for furniture.

April 7. All morning Julie and I shopped for dining-room furniture and a silver tea-set. I think I will design a silver tea-set for myself to match Grandma Cunningham's beautiful antique sugar bowl. (I did and it was made for me by Shreve, Crump and Low.)

April 21. Mrs. Taylor lent us her big Packard automobile and chauffeur and H. and I had a wonderful drive all around the countryside this beautiful spring afternoon. It was a deliciously restful thing to do.

April 26. Fearfully rushing day. Twenty notes behindhand.

May 2. Many came to see the presents. I love fixing up the present room and it looks *wonderful* and elicits screams of admiration from everyone who enters it—the things are so gorgeous.

May 6. Harold's parents arrived from Europe and we went around to see them at the Victoria Hotel. In the evening we and they and also old Mr. Peabody dined at Aunt Lizzie's. They were all so nice.

May 7. A bombshell arrived at breakfast in the shape of a short note from Carrie telling of her engagement to Gus Parker! Coming out today—I was speechless with surprise. Everything else went out of my head, even my own wedding. She came in after breakfast and we just jabbered.

May 8. Perfect day for the wedding for which we are all grateful. In the morning H. came in with a beautiful diamond spray pin which his father had got out of the bank for him. It had belonged to his mother—a great surprise. Also a box came from the White House—but it was roses and we certainly had enough of those. Presidents should send something solid so it can be kept as a memento. We all ate lunch in the parlor and I didn't feel at all excited, though H. was very much so. Angela said it was a good sign.

While I was dressing, Carrie came in with a spray of orange blossoms. She telephoned this morning that she can't come to the reception. Stevie Chase's mother, a distant cousin of hers, died and her father wouldn't let her go to the reception or sit in her pew at church. It was an awful disappointment to both of us and seemed so unnecessary. She was on the point of tears and I have never seen her show so much emotion as she did while with me this morning and I was much touched. Gus was in a hack waiting for her and waved as they drove off to church with a message to be put in the middle of the front row of the back gallery —previously reserved for the Lawrence Club.

Uncle Amory, Miss Murphy the hairdresser, and I had a quiet little drive to the church together. My wedding dress of heavy white satin and lace made me look very tall and slender (I have never been thinner) and Aunt Harriet's beautiful long rose point veil was gorgeous (she lends it to all the family who want it). It was caught on with Carrie's orange blossoms and my diamond pin. There was a large crowd waiting as we left the carriage. In the vestibule was the choir, and all the ushers and we got ourselves in line. The choir went in singing a hymn and I felt only pleasantly excited while we waited. When the hymn was over and the choir started singing the Lohengrin Wedding March (which I love to hear) Mr. Haynes threw open the doors and we started up the aisle. Mamma—and maybe others—had wondered why I didn't walk up with Ap, but it seemed to me ridiculous to have a boy of sixteen giving away a sister fourteen years older, hence my choice fell on Uncle Amory, who seemed much pleased and looked very fine. I felt comfortable and pleased about joining Harold at the top. He and Jim looked calm and tall and very pale and he took my hand and led me up very solemnly, *his* hand shaking so badly I had to grip it hard to give him confidence. Cousin Cottie Peabody, Dr. Worcester, and Papa divided the service, Papa having the most and last. It took a surprisingly short time before Dick Lawrence was twirling me around by my very long train and we were walking down again to the Mendelssohn March and I felt very pleased with everything and comfortable and safe and settled. Carrie in front of me up in the organ loft said later she wouldn't worry about me any more as she never saw any couple look so happy.

I did not half appreciate all that was done for me. I had been spoilt and still wanted everything the way I wanted it— the church, which is beautiful, decorated just so, the choir to sing the wedding march, etc., and etc. There was a big reception at 122. We were sent off in a shower of rice and the next day sailed for England, which we both loved. I felt happy and contented and had given up fighting fate.